THE ELUSI MESSIAH

THE ELUSIVE MESSIAH

*A Philosophical Overview of
the Quest for
the Historical Jesus*

RAYMOND MARTIN

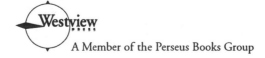
A Member of the Perseus Books Group

Copyright © 2000 by Raymond Martin

Published in 2000 in the United States of America by Westview Press, 5500 Central Avenue, Boulder, Colorado 80301-2877, and in the United Kingdom by Westview Press, 12 Hid's Copse Road, Cumnor Hill, Oxford OX2 9JJ

Library of Congress Cataloging-in-Publication Data
Martin, Raymond, 1941–
    The elusive Messiah : a philosophical overview of the quest for
the historical Jesus / Raymond Martin.
        p.   cm.
    Includes bibliographical references and index.
    ISBN 0-8133-9148-2
    1. Jesus Christ—Historicity.   2. Faith and reason—Christianity.
I. Title.
BT303.2.M384   1999
232.9'08—dc21   99-17104
                                                                    CIP

Design by Heather Hutchison

The paper used in this publication meets the requirements of the American National Standard for Permanence of Paper for Printed Library Materials Z39.48-1984.

10   9   8   7   6   5   4   3   2   1

To Brittany and Louis

CONTENTS

Contents

PART FOUR
RESPONSES

PREFACE

IN THE PAST SEVERAL DECADES, there has been an explosion of interest in the quest for the historical Jesus. This renewed interest has generated a fierce debate among historians, partly about who Jesus was, partly about what evidence should be used in determining who Jesus was, and partly about what methods should be used in interpreting whatever evidence is used. The debate among historians has sparked another, equally heated, debate among historians, theologians, and interested onlookers about how Christians can best respond to the challenge that this recent scholarship poses to their traditional beliefs.

Virtually all of the books that have been published in these debates have been written by participants in order to advance their own proposals. For instance, in the first debate, historians have argued that their portraits of Jesus are preferable to competing portraits, or that their evidence or methods are preferable to alternative evidence or competing methods. In the second debate, historians, theologians, and philosophers have argued that recent historical Jesus studies have or lack certain implications for traditional Christian beliefs. In each of these debates there are so many participants, of so many different sorts, saying so many different things, that for ordinary people who are not experts in history, theology, or philosophy but who are interested in following the debates, it can all be a little confusing. The present book is addressed primarily to ordinary people rather than to scholars, and its goal is to inform ordinary people in a way that reduces the confusion. To this end, the scholars whose views I consider are those who, in my view, ordinary people most need to know about for an accurate overview of the contemporary controversies. And for the sake of readers who may not be familiar with the views of these scholars, I give summaries of their views that are much more detailed than what would otherwise be required.

In providing these summaries, I try to provide an evenhanded, neutral overview of debates among historians over *who Jesus was* and over *what evidence should be used to determine who he was.* That is, without taking a stand about who is right, I try to provide an overview that fairly traces the main contours of the debate. For instance, I provide representative sketches of "conservative" and "liberal" portraits of Jesus without suggesting that either conservative or liberal historians have the upper hand. On the dispute among historians over methods, however, which is not one that splits along conservative and liberal lines, I take a stand. With some qualifications, I side with those who reject narrowly naturalistic approaches to interpreting Jesus and subscribe instead to more expanded approaches. Finally, I use my view about which methods it is appropriate to use in historical Jesus studies to try to shed some light on the question of how Christians can best respond to the challenge posed to their beliefs by these studies, but I do not then conclude by recommending any of the three main responses considered over any others.

Although this book is addressed primarily to those who are not experts in historical Jesus studies, I hope that it will also interest scholars of the subject. On the question of historical methods as well as on that of the implications of historical Jesus studies for what Christians should believe, I not only characterize but also critique the arguments of several historians, theologians, and philosophers who are prominent participants in the current debates.

Many readers, quite properly, will be skeptical that my overview of historical Jesus studies and review of the question of how Christians should respond will be as neutral as I have said it will be. They are right to be suspicious. In any book that addresses religious or political questions, it is natural, even healthy, for readers to be suspicious. So, I want to begin by laying my cards on the table.

I am a philosopher. By training and temperament, I am a specialist in the philosophy of historical methodology. What that means is that I am a specialist in assessing, on general grounds, the arguments that historians use to try to convince other historians and the rest of us of their views. So, for instance, whereas a New Testament scholar's area of expertise will be some aspect of the world at a certain place and time—say, religion in Israel in the first century C.E.—my area of expertise is historians' arguments. I am not a New Testament scholar or a theologian. I am not a historian of Jesus. I have no view about which historian, or group of historians, has the inside track in figuring out who Jesus was. I have no particular religious or antireligious beliefs, and nothing against those who do have one or the other, so long as they are tolerant and respectful of those who, while tolerant themselves, have beliefs or lifestyles different from their own. If I subscribe to anything that deserves to be called a creed, it is simply this: Live and let live.

As will be apparent especially in the last chapter of the book, the distinction that is emotionally and intellectually most salient for me is not between Christian and non-Christian, or religious and nonreligious, or conservative and liberal historian of Jesus, but between "open" and "closed." In my view, how open or closed people are depends much less on what they believe than on how they relate to their beliefs. Open people tend to be less emotionally attached to their beliefs than are closed people. They tend to depend less than do closed people on their beliefs for a sense of personal security. And it tends to be easier for them to set aside their beliefs and enter sympathetically into the points of view of others whose beliefs are different. In my experience, whether a person is religious or not, Christian or not, or conservative or liberal has very little to do with whether he or she is open or closed. The proportion of religious (or Christian, or conservative) people I have known who are open (and closed) is about the same as the proportion of nonreligious (or non-Christian, or liberal) people I have known who are open (and closed). So, to me, whether a person is religious or not, Christian or not, or conservative or liberal has very little significance.

Nevertheless, in writing this book I do have a personal agenda. It is that I want to use the quest for the historical Jesus as a way of exploring the relationship between the methods people use in investigating the world and what they take to be the results of their investigations. For reasons that will become clear as this book progresses, the recent debate over the historical Jesus and its companion debate over how Christians should respond to historical Jesus studies are nearly ideal for studying philosophically the relationship between methods and results. That is primarily why I am interested in these two debates. An additional reason is that, like you perhaps, I would like to know who Jesus was, what his message was, and why he made such a strong impression on so many people.

I want to express my deep appreciation to a number of people who in different ways helped me enormously in writing this book: for useful discussions and suggestions, John Barresi, of Dalhousie

University, Charles Manekin, Fred Suppe, and Allen Stairs, of the University of Maryland, and Ken Feigenbaum; for tough questions and objections, those who attended my "Jesus talks" at Dalhousie University; for artistic and technical assistance in composing the figures in Chapter 2, Eric Marchais; for assistance in tracking down and procuring books, articles, and bibliographic information, Nancy Hall; and for their extraordinary patience and good humor as well as helpful questions and objections, several generations of students in philosophy of religion and philosophy of historical methodology classes I have taught over the years (even decades!) at the University of Maryland, Dalhousie University, and the University of Auckland.

Finally, I thank everyone at Westview Press who worked on this book for being so extraordinarily competent and helpful, in particular, my acquisitions editors, Laura Parsons and Cathy Murphy, my copy editor, John J. Guardiano, and my project editor, Lisa Wigutoff.

Raymond Martin

INTRODUCTION

WHO WAS JESUS? WHAT WAS HIS MESSAGE? Why was he killed? Why did he have such an enormous impact? What, if anything, did he think was the meaning of his life? What, if anything, should *we* think was the meaning of his life?

These are questions about Jesus that many of us would like to be able to answer. Some think they already know the answers. But, as we shall see, the so-called authorities—primarily historians and theologians—disagree with each other about how to answer these questions. If these authorities, who know so much more about the relevant historical evidence than most of the rest of us, cannot agree on the answers, on what basis can the rest of us plausibly claim to know?

The first five of these questions—Who was Jesus? What was his message? Why was he killed? Why did he have such an enormous impact? What, if anything, did he think was the meaning of his life?—are about what actually happened historically and why it happened. The sixth question is about what *we* should decide is the *meaning* of what happened. We could arrive at answers to the historical questions about what happened and why without also answering the sixth question, about meaning. But it is hard to see how we could fully answer this question about meaning without first answering at least some of the historical questions. If we do not know what happened, or why it happened, we are not well positioned to understand what it should mean to us that it happened.

Professional historians have been trained to figure out what happened and why it happened. They have specialized knowledge and skills that most of the rest of us lack. Later we will examine some of the specialized knowledge and skills that historical Jesus scholars in particular have that are relevant to figuring out, in the case of Jesus, what happened and why. For now, it is enough to acknowledge that when it comes to figuring out what happened in the remote past and why it happened, professional historians are the experts and, by comparison, most of the rest of us are amateurs.

In the past several decades, many prominent contemporary historians—all acknowledged experts—have proposed interpretations of Jesus that conflict with what many Christians believe. This is not the first time this has happened. But, as we shall see, the care and expertise with which contemporary historians have surveyed and assessed the relevant evidence far exceeds those of their predecessors. Yet, in important ways, these contemporary historians have been unable to agree among themselves. So how seriously, if at all, should Christians take these historians? How seriously, if at all, should anyone take them? In the case of Jesus, how should the ordinary person decide what to believe about what happened and why? These are some of the main questions that I want to consider in this book. I shall not attempt to answer them. My goal is to help interested readers to answer them for themselves.

The debate among historians on the question of who Jesus was and what he was about has been between those who subscribe to more or less traditional portraits of Jesus—I call this group *conservatives*—and those who subscribe to highly revisionist accounts, whom I call *liberals*. The conservatives tend to base their portraits of Jesus primarily on literary evidence derived from the New Testament, supplemented by writings from the Jewish historian Josephus and by contextual information, derived from the social sciences, about what life must have been like for any Jewish peasant living in Israel in the first century C.E. The liberals tend to base their portraits of Jesus on the same evidence that the conservatives use *plus* other literary evidence from the period—the so-called (New Testament) *apocrypha*. The apocrypha consist mostly of documents that purport to convey sayings of Jesus or that were written by early Christians about Jesus, but were not included in the New Testament. As we shall see, there are substantial differences of opinion among scholars about when many of these apocryphal documents were written. Differences of opinion on this question form the basis for differing views about how important the apocrypha are as evidence to be used in sketching a portrait of Jesus.

In addition to this debate among historians over what evidence should be used in determining who Jesus was, there is also a debate among historians over the methods that should be used in interpreting *whatever* evidence is used. Here the most important difference of opinion is not between conservative and liberal historians, but between the conservatives and liberals who subscribe to narrowly naturalistic approaches to interpreting Jesus and those who subscribe to more expanded approaches.

Finally, in addition to these debates among historians over evidence, methods, and competing portraits of Jesus, there is another debate among historians, theologians, philosophers, and interested onlookers over how Christians can best respond to the challenge posed recently by historical Jesus studies to traditional Christian beliefs.

My goal in this book is to help ordinary readers understand this challenge to traditional Christian beliefs and to figure out how Christians might best respond to it. Central to this project is the consideration of a claim that is regularly made by secular historians. It is that their interpretations of Jesus, unlike interpretations that are theologically motivated, derive solely from the rational evaluation of historical evidence, without appeal to faith of any kind. I reject this claim. I think that even secular historians are committed to a kind of faith, similar in important respects to religious faith. In my view, the clash between historical scholarship and religious belief is not merely a clash between reason and faith but also one between secular and religious faiths. As we shall see, this dimension of the conflict makes a huge difference in how Christians might respond to the challenge to their beliefs posed by secular scholarship.

In my view, Christians have just three possible responses to the challenge to their beliefs posed by secular scholarship. In the last three chapters, I devote a chapter each to considering these responses in turn. For the most part, I consider what is to be said on behalf of each response by examining the views of the most influential scholars who have defended the responses. But in the final chapter I also reopen the question of whether it is even possible to approach the question of who Jesus was and what he was about without allowing faith—either religious or secular—to bias one's analysis and conclusions. I argue that it is possible. In describing how, I explain what it would mean in the case of the controversy over the historical Jesus to have a genuinely open mind.

Where to begin? The first step is to try to understand the nature of the challenge posed to Christian belief by secular historical Jesus studies. As I admitted in the Preface, when it comes to recovering the history of Jesus, I am not an expert. The other side of that admission is the acknowledgment that on this question there are experts. To understand the challenge posed to Christian belief by historical scholarship, we need to understand what both conservative and liberal expert historians have said, and also why they have said it. For that, we have to survey a representative sample of the best of both sorts of scholarship. As we shall see, many of these same scholars have written not only about the history of Jesus but also about the challenge to Christian belief posed by their scholarship, as well as about how Christians might respond to that challenge. It is important to recognize that on these latter issues these historians are not experts. In simple terms, what we really need to know from historians, insofar as they can speak from their expertise to the issue, is the answer to four questions: Who was Jesus? What was his message? Why was he killed? What happened then?

Initially there may be some tendency, even among thoughtful Christians, to resist broaching the question of how they should respond to the challenge posed by historical scholarship to traditional Christian beliefs. It may seem that by asking this question they merely help to validate the importance of the challenge and that if the question is ignored, in time it will go away. For reasons I shall explain, I think it is unlikely that this challenge is going to go away. On the contrary, it is likely that over the next several decades it will intensify. If I am right that the challenge posed by historical Jesus studies is not going to go away—any more than any other challenge posed by science to religious belief has ever gone away—then how thoughtful Christians of today and of tomorrow respond or fail to respond to it may well have momentous consequences for the future of Christianity.

THE ELUSIVE MESSIAH

Part One

CHALLENGES

1

SCIENCE

God said, 'Let there be light.'
—*An author of* Genesis *(circa 700 B.C.E.)*

God said, Let Newton be! *and all was light.*
—*Alexander Pope (1688–1744)*

FROM THE FOURTH TO THE SIXTEENTH CENTURY C.E. in Europe, philosophy and science were in the service of Christianity. The view of the world to which most thinkers subscribed was a theological version of the views of the pagan philosophers Plato and Aristotle. In the sixteenth century, modern physical science made its first appearances. Then in the seventeenth century, in the monumental achievement of Isaac Newton, modern science fully arrived.

For the first time, educated Europeans began to believe—not all of them, but many—that by exercising their reason alone, without appeal to religious revelation, they could penetrate to the ultimate nature of things. Previously, in matters of belief, faith, informed by divine revelation and interpreted by philosopher-theologians, had stood almost alone as a source of authority. Henceforth, in the minds of educated people, faith would have to compete with science.

The arrival of modern physical science, and with it the transition from faith alone as a source of authority to faith together with secular

3

reason as dual sources of authority, was the most momentous intellectual change in the history of Western civilization. But the change was
not just intellectual. As the philosopher Francis Bacon (1561–1626)
perceptively observed, knowledge is power. Although the full significance of Bacon's observation would not become apparent for hundreds of years, he was right. Ultimately science spawned an awesome
technology. And importantly because it did, it became a technique for
both understanding and controlling the world, and even ourselves.
This technique then threatened, and still does threaten, to marginalize
if not eliminate every other avenue of understanding.

With science and religion each proposing their own versions of the
truth, sooner or later they were bound to contradict each other. The
first major conflict came in the sixteenth century and was centered
on astronomy. Previously Europeans had thought that Earth was the
center of the universe. This seemed to be true observationally, and
almost everyone accepted it as the way things should be. After all,
God had created the universe as a home for human beings. That was
its purpose, and so human beings *belonged* at the center. Any other
location made no sense. Yet the Polish astronomer Copernicus
(1473–1543) theorized that our local region of the universe is actually a solar system, that is, that the planets, one of which is Earth,
orbit around the Sun. But if that were true, it cast doubt on whether
human beings were at the center of the universe. Copernicus's own
view was that our sun was at rest close to the center of the universe.
Although today it is difficult to appreciate, at that time this suggestion was extremely troubling to many people. However, shortly after
the publication of Copernicus's theory, the Italian philosopher Gior-
dano Bruno (1548?–1600) made an even more troubling suggestion.

According to Bruno, the new astronomy showed not only that
Earth is not the center of the universe but also that it is meaningless
even to speak of a center. Bruno claimed that the universe, which is
centerless, projects from every point to infinity, a thought that filled
him with awe and wonder. The Church had a different reaction. In
1592 the Inquisition tried Bruno for heresy. Then, supposedly so
that he could be further questioned, he was imprisoned in Rome for
eight years. He refused to recant his theories, and Church authorities
had him burned at the stake. That took care of Bruno, but questions
lingered. The Church then vigorously intimidated into silence anyone, including Galileo, who was bold enough to claim that Earth
moved. Naturally, some continued silently to entertain subversive

thoughts. In particular, some wondered, assuming that Earth is not the center of the universe, what then could be the universe's purpose? To that question, and to all similar questions about purpose, the new science, unlike the philosophical/theological theories that it had begun to replace, gave no answer.

Toward the end of the seventeenth century, science—this time, physics—again challenged Christianity. This time the challenge was both more subtle and more profound. Isaac Newton (1642–1727), who was himself deeply religious, had shown that the movements of all inanimate objects in the universe could be understood in terms of three laws of motion and a law of universal gravitation. The last thing Newton wanted was for his theory to challenge Christianity. But, in the minds of many, it did just that. Previously, among many educated people, it had been considered common knowledge that God's constant intervention was needed to keep the natural world going. Without intending to do so, Newton had shown that Nature, without God's intervention, could work quite well on its own. His theories had the effect of marginalizing God in His role as director of the universe. God was still needed, almost everyone assumed, to get the universe going in the first place, and perhaps also to create human beings and each of the separate species of animals; but once the universe was up and running and each of these elements was in place, God was unnecessary.

This minimalization of God's role as director of the universe was reinforced by a closely related philosophical development. John Locke (1632–1704), who, like Newton, was a devout Christian, proposed a new theory about how knowledge is acquired. (Such theories are called *epistemologies,* from the Greek words *episteme,* which means *knowledge,* and *logos,* which means *theory.*) According to Locke's epistemology, which he proposed in response to the emergence of modern physical science, knowledge about the world is acquired *only* on the basis of empirical (sensory) evidence, especially from vision and touch. Although Locke himself did not draw the conclusion that faith and creeds are therefore not sources of knowledge (in fact, he seems to have believed that they were), others soon did. By the mid–eighteenth century, this more consistent version of Locke's empiricist epistemology had become widely accepted. Eventually it became a centerpiece of the Enlightenment.

Once again, the moral was clear. Henceforth, in the minds of many educated people, any believable view about how things are would have to be supported by empirical evidence. And since new evidence could always overturn old theories, all views could at best merely be probable and, hence, provisional. No longer could one ever be sure that one had arrived at the final truth. One always had to be prepared, in the light of new evidence, to change one's views. But what, then, of insights from religious revelation into the nature of things? What of the total commitment required by faith? In the eighteenth century, leading European intellectuals, almost all of whom remained Christians, pondered these questions, often with uneasy minds. To many, it was as if they had been dragged to the edge of a cliff and forced to peer over into an abyss. What they saw frightened them.

In Europe, prior to these scientific challenges to religious belief, the only intellectual competition that Christianity had faced had come from other religions. But unless one or another of these had been imposed militarily—which, in the fifteenth century, Islam almost was—they were no real threat. With the appearance of modern physical science, suddenly there was a new competitor for the minds of educated people. Christianity now had a worthy opponent, one that, unlike Islam, had been homegrown. Like a dangerous virus, the new ideal of secular rationality—essentially Locke's empiricist epistemology—quickly penetrated to the core of the Western psyche. But for Christianity the worst was yet to come. It came in the mid-nineteenth century, when science unveiled its next major challenge.

Charles Darwin's (1809–1882) theory of evolution rocked the minds of educated Christians. Not only did it blur the line between human beings and "brutes," but also, more insidiously, it gave powerful support to the view that human beings appeared on Earth as a consequence not of intelligent planning, but rather of unthinking material causes, operating blindly, with no prevision of their results. If this new idea were accepted, God would be deprived of yet another of His traditional chores, that of creating intelligent life on Earth and each of the separate species of animals, and hence would be marginalized even further in His role as director of the universe. As it turned out, this is exactly what happened.

By the dawn of the twentieth century, scientific challenges to Christianity had provided the basic framework for a secular alternative not only to Christianity but also to religious belief altogether. To many educated people it seemed that science had shown that, for all we know, the physical universe may have existed forever and that without God's help it can run perfectly well on its own. It also seemed that science had shown that human beings are not nearly as special as most people—and all Christians—had previously supposed. These were heavy lessons for Western society. It seemed to many that religion was on the way out—that it was only a matter of time.

In 1902 Bertrand Russell (1872–1970) published an essay entitled "A Free Man's Worship." For many educated people Russell's essay captured the spirit of the times. It was—and still is—widely read. In it, Russell wrote:

> Such, in outline, but even more purposeless, more void of meaning, is the world which Science presents for our belief. Amid such a world, if anywhere, our ideals henceforward must find a home. That Man is the product of causes which had no prevision of the end they were achieving; that his origin, his growth, his hopes and fears, his loves and his beliefs, are but the outcome of accidental collocations of atoms; that no fire, no heroism, no intensity of thought and feeling, can preserve an individual life beyond the grave; that all the labours of the ages, all the devotion, all the inspiration, all the noonday brightness of human genius, are destined to extinction in the vast death of the solar system, and that the whole temple of Man's achievement must inevitably be buried beneath the debris of a universe in ruins—all these things, if not quite beyond dispute, are yet so nearly certain, that no philosophy which rejects them can hope to stand. Only within the scaffolding of these truths, only on the firm foundation of unyielding despair can the soul's habitation henceforth be safely built.[1]

In short, it seemed to Russell, and subsequently also to a host of antireligious intellectuals, that religion could not long withstand the assaults of science.

Ironically, in the twentieth century, even many Christian intellectuals added their voices to this chorus. The influential Lutheran theologian Rudolf Bultmann (1884–1976) is a case in point. Strongly influenced by the philosopher Martin Heidegger (1889–1976), Bultmann argued that the Bible, and especially the New Testament Gospels, need to be "demythologized." That is, he argued that to be believable, the Bible has to be purged of those mythological elements in it that, as relics of prescientific worldviews, have no relevance to contemporary concerns except as a window that opens onto primitive beliefs. In an influential paper published in the 1940s, Bultmann wrote, "It is impossible to use electric light and the wireless and to avail ourselves of modern medical and surgical discoveries, and at the same time to believe in the New Testament world [of] miracles."[2] This idea maintains a strong currency among educated Christians. For instance, John Spong, currently Episcopal bishop of Newark and the author of several best-selling books, has written recently that "unless theological truth can be separated from pre-scientific understandings and rethought in ways consistent with our [current, scientific] understanding of reality, the Christian faith will be reduced to one more ancient mythology that will take its place alongside the religions of Mount Olympus."[3]

In sum, to many intellectuals, including many Christian intellectuals, the long, lingering war of attrition between science and traditional Christianity had drawn to a close, with science emerging decisively as the victor. To Russell and many others, it seemed that religion was destined to fade away. Yet it has not worked out that way. And things do not even seem to be moving in that direction.

Christian religious belief has not only survived, it has flourished. In a Gallup survey published in 1989, Americans were asked whether they thought that "even today, miracles are performed by the power of God." Eighty-two percent replied yes, and only 6 percent said they completely disagreed.[4] Even among intellectuals religious belief seems to be gathering steam. Twenty years ago in the United States it was hard to find more than a few well-known, highly respected secular academic philosophers who would admit to being religious, let alone Christian. Today it is easy. They have gone public, and they are everywhere.[5] In the West, for the last several hundred years, academic philosophy often has been ahead of the cultural wave, a kind of harbinger of things to come. If in this case it is, then in secular universities and also in the larger culture of university-educated people, religion in general, and Christianity in particular, are on the way back.[6]

To some this is a puzzling development. Why has the challenge to Christianity from science been so ineffective? Part of the reason, it seems, is that until recently science had challenged only the periphery of traditional Christian religious beliefs. Whatever initial discomfort these challenges may have caused, Christians thinkers have been able to accommodate. In fact, in our own times, so comfortably have they been able to accommodate that many scientific discoveries that formerly were viewed as serious challenges to Christianity now seem merely quaint. Galileo, for instance, upset religious authorities by claiming to have seen through a telescope that there are mountains on the moon. Theologians of the time had reasoned that if there were mountains on the moon, the moon would be imperfect, and God would not have created an imperfect moon. Instead God would have created—and, hence, did create—a flawless moon: a perfect crystalline sphere. From our perspective, the theologians may as well have said that the moon is made of green cheese.

Other scientific challenges, such as the displacement of human beings from the center of the universe, were more severe. Yet, early in Christianity's struggle with science, Christian thinkers hit upon a two-stage response to scientific challenges to their religious dogmas. First, deny the truth of what the scientists have asserted; then, when that ceases to be convincing, reinterpret Christian belief so as to make room for the new scientific truth. For instance, whereas initially Christian theologians resisted Darwinian evolutionary theory, today most accept it with the proviso that God created the mechanisms of evolution. Such strategies of accommodation have been remarkably successful. In retrospect, however, it would seem that part of the reason they have been so successful is that traditionally science has left Christianity with plenty of room for accommodation.

What if science, in its search for truth, arrived at results that conflict not only with peripheral but also with central Christian beliefs? Among these are two fundamental beliefs about what happened historically: that God, in the person of Jesus of Nazareth, intervened directly in human history in order to atone for human sin (the doctrine of the Incarnation); and that the account of Jesus' words and actions in the New Testament more or less accurately tells the story both of God's main intervention in human history and of His message to human beings. If scientific findings were to conflict with either of these two central beliefs, there would, it seems, be little room for accommodation.

Christians could always respond, as Bultmann had, by withdrawing their belief in the literal truth of their core beliefs and espousing a "demythologized" version of their faith. That is, they could respond by giving up their conviction that the account of Jesus in the New Testament is reliable and simply admitting that it is myth. After all, New Testament stories, even if not literally true, might still be "spiritually true." Many sophisticated adherents of other religions—Hindus and Buddhists, for instance—have successfully adopted this attitude toward the stories in their own religious scriptures, so why not also Christians?

The short answer is that Christians cannot easily take this path because Christianity is different. The core religious beliefs of Hindus and Buddhists, for instance, are claims not about history but about the ultimate nature of things. The core religious beliefs of Taoists and Confucianists are claims not about history but about how to live. In short, historical beliefs are not central to major Asian religious traditions. They are central to Christianity, however. Traditionally Christians have believed that God so loved human beings that He assumed a human form and entered into human history and, in His human form, suffered and died on a cross to atone for human sin. If the historical stories that sustain these beliefs are not true, then it would seem that Christianity is, at best, merely a generator of pious myths and, at worst, a fraud. Of course, historical beliefs have also been central to Judaism, but Jews have ethnic ties and a poignant, shared, this-worldly history to undergird their identity as Jews. Historical criticism of Islamic religious beliefs, which is just beginning in earnest, has until recently been muted, since it can be so personally dangerous to be a critic of Islam. Historical criticism of traditional Christian beliefs, on the other hand, is not only permitted, but strongly encouraged by entrenched Western institutions, such as the university system.

The only way most Christians claim to know that God suffered and died on a cross in order to atone for human sin is through the stories in the New Testament. Suppose, for the sake of argument, that Christians were to admit that the New Testament accounts of Jesus that relate these events are just pious stories written by superstitious men. Then, except for their feeling more comfortable with their own religious imagery, Christians would have no particular reason to remain Christians, rather than to join some other religion or to become irreligious. As a consequence, Bultmann's response, which was popular initially among Christian intellectuals, has not worn well. A "demythologized" version of Christianity has always been too thin for the vast majority of ordinary Christians. Increasingly, there are signs that it is too thin even for many Christian intellectuals.[7] And, as we shall see, Bultmann's account of Christ's message does not sit well with recent developments in historical Jesus studies.

It would seem, then, that if scientific findings were to conflict directly with Christianity's core historical beliefs, there may be little room for accommodation. In that case, the fate of Christianity, at least among educated Christians, might hinge solely on its ability to resist the challenge. Yet, in the past, Christian resistance to scientific challenges has worked only temporarily, giving theologians time to figure out how best to accommodate. Educated Christians have never been able to resist science in the long run. Could they successfully resist science now, not just as a temporary strategy, but as their final response?

We may find out. Today there is a new scientific challenge to Christianity. This time the challenge comes from historical studies, and as we enter a new millennium, it appears to be gathering momentum. Unlike previous scientific challenges, it takes direct aim at Christianity's core historical beliefs and denies their truth. In this respect, this one is more menacing to Christians than previous scientific challenges. And unlike previous challenges to Christianity from historical studies, this new challenge is supported by much better scholarship and is being attractively disseminated to the general public.

Yet, in two important respects, even this new challenge from historical studies is less menacing than the old challenges from science. First, the scientific credentials of historians are more debatable than those of physical scientists. And second, historians have not been able to agree among themselves on a story about Jesus to replace the one presented in the New Testament. Hence, unlike in the case of previous scientific challenges, in which scientists who are acknowledged to be highly competent have agreed on something that Christianity has denied, the challenge from historical studies is more ambiguous. Even so, as we shall see, the academic credentials of those historians whose work is fueling the current challenge to Christianity are impressive. And they agree well enough on important aspects of their collective challenge to Christianity to make many educated Christians uncomfortable.

2

HISTORY

THE CHALLENGE TO CHRISTIANITY posed by contemporary historical Jesus studies has two parts. One is that on the basis of historical evidence alone, ordinary people can know little about what Jesus said and did, and even less about what he meant by what he said and did. This part of the challenge can be summed up in one word: *skepticism*. The remainder of the challenge is that much of what ordinary people can know conflicts with what many Christians have been taught to believe. I shall call this part of the challenge *revisionism*.

How deeply does the skepticism cut? In my view, it cuts pretty deeply. Take, for instance, the question of whether we can know what Jesus was like as a person. Many Christians assume that we do know. But if we base our beliefs about Jesus on historical evidence alone, there are reasons for being doubtful. First, virtually all secular historians would agree that we do not know enough about Jesus before he began his public career to construct even a sketchy biography of his life.[1] We do not know what his family life was like, what sort of education, if any, he received, how while growing up he responded to various events, even what languages he spoke.[2] There are no accounts, written by him, of his private thoughts, such as a diary or letters to a close friend or relative. There are not even any accounts written by people who knew him. And even after Jesus went public, our knowledge about what he was like as a person is quite slender. As we shall see, historians agree that many of the words attributed to Jesus in the New Testament are not actually his words but rather the invention of the Gospel writers or later scribal additions to the text. They also agree that often these words do not even express views that Jesus held. But they disagree with one another about *which* of Jesus' alleged sayings are authentic, many doubting that the question will ever be resolved to the satisfaction of most scholars.[3] And in most of those cases in which historians think they do know what Jesus said, they still know next to nothing about the specific context in which he said it, and so often can do little more than hazard a guess about what he may have meant.

Historians also agree that much of what the New Testament reports Jesus to have done he never really did, and much of what is reported to have happened to him never really happened. That is, they agree that the authors of the New Testament Gospels not only rearranged but also revised material they inherited from earlier sources, and even made things up.[4] Of course, New Testament scholars who espouse these views may be mistaken. But even if these views are mistaken, the fact that they are so widely held should, I think, give one pause. If our goal is to determine on the basis of historical evidence alone who Jesus was and what he was about, apparently it is not going to be easy.

The Problem for New Testament Scholars

Why do we seem to know so little on the basis of historical evidence alone about Jesus? There are several reasons:

- The evidence is meager. There are few sources of information about Jesus, primarily just the four New Testament Gospels and the letters of Paul.[5]
- We do not have original copies of the most important literary evidence. The oldest surviving copies of the four New Testament Gospels date from about 200–210 C.E., no two of them are identical, and they are all in Greek, which may not have been the language in which Jesus taught or in which some of the Gospels were originally written.[6]
- We may not have reports about Jesus written by eyewitnesses. Although Jesus died about 33 C.E., the earliest New Testament Gospel, which most scholars believe is Mark, was probably not written before 50 C.E. and may have been written as late as 70; the latest, that of John, probably was written around 90 C.E. and may have been written as late as 120.

- We do not know who the authors were of any of the New Testament Gospels, which were untitled until the second half of the second century. In the midst of a heated controversy among different groups of Christians about which Gospels were authentic, names suddenly appeared on the Gospels.[7] Many scholars believe that these names were assigned to the Gospels not because anybody actually knew who wrote them, but simply to bolster the case that the Gospels named were authentic (some historians even suspect that the Gospel of Mark may have been written by a woman).[8]

- We know almost nothing about the history of the New Testament Gospels from the time of their creation to the production of our oldest surviving copies of them. That means that there is a gap of about 175 years between Jesus' saying and doing whatever it was he said and did, and the production of the first surviving copies of the New Testament Gospels. To get a feeling for what such a gap might mean, simply imagine how much confusion there might have been about the original Declaration of Independence if the oldest copies of it that we possess were produced in 1950 and we did not know, for the period from 1776 to 1950, how many copies of the document were made, or by whom, or under what conditions, or with what motivations, and so on.[9]

- The New Testament Gospels were not written independently of one another and thus do not provide independent corroboration of the events they jointly depict. Scholars agree that many parts of the Gospels that were written second and third—presumably Matthew and Luke—were copied verbatim from the earliest New Testament Gospel—presumably Mark. They believe that other parts of Matthew and Luke were copied from a document or recorded from a well-defined oral tradition, which historians have named Q.

- The problem of working out the relations of literary dependence among the Gospels of Mark, Matthew, and Luke (scholars agree that John was written later) is notoriously problematic. For most of the twentieth century, a majority of New Testament scholars have agreed that the solution to this problem, which is known as the *Synoptic Problem,* is what is called *the Two-Document Theory* or, sometimes, *the*

Two-Source Theory (which is explained later). Yet scholars are divided as to which version of this theory to accept, and a significant minority of New Testament scholars subscribe to entirely different solutions to the problem.

- The literary evidence is ambiguous. Almost all historians think that there are important disagreements among the four New Testament Gospels that are due not to anybody's inability to remember, but to the fact that each of the authors of the Gospels is interpreting from the point of view of his own theology.[10] John P. Meier, who has a relatively optimistic view of the reliability of the four New Testament Gospels, nevertheless concedes that they "aim first of all at proclaiming and strengthening faith in Jesus as Son of God, Lord, and Messiah" and that "their presentation from start to finish is formed by their faith that the crucified Jesus was raised from the dead and will come in glory to judge the world." Meier says that "we know next to nothing" about the true historical sequence of the events that are related in the New Testament. Rather, each author has rearranged the material "to suit his own theological vision." And, Meier says, "to compound the confusion, in the Fourth Gospel John largely goes his own way, concentrating Jesus' ministry not in Galilee, like the Synoptics, but rather in Judea and Jerusalem."[11]

- There is important potential evidence the relevance of which is under dispute. For instance, some, but not all, scholars believe that at least one of the Gnostic Gospels, the Gospel of Thomas, is based in part on sources as old as or perhaps even older than those on which the earliest New Testament Gospel—presumably Mark—is based. Thomas contains 114 sayings and parables that are ascribed to Jesus, 65 of which are unique to it, including sayings that some think are crucial to determining Jesus' views. For instance, in response to the disciples' asking, "When will the kingdom of God arrive?" Jesus answered, "It will not come by watching for it. It will not be said, 'Look, here!' or 'Look there!' Rather, the kingdom of God is spread out upon the earth, and people don't see it." Some scholars believe that this saying is evidence that in Jesus' view the kingdom of God was already present, rather than something that would happen in the future, perhaps at the end of the world.

- Gnostic texts portray Jesus rather differently than do the New Testament Gospels. In Chapter 4, in my summary of Meier's views, I review the problem of assigning a date of origin to the most plausibly authentic sayings of Jesus in the Gospel of Thomas. As we shall see, whether any of these sayings are actually authentic—that is, whether Jesus really said them or something fairly close to them—is a difficult question, about which reasonable, highly competent scholars disagree. Yet how one decides this question can make a huge difference. For instance, if one decides that the oldest sayings from Thomas are likely to be authentic, it is much easier to argue plausibly that Jesus was primarily a this-worldly social and political reformer, rather than an other-worldly apocalyptic prophet.

The Case for Copying

In the eighteenth century G. E. Lessing (1729–1781) and J. G. von Herder (1744–1803), among others, argued that there had been extensive copying among the authors of the Gospels of Matthew, Mark, and Luke. The basis for their argument was a careful textual comparison of these Gospels, which they conducted by printing them side by side, in columns. It was immediately apparent that three of the Gospels—Mark, Matthew, and Luke—are very similar. These then became known as "the Synoptics," which literally means *seen together*. Subsequently virtually all secular New Testament scholars have concurred that it is too hard to explain the great many verbatim similarities among the New Testament Gospels of Matthew, Mark, and Luke on the supposition that they were written independently. In addition to these three-way agreements, Matthew and Mark have many words in common that are not in Luke, but Matthew and Luke have only a few words in common that are not in Mark. Conceivably, a well-defined, oral tradition transmitted by schools of professional or semiprofessional memorizers might account for agreements in the Synoptic Gospels. But virtually all secular scholars believe that extensive, direct copying is, by far, the more plausible explanation.[12] If we had three independent accounts of the same events and the accounts agreed with one another, that would be strong evidence that the events as reported actually took place; but if we have only one such account, that is much less evidence. The case for copying weakens the historical credibility of all of the Gospels.

What about the Gospel of John? It is radically different in style and content from the other three Gospels, in ways that have left virtually all scholars convinced that it was written much later.[13] In the Synoptic Gospels, Jesus often teaches in short epigrams (or proverbs); for instance, in Mark 4.25 Jesus says, "For to him who has, will more be given; and from him who has not, even what he has will be taken away."[14] In the Synoptics, Jesus also teaches in parables, such as the stories of the Good Samaritan, the Prodigal Son, and the Sower and his Seed.[15] In John, on the other hand, Jesus' teaching style is different. Gone are most of the short, pithy epigrams and parables, and in their place are long, abstract discourses. For instance:

> Jesus answered them, "Do not murmur among yourselves. No one can come to me unless the Father who sent me draws him; and I will raise him up at the last day. It is written in the prophets, 'And they shall all be taught by God.' Everyone who has heard and learned from the Father comes to me. Not that any one has seen the Father except him who is from God; he has seen the Father. Truly, truly, I say to you, he who believes has eternal life. I am the bread of life. Your fathers ate the manna in the wilderness, and they died. This is the bread which comes down from heaven, that a man may eat of it and not die. I am the living bread which came down from heaven; if any one eats of this bread, he will live for ever; and the bread which I shall give for the life of the world is my flesh (John 6.43–51).

And again:

> I am the true vine, and my Father is the vinedresser. Every branch of mine that bears no fruit, he takes away, and every branch that does bear fruit he prunes, that it may bear more fruit. You are already made clean by the word which I have spoken to you. Abide in me, and I in you (John 15.1–4).

And so on. While some of the ideas in these passages parallel those in the Synoptics, it is obvious that in John the ideas are developed much more abstractly.

Between the Synoptics and John there are also dramatic differences in content. In the Synoptics, Jesus talks a lot about the kingdom of God and hardly at all about himself. In John, Jesus talks a lot about himself and hardly at all about the kingdom of God. For instance, Jesus uses the word "kingdom" 18 times in Mark, 47 times in Matthew, 37 times in Luke, and 5 times in John; he uses the word "I" 9 times in Mark, 17 times in Matthew, 10 times in Luke, and 118 times in John. And the differences are not just statistical. When Jesus uses the word "I" in the Synoptics, almost all of his self-references are of a conventional kind. In John, by contrast, Jesus regularly makes staggering statements about himself, such as "I am the bread of life" (6.35), "I am the light of the world" (8.12), "I am the way, and the truth and the life" (14.6), and "Before Abraham was, I am" (8.58). There are possible ways to explain these and other differences that would preserve for John an early date of origin. However, most scholars agree that all of these explanations are farfetched. They have concluded that John, who claims to have been an eyewitness to the events he describes, wrote much later than Matthew and Luke and elaborated for theological reasons what he believed Jesus to have said. In other words, John used Jesus as the spokesman for John's own interpretation of who Jesus was.

The Synoptic Problem

There are many patterns of agreement and disagreement in the Synoptic Gospels, all of which need to be explained. The chief ones are these:

- Most of the subject matter of Mark—about 90 percent—is also in Matthew.
- Much of the subject matter of Mark—about 50 percent—is also in Luke.
- Very little of the subject matter of Mark is not also in either Matthew or Luke.
- Matthew and Luke contain much subject matter that is not in Mark.
- Subject matter that is in all three Gospels usually occurs in the same order.

- When common subject matter is ordered differently in Matthew than in Mark, Luke's order tends to agree with the order in Mark.
- When common subject matter is ordered differently in Luke than in Mark, Matthew's order tends to agree with the order in Mark.
- Matthew and Luke, in the subject matter they share with Mark, but only in that subject matter, are often similar in wording.
- Frequently Mark and Matthew share the same wording while Luke diverges, or Mark and Luke share the same wording while Matthew diverges.

In short, the agreements and disagreements that most need to be explained are of *subject matter* (the first four listed), of the *order* in which subject matter is presented (the next three), and of *wording* (the final two). Virtually all New Testament scholars believe that these agreements and disagreements are not coincidental, but rather are explicable only if there has been extensive copying among the authors of these three Gospels. The *Synoptic Problem* is the problem of figuring out who copied from whom (or what), and what they copied.[16]

From the late eighteenth to the late nineteenth century, theologians and historians proposed hundreds of solutions to the Synoptic Problem. So numerous and varied were the proposed solutions that it seemed for a while as if scholarly chaos might prevail. But by the end of the nineteenth century, the debate had become more focused. Then, over the next two or three decades, opinion gradually converged on a single solution: the *Two-Document Theory*. Some scholars question whether one of the two sources in question was literally a document (as opposed to an oral tradition). In order to leave this question open, today this hypothesis is often called the *Two-Source Theory*.

In *The Four Gospels* (1924), B. H. Streeter presented the classic formulation of the Two-Document Theory.[17] In his account, the authors of Matthew and Luke used a written version of Mark virtually identical with our own, from which they drew much of the subject matter for their own Gospels; and they also used a common source, which historians have named *Q* (from *Quelle*, in German, which

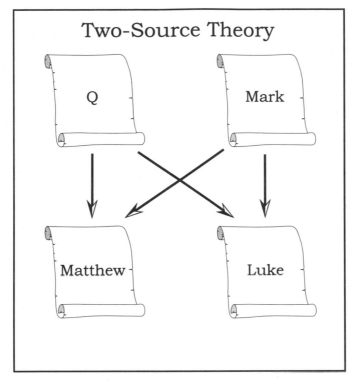

FIGURE 2.1 *The Two-Source Theory. The Two-Source Theory is the view the Matthew and Luke, in composing their Gospels, made use of two (probably) written sources—Mark and the Sayings Gospel Q.*

means *source*), from which they drew most of the additional material they included in their Gospels (Figure 2.1).

The *Mystery of the Double Tradition* is the problem of explaining the close parallels in Matthew and Luke that have no counterpart in Mark. It would seem that either the author of Matthew copied from Luke, or the author of Luke copied from Matthew, or both copied from a third source: Q. Most historians believe that neither of the authors of Matthew or Luke copied from the other, since the agreements between Matthew and Luke begin where Mark begins and end where Mark ends. For instance, although Mark begins with John the Baptist and Matthew and Luke each begin with birth narratives, their birth narratives differ. Matthew and Luke begin to agree with each other when they begin to agree with Mark. Mark ends with the women fleeing from the empty tomb. Matthew and Luke continue beyond that point to give resurrection accounts, but their resurrection accounts also differ.

Though it is rarely suggested that Matthew copied from Luke, some scholars argue that Luke copied from Matthew. However, it counts heavily against the idea that either copied from the other that when all three of Matthew, Mark, and Luke have material in common, Matthew and Luke never agree with each other against Mark. Had either the author of Matthew copied from Luke or the author of Luke copied from Matthew, then it seems that Matthew or Luke at least sometimes would have agreed with the other against Mark, either in wording or in inserting the same new material in the same place. This never happens. In addition, in the non-Markan material that Matthew and Luke have in common, there is quite a bit of verbal agreement but no agreement in the order in which material is presented. Most scholars believe that if either the author of Matthew or the author of Luke had copied from the other, then it is likely that there would have been some agreement in the order in which material is presented.[18]

Quite a few scholars subscribe to a more complicated "Four-Source" elaboration of the Two-Source Theory (Figure 2.2). According to this view, the authors of Matthew and Luke, in addition to drawing material from Mark and Q, also drew material from their own special sources, M and L, respectively. There are many variations of this four-source theme, to which one or another scholar subscribes. Some of these variations are amazingly complex (Figure 2.3).[19]

It is often said that among New Testament scholars there is a near consensus on the Two-Source Theory. But there are a great many variations on that theory that scholars take seriously. According to some experts, most New Testament scholars, often without admitting it openly, have rejected parts of the Two-Source Theory.[20] In addition, some scholars subscribe to different views altogether. W. R. Farmer, for instance, is a champion of the *Griesbach Hypothesis,* according to which the author of Matthew wrote first, the author of Luke wrote second and used Matthew as a source, and the author of Mark wrote third and used both Matthew and Luke as sources.[21] With this hypothesis, there is no need to suppose that there was a Q, which is appealing, since no known ancient source records anyone

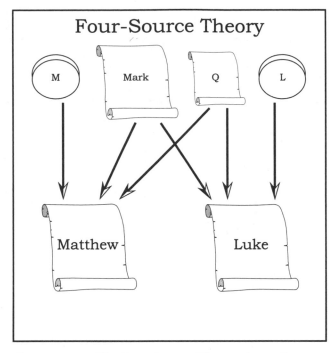

FIGURE 2.2 *The Four-Source Theory. According to the Four-Source Theory, Matthew used Mark, Q, and his own special source called M. Luke also used Mark and Q, but he had another source called L, which Matthew did not have. The material in M and L probably came from oral tradition.*

ever having seen Q.[22] Although it is difficult to know what proportion of New Testament scholars favor the Griesbach Hypothesis, some estimate that it may be as high as 10 percent.[23] If it were 10 percent, that would make it a very popular minority view.

The Problem for Students of New Testament Scholarship

These, then, are the main problems that New Testament *scholars* have to face. Dealing with them in the best way possible requires specialized knowledge and training in languages, ancient history, anthropology, the techniques of historical scholarship, and so on. Every competent New Testament scholar has received a great deal of

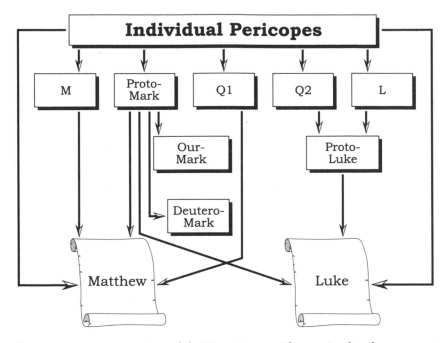

FIGURE 2.3   *A variation of the Four-Source Theory. In this diagram, "Proto-Mark" and "Proto-Luke" indicate earlier versions of Mark and Luke than the New Testament Gospels. "Deutero-Mark" indicates a later version. "Q1" and "Q2" indicate alternative versions of the Q material.*

specialized training in each of these areas. Relative to almost all of the rest of us, they know a tremendous amount about the ancient world, and they are much better qualified to assess competing hypotheses about what really happened. That is why they are the *experts,* and we are not.

Our amateur status does not mean, however, that we cannot ever pass judgment on the views of New Testament scholars. In certain cases, we may be able to see better than a historian that he or she is in the grip of a distorting theory. Even so, we must give expertise its due. In my view, when it comes to trying to decide what to believe on the basis of historical evidence alone, the distinction between experts and amateurs is crucially important. Roughly speaking, the rule for *experts* is this: Base your views directly *on the primary evidence;* although the opinions of other experts cannot be ignored, you can override their opinions by your own reading of the evidence. The rule for *amateurs,* on the other hand, is this: Base your beliefs mainly *on the views of the experts;* if a sizable majority of the experts agree among themselves, then accept what they say; if they disagree, then suspend judgment.

That something like this should be the rule for amateurs is obvious in the case of a highly technical field, such as physics. Suppose, for instance, that physicists were divided into two equal camps about some detail of the second law of thermodynamics. Technically illiterate amateurs would *not* be rationally entitled, on the basis of scientific evidence alone, to side with either group of disagreeing physicists. After all, if the physicists, with all of their expert knowledge and training, cannot decide an issue, who are we, the amateurs, to say which group of physicists is correct?

Since historical studies tend not to be as technical as the sciences, it is tempting to suppose that if we—the amateurs—apply ourselves, then in historical studies we can follow the argument as well as the experts can follow it. In my view, this supposition is a big mistake. Hence, I also think it is a big mistake to suppose that in general amateurs are qualified to arbitrate disputes among expert historians. Granted, one's vision can be blurred by standing too close; an intelligent, literate amateur, standing above the fray, may sometimes see aspects of a controversy that even experts miss. And in historical studies, unlike in the sciences, common sense and sound practical judgment constitute a kind of expertise, and one need not be a historian to have either of these. Thus, so far as the distinction between experts and amateurs is concerned, the sciences and historical studies are not completely analogous. Yet neither are they so unlike each other that in historical studies amateurs are often entitled to arbitrate disputes among experts. When in historical studies the experts disagree, then in most cases an amateur, who would form his or her opinion on the basis of historical evidence alone, is required to suspend judgment. Since in historical Jesus studies the experts often disagree, amateurs are often required to suspend judgment.

The Problem for Christian Students of New Testament Scholarship

We have seen what the main problems are for New Testament historians. We have seen the additional problem for amateur students of

New Testament scholarship. Amateur students of New Testament scholarship who also happen to be Christians have one more problem to face.

To see what this last problem is, suppose, for the sake of argument, that you are a Christian, and ask yourself the following question: If I know what Jesus said or did, in the sense that I know what words he uttered and what actions he performed, should I interpret his words and actions as those simply of a first-century Jew—which, it may seem, is the only way they can be interpreted by responsible secular scholars—or should I interpret them as those of God or of one who has been specially divinely empowered?

The first way of proceeding is to treat Jesus like any other historical figure—say, like Socrates or Galileo—and to base your interpretation of what Jesus probably meant by what he said and did on the best available historical evidence, purged of all theological presuppositions. This evidence then would consist largely of contextual considerations: what we know about first-century Israel and also about Jesus' specific circumstances. In this way of proceeding, it would seem that you could in principle determine, without invoking theology, what it is most reasonable to believe. A seeming advantage of this way of proceeding is that disputes over how Jesus' words and deeds should be interpreted could be settled, in principle, by appeal to historical evidence alone. However, from the point of view of a Christian, there is a problem with this way of proceeding: You must presuppose for the sake of the inquiry something you believe to be false. That is, you must presuppose that Jesus was neither God nor specially divinely empowered, and then interpret his remarks accordingly. But if you are a Christian, why would you want to do *that?*

The second way of proceeding is to regard Jesus as God or as specially divinely empowered. The advantage of this way, from the point of view of a Christian, is that you do not have to presuppose something you believe to be false. The problem with this way is that disputes over how Jesus' words and deeds should be interpreted cannot now be settled by appeal to historical evidence alone. In fact, in this way of proceeding it becomes unclear, in trying to settle disputes over what Jesus probably meant by what he said and did, what role, if any, there is for historical evidence.

In this second way of proceeding, in which historical evidence would have only limited relevance in determining what Jesus meant by what he said and did, one would face the task of determining what sort of relevance historical evidence has, and how much it has. How would you decide? To whatever extent historical evidence were irrelevant in determining what Jesus meant by what he said and did, then it might be largely arbitrary how you interpreted Jesus' remarks. Put differently, in this way of proceeding, the project of interpreting Jesus' remarks is not an ordinary historical project but a theological-historical one, and it is unclear what the constraints are on theological-historical interpretations. I shall return to this issue in Chapters 6 and 7.

So much for the preliminaries. The bottom line is that a new and perhaps the final major scientific challenge to Christian religious belief has arrived. It is a product of the maturation and public dissemination of the results of a recently renewed and highly professional quest for the historical Jesus. For the purposes of the present chapter, an important part of the challenge posed by historical Jesus studies can summed up in one word—*skepticism*. There is another part of the challenge, which I called *revisionism,* to which we now turn.

3

THE QUEST

IN 1906 ALBERT SCHWEITZER (1875–1965) published his *Quest of the Historical Jesus*. It became an instant classic. It not only profoundly affected New Testament scholarship but also was widely read and admired by the general public. Yet in his analysis, Schweitzer's assessment of the work of the German historian Herman Samuel Reimarus (1694–1768), whom he regarded as having originated the quest for the historical Jesus, is surprisingly naive. Schweitzer wrote that Reimarus had no "predecessors," and that his account of Jesus was "one of those supremely great works which pass and leave no trace, because they are before their time."[1] Ever since, most New Testament historians have begun their surveys of the quest for the historical Jesus with Reimarus.

But, contrary to Schweitzer's assessment, Reimarus, who was a child of the Enlightenment, was not before his time, but right on time. A host of thinkers—Spinoza, Pierre Bayle, the English Deists, and others—had paved the way for what Reimarus accomplished. Admittedly, what he did accomplish is impressive. He reconstructed the life of Jesus, more thoroughly than anyone had before, on thoroughly naturalistic assumptions. But Reimarus did not invent naturalism, or its application to historical studies, or even its application to the New Testament. Well before Reimarus put pen to paper, naturalism—roughly speaking, the idea that in principle everything can be explained scientifically—had already become the prevailing worldview of the Enlightenment.[2] So far as the study of biblical history is concerned, prior to Reimarus the focus had been on stories of miracles and prophesy fulfilled. Since these stories posed the greatest challenges to naturalism, they had to be discredited. Once they were discredited, the way was open for someone to write a naturalistic history of Jesus. This is what Reimarus was the first to do.

The Proto-Quest (1670–1750)

The Dutch rationalist philosopher Baruch (or Benedict) Spinoza (1632–1677) wrote one of the earliest Enlightenment critiques of miracles and prophesies. An excommunicated Jew, Spinoza was a champion of reason and a severe critic of what, in his view, faith had become in his own times: "a mere compound of credulity and prejudices," which "degrade man from rational being to beast" and "completely stifle" the power of his rational judgment.[3] In the interpretation of Holy Scripture, Spinoza stressed the importance of historical context. For instance, he questioned whether "the reasoning by which the Lord displayed His power to Job" really was a revelation from God, rather than the author of Job merely "rhetorically adorning his own conceptions." And he claimed that even if what it is written that God said to Job was a genuine revelation, what God said was "adapted to Job's understanding, for the purpose of convincing him" and not for "the convincing of all men."[4] Spinoza said that in interpreting Scripture the "universal rule is to accept nothing as an authoritative Scriptural statement which we do not perceive very clearly when we examine it in the light of its history." For this purpose, he said, "it is important to be acquainted with the life, the conduct, and the pursuits" of the author of the scriptural account and even, if possible, "to have intimate knowledge of his genius and temperament." In addition, he stressed that to avoid confounding "precepts which are eternal with those which served only a temporary purpose or were only meant for a few, we should know what was the occasion, the time, the age, in which each book was written, and to what nation it was addressed." Finally, we need to be sure not only that the work as a whole is "authentic" but also "that it has not been tampered with by sacrilegious hands" so that "errors can have crept in." If errors have crept in, he said, then we need to be sure that "they have been corrected by men sufficiently skilled and worthy of credence."[5]

Spinoza denied the reality of miracles, reasoning as follows: A miracle, were one to occur, would be a violation of a universal law of nature; for something to be a universal law of nature, it must be necessarily true; for something to be necessarily true, it must be "by Divine decree"—that is, it must follow "from the necessity and perfection of the Divine nature"; yet a miracle, were one to occur, would also be by Divine decree; therefore, a miracle, were one to occur, would both be by Divine decree and violate laws of nature that are also by Divine decree; hence, a miracle, were one to occur, would involve God's acting against His own nature, which would be a kind of Divine inconsistency, and it is absurd to suppose that God could or would act inconsistently.[6]

Spinoza's argument against miracles, unlike the arguments against miracles of many who would come later, was thus based not on atheism, but on theism. He argued that miracles cannot occur not because there is no God, but because there is one. His aim, however, was not primarily to make a positive contribution to theology, but to lay the foundations for a thoroughly naturalistic approach to historical studies. To do that, miracle stories had to be disposed of, and hence Spinoza tried to dispose of them not one at a time, but all at the same time. The idea that this could be done was his great contribution to the philosophical discussion of miracles. In his view, historians who employ proper methods do not *emerge from* the examination of history with the *discovery* that no miracles have occurred, but rather *bring to* the study of history the certain knowledge that none has occurred. Hence, in his view, any claims made by ancient authors that miracles have occurred should be rejected out of hand, and explained naturalistically. The important question historically, he said, is not whether a miracle story is true, but why an ancient author reported a false story. Was the ancient author deluded? Was he credulously passing on something he had read or heard? Was the miracle story his mythical way of saying something that could be understood, in different terms, naturalistically?

Pierre Bayle (1647–1706), a French philosopher and critic, is famous primarily for having written the multivolume *Dictionnaire historique et critique*.[7] Earlier Bayle had been dismissed from his position as professor of philosophy and history at the Protestant academy of Rotterdam because he was suspected of having encouraged the questioning of religious dogma. Subsequently he strongly supported an emerging movement among many intellectuals in favor of complete freedom of thought and speech in intellectual contexts. So far as scriptural interpretation itself is concerned, his greatest influence stemmed from his claim that one cannot make rational and scientific sense out of Judeo-Christian revelation. He argued, for instance, that whereas reason teaches that nothing comes from nothing, Genesis says that through God's agency the world came from nothing. By implication, he also rejected New Testament stories of miracles and prophesies fulfilled. Renowned primarily as a skeptic not only of religious beliefs but even of reason itself, he wrote, perhaps tongue in cheek, that one should escape skepticism by taking refuge in blind, irrational faith. But later thinkers saw him not as a defender of faith, but as a deist who scoffed at all historical religions.

From at least the time of Lord Edward Herbert of Cherbury (1583–1648), there was a long tradition of English Deism, which profoundly affected the quest for the historical Jesus. Deists held that whatever can be known religiously can be known only on the basis of reason. Thus they denied the validity of religious claims based on revelation or on the teachings of any church. They accepted that there is a God, but denied that God intervenes in the world, so they rejected, except as potentially instructive myths, all New Testament stories of miracles and prophesies fulfilled.

Perhaps the most notorious Deist of the time was John Toland (1670–1720), author of *Christianity Not Mysterious, Showing That There Is Nothing in the Gospel Contrary to Reason, Nor Above It; And That No Christian Doctrine Can Properly Be Call'd a Mystery* (1696). He argued that the deliverances of faith, including interpretations of Scripture that are inspired by faith, are not worthy of being believed unless they are confirmed by reason.[8] For his trouble, he was condemned by the Irish Parliament, who ordered that his book be burned and that he be arrested.[9]

Anthony Collins (1676–1729), a friend and disciple of John Locke, was strongly influenced by Toland. In two books Collins denied messianic claims on behalf of Jesus that were reported in the New Testament. He said that all such claims were based exclusively on prophesies fulfilled, and that New Testament authors simply invented the idea, and the evidence to support the idea, that Jesus' life fulfilled prophesies. But, said Collins, in doing this they were merely following a time-honored and highly respected rabbinical practice and hence were not doing anything improper. Even so, he concluded, their claims of prophetic fulfillment are false.[10]

In addition to Toland and Collins, there were other English Deists whose work had been translated into French and German and had been widely discussed in Germany in the half century preceding Reimarus's work. In 1720–1721 Reimarus actually studied in both Holland and England and thus could even have encountered the ideas of these thinkers at their source.[11] And about the time Reimarus was composing his history, the Scottish philosopher and historian David Hume (1711–1776) was arguing against miracles, not on theistic grounds, as had Spinoza, but on the basis of an assessment of what would have to obtain *evidentially* for anyone to be rationally entitled to conclude that a miracle had occurred.[12]

As a philosopher, Hume is renowned primarily for developing the empirical philosophies of John Locke and George Berkeley to their logical, skeptical conclusions. As a historian, he is renowned for writing a famous history of England. So far as his thoughts on miracles are concerned, he conceded that a miracle might occur, but he denied that anyone could ever have good reason to believe that one had occurred. For someone to have good reason to believe that a miracle had occurred, Hume argued, he would have to know that the law of nature that the so-called miraculous event supposedly violated really was a law of nature; and to know that, he would have to have a great deal of evidence that nature, without exception, works contrary to the supposed miracle. But all of his evidence that nature works contrary to the supposed miracle would then count against there having been a miraculous exception to the law of nature.

In short, Hume said that in considering whether there is evidence sufficient to believe in a miracle, one has to consider all of the relevant evidence, and that if one does, there are only three possible outcomes:

- The evidence that the alleged law of nature that was supposedly violated really is a law of nature outweighs the evidence that the alleged miraculous event actually occurred, in which case, Hume said, the claim that the miraculous event occurred is inadequately supported by evidence and should be abandoned.
- The evidence that the alleged miraculous event actually occurred outweighs the evidence that the alleged law that was supposedly violated really is a law, in which case the claim that the alleged miraculous event was really miraculous is inadequately supported by evidence and should be abandoned.

- The evidence that the alleged miraculous event actually occurred and the evidence that the alleged law that its occurrence supposedly violated really is a law are equally weighty, in which case one should suspend judgment about whether the alleged miraculous event both occurred and really was miraculous.

In none of these outcomes, Hume argued, is one entitled on the basis of evidence to conclude that a genuine miracle has occurred.

Hume's argument has been enormously influential, so it is worth pausing briefly to illustrate what he had in mind. Imagine, for instance, that someone reports that through prayer and faith she has been cured of a supposedly incurable disease, say, an advanced cancer of some sort. Initially, a Humean might be skeptical that the report is true, that is, that the alleged faith-healing actually occurred. However, were the evidence very strong that it did occur, then the Humean would deny that we know that the supposed laws of nature that allegedly were violated by the faith-healing actually are genuine laws of nature. In other words, he would admit that the unusual event—the faith-healing—occurred, but deny that its occurring is evidence of God's intervention in the natural world. Rather, he might argue, its occurring is merely evidence of the extraordinary power of mind over matter, a natural phenomenon that someday may be scientifically understood. What the Humean would never admit is that we have adequate evidence that a law of nature has actually been violated.

Hume thus claimed that on the basis of evidence alone, we are never entitled to conclude that a genuine miracle has occurred, and that we can know this in advance of even examining the evidence for an alleged miracle. It follows from Hume's argument, then (as it had also from Spinoza's), that no one needs to examine the historical evidence for some miracle story in order to determine whether the story is worthy of being believed. On the assumption that genuine prophesies, were they to occur, would be miracles, Hume's argument is also an argument against the validity of prophesies. To this day, there are philosophers and historians who staunchly defend Hume's argument.[13]

In sum, before the middle of the eighteenth century, it was widely believed by secular intellectuals that there is insufficient evidence both that Jesus performed miracles and that events in Jesus' life fulfilled prophesies in the Hebrew Scriptures. An important assumption that remained to be questioned was that the New Testament Gospels present mutually corroborative eyewitness accounts of the same events. Soon this assumption too was rejected. As we have seen, all but conclusive evidence was discovered that the New Testament Gospels were not written independently of one another and, hence, could not corroborate each other. This evidence also tended to count against the claim that any of the New Testament Gospels were written by an eyewitness.

The First Quest:
From Reimarus (1788) to Schweitzer (1906)

From 1774 to 1778, G. E. Lessing published a series of supposedly anonymous "fragments" of a text that he said had been found in the Wolfenbuttel Library in Hamburg, Germany. The text from which the excerpts were selected had been written by Reimarus, who had decided not to publish, for fear of the consequences for him and his family. However, when he died, his daughter gave the text to Lessing to publish as he saw fit.[14]

In the seventh and final fragment that Lessing published, which is entitled *The Intention of Jesus and His Disciples* (1788), Reimarus distinguished sharply between Jesus as he actually was and as he had been portrayed in the New Testament.[15] Reimarus claimed that actually Jesus had been a teacher of rational, practical religion, who may have thought of himself as a political messiah, but did not think of himself as divine; rather, he was a faithful Jew, who intended that his followers should also remain Jews. According to Reimarus, Jesus' message was about the coming of the kingdom of God and the ensuing liberation from Rome. There were no "mysteries" in his teaching. But since Jesus left no written record of his own, he was at the mercy of those who did, and it was his misfortune that those who wrote about him were motivated primarily by financial gain to distort his message almost beyond recognition. Their coup de grâce was the story of the resurrection, which they simply invented. What actually happened, Reimarus claimed, is that within twenty-four hours of Jesus' burial, his disciples stole his body from the tomb. Several weeks later, they proclaimed him as the resurrected Lord. And then, later still, they invented the idea that Jesus is the Savior of the world and will imminently return.[16]

Reimarus thus is rightly credited as the first to express a theme that has always been a centerpiece of New Testament criticism, namely, that the authors of the New Testament, for reasons of their own, created a Christ of faith where before there had been only a Jesus of history. In other words, Reimarus claimed that the authors of the New Testament, rather than writing a historical account, had written a theological interpretation. The cornerstone of this interpretation is that Jesus was both the hoped-for Messiah and also the Son of God. In Reimarus's view, the New Testament authors presented their accounts in "intentional, deliberate fabrication," as if they were straight history.[17]

Reimarus had a surprisingly modern view of Jesus' eschatological convictions. He tried to locate Jesus squarely in what he took to be the Jewish context out of which Jesus came. In Reimarus's view, this meant that Jesus looked forward not to a spiritual or apocalyptic intervention but to a thoroughly temporal and political one. In other words, Jesus looked forward not to the end of the world but to the defeat, with God's help, of the Romans by the Jews. Although subsequently Schweitzer, and then a whole generation of twentieth-century New Testament scholars, rejected Reimarus's understanding of first-century Jewish eschatology, it is widely accepted today.

After Reimarus's work was published, there followed a series of lives of Jesus by writers in Germany. Some of them were unwilling to abandon completely, as had Reimarus, the idea that Jesus had worked miracles and that events in his life had fulfilled prophesies. But the primary emphasis of almost all of these lives was to recover Jesus as an ethical teacher whose message had relevance to the present day.[18] One of the most comprehensive and influential accounts in this genre was K. F. Bahrdt's eleven-volume work *An Explanation of the Plans and Aims of Jesus* (1784–1792). Another was K. H. Venturini's four-volume work *A Non-supernatural History of the Great Prophet of Nazareth* (1800–1802). Bahrdt and Venturini both tried to explain away the miracle stories in the Gospel accounts. Venturini, for instance, suggested that Jesus' healings were due to his skillful use of medicine, which he carried from place to place in a "portable medicine chest"; he also claimed that Lazarus was not raised from the dead, but merely awakened from a coma, and that at the wedding at Cana, Jesus did not turn water into wine, but merely brought several extra bottles of wine as a wedding gift to the bride and groom. In the case of the resurrection, both Bahrdt and Venturini claimed that Jesus did not die when he was crucified, and hence did not rise from the dead, but was merely revived in his tomb. In the same vein, H.E.G. Paulus, in his two-volume work *The Life of Jesus As the Basis of a Purely Historical Account of Early Christianity* (1828), echoed the earlier explanations of Jesus' healings in terms of his unusual knowledge of folk medicine. Paulus explained away Jesus' alleged nature miracles. For instance, according to Paulus, Jesus did not really walk on water, but was merely walking in the shallows near the shore, and the disciples mistakenly supposed that he was in deeper water.[19]

In 1835 David Friedrich Strauss (1808–1874) published *The Life of Jesus Critically Examined.*[20] At the time, Strauss was twenty-seven years old. His book was the first influential history of Jesus and clearly the most important one published in the nineteenth century. In the first edition of the book, Strauss examined each episode in the New Testament, one by one, but devoted little time to the question of literary sources, presumably because he thought that Griesbach had already "clearly demonstrated" that "our second Gospel [Mark] cannot have originated from recollections of Peter's instructions," since "it is evidently a compilation" from "the first and third Gospels." Subsequently F. C. Baur criticized Strauss on the grounds that the work was "a critique of Gospel history without any critique of the Gospels." Hence in the second edition of his work, which was published in 1864, Strauss cited literary evidence to support his interpretation along with arguments on behalf of his literary evidence. It is largely these latter arguments that account for Strauss's extraordinary influence on the subsequent course of the quest for the historical Jesus.[21]

Strauss proposed that any narrative should be rejected as nonhistorical if it is inconsistent with itself or with other equally credible accounts, or if the events depicted in it violate known natural laws. He thus concluded that it is patently absurd to accept at face value the miracle stories in the New Testament. Others had made this point before. But Strauss also rejected as "ridiculous" the proposals made by many earlier thinkers to explain the so-called miracles naturalistically. In his view, the Gospels are so filled with incredible stories and so riddled with irresolvable contradictions that they can be explained plausibly only by supposing that their authors never intended them to be historical accounts.[22]

Strauss's alternative approach was to accept the Gospel narratives as a whole, but to regard them not as "true history" but as "sacred legend." In other words, so far as the miracle stories are concerned, he rejected the idea that the Gospel writers had mistaken for miracles events that have a natural explanation, in favor of the view that they made up the miracle stories in order to convey what they regarded as spiritual truths. He called his alternative approach "the mythical view" and claimed that once one admits that the miracle stories are myths, "the innumerable and never otherwise to be harmonized discrepancies and chronological contradictions in the gospel histories disappear, as it were, at one stroke."[23]

Like Collins before him, but unlike Reimarus, Strauss thus devised a strategy for having it both ways. In support of his view, Strauss distinguished among several kinds of primitive myths and then illustrated each kind by finding instances of it in the New Testament and other ancient literature. He tried to reconcile his interpretation with Christianity mainly by trying to understand the significance of New Testament myths about Jesus in the context of the global understanding of world history propounded by the philosopher G.W.F. Hegel. For instance, he suggested that the story of the Incarnation can be understood as a myth that foreshadows the union of God with world history that, in Hegel's view, is the goal of the historical process. There were few buyers. Strauss was fired from his job at the University of Tübingen. Later he was offered a teaching post in Zurich, but the offer was rescinded when 40,000 people signed a protest petition. He never held another teaching position.

Reimarus and Strauss thus had radically different views of the intentions of the authors of the New Testament Gospels. Reimarus assumed that they intended to be writing histories, or at least intended that their Gospels be read as histories. His explanation of why they said false things, such as that Jesus worked miracles when in fact he did not, was that they were lying. Strauss, on the other hand, rather than accusing the New Testament authors of lying, simply rejected the assumption that they intended to be writing histories. His view was that they intended to be writing "sacred myth." His explanation of why they said things that they knew were not literally true was that they were intentionally creating a mythology in order to convey a deeper spiritual truth.

Strauss eventually explicitly acknowledged that his historical work was guided by philosophical presuppositions, in particular, by his commitment to Hegel's views. In an article published later in his life, Strauss wrote, "I am no historian; with me everything has proceeded from a dogmatic (or rather anti-dogmatic) concern." His "anti-dogmatic" concern was to replace the traditional Christian view of a transcendent yet personal God with the Hegelian notion of an "impersonal but person-shaping All." Strauss said that this Hegelian notion formed the "the ultimate point of departure" of his "Cosmic conception."[24]

Throughout the latter half of the nineteenth century, the quest for the historical Jesus continued in separate streams. Several writers followed Strauss in embracing radical skepticism about the historical reliability of the New Testament accounts. In the work of Bruno Bauer (1809–1982) this skepticism reached a limit of sorts. In his *Criticism of the Gospels and History of Their Origin* (1850–1851), Bauer accepted the increasingly popular view that Mark was the earliest gospel and that others had copied from him, but then Bauer totally rejected the historical reliability of Mark's account. In Bauer's view, Mark's account was a literary creation, pure and simple. Bauer concluded that the historical Jesus probably never even existed.[25]

A few decades later, in France, E. Renan (1823–1892) wrote what was until recently one of the most popular accounts of Jesus ever written. In *The History of the Origins of Christianity* (1863) he recounted how Jesus began innocently enough as a wise and gentle teacher of ethical precepts and God's love, but then, in spite of himself, was drawn into a radicalizing and self-alienating process, the result of which was that, almost against his will, he was cast into the role of apocalyptic prophet and would-be messiah.[26] Renan discounted the miracle stories but avoided trying to explain them naturalistically. However, he attributed the story of the resurrection to "the strong imagination of Mary Magdalene."

In England, some prominent British scholars tried to write lives of Jesus not from the perspective of naturalism, but from that of Christian faith. One of the best known and most impressive contributions of this sort is F. W. Farrar's *Life of Christ* (1874).[27] Typical of Farrar's approach is his account of the wedding feast in Cana, which he began with the observation that in the East any newly wedded couple would have felt a solemn obligation to provide for their guests and would have been deeply mortified to have run out of wine. He then pointed out that Jesus may well have been responsible for the hosts' running out of wine, since the companions that Jesus brought with him had not actually been invited to the wedding: "The youthful bridegroom in Cana of Galilee [could not] have been aware that during the last four days Jesus had won the allegiance of five disciples." Farrar says that under these circumstances:

> There was a special reason why the mother of Jesus should say to Him, "They have no wine." The remark was evidently a pointed one, and its import could not be misunderstood. None knew, as Mary knew, who her Son was; yet for thirty long years of patient waiting for His manifestation, she had but seen Him grow as other children grow. He had lived in sweetness, indeed, and humility and grace of sinless wisdom, like a tender plant before God, but in all other respects as other youths have lived, preeminent only in utter stainlessness.

"But now," Farrar continues, Jesus

> was thirty years old, and the voice of the great Prophet, with whose fame the nation rang, had proclaimed Him to be the promised Christ. He was being publicly attended by disciples who acknowledged Him as Rabbi and Lord. Here was a difficulty to be met; an act of true kindness to be performed; a disgrace to be averted from friends whom He loved—and that, too, a disgrace to which His own presence and that of His disciples had unwittingly contributed. Was not His hour yet come? Who could tell what He might do, if He were only made aware of the trouble which threatened to interrupt the feast? Might not some band of hymning angels, like those who had heralded His birth, receive His bidding to change that humble marriage-feast into a scene of heaven? Might it not be that even now He would lead them into His banquet-house, and His banner over them be love?[28]

And so on. At the time of its publication, and for several decades thereafter, Farrar's account was quite popular among educated Christians. But it was swimming against the intellectual currents of the times. It had no effect on the form the quest for the historical Jesus would take thereafter.

More in keeping with progressive developments, Johannes Weiss argued in 1892 that Jesus was a preacher of apocalyptic doom who thought that the end of human history was coming to pass in his own lifetime.[29] This sort of interpretation is called *apocalyptic eschatology*. Albert Schweitzer subsequently organized his own interpretation around Weiss's claim that the core of Jesus' message was that God would very soon intervene in human history, establish the kingdom of God promised in Hebrew Scripture, and install Jesus to rule over it.[30] Schweitzer also argued that Jesus kept his messiahship a secret, revealing it only to his disciples and then commanding them to tell nobody, and that Judas betrayed this secret to the chief priests. In Schweitzer's view, Jesus expected the Son of Man to appear, was disappointed, and went to his death in order to bring down upon himself the "Messianic woes," so that his people might be delivered.

Schweitzer's *The Quest of the Historical Jesus* was so influential that until the 1970s, understanding Jesus within the framework of apocalyptic eschatology was widely regarded by scholars as an "assured result" of New Testament scholarship.[31] But apocalyptic eschatology posed an obvious theological problem. Whatever else Christians might accept *on faith* about Jesus, those Christians who accepted from *historical studies* that Jesus had a mistaken view about world history had something to explain—how Jesus could have made such a mistake.[32] Schweitzer's own solution to this problem was to retreat into mysticism, which in the context of historical Jesus studies is nowhere more eloquently expressed than in the closing paragraph of his book:

> He comes to us as One unknown, without a name, as of old, by the lake-side, He came to those men who knew Him not. He speaks to us the same word: "Follow thou me!" and sets us to the tasks which He has to fulfill for our time. He commands. And to those who obey Him, whether they be wise or simple, He will reveal Himself in the toils, the conflicts, the sufferings which they shall pass through in His fellowship, and, as an ineffable mystery, they shall learn in their own experience Who He is.[33]

Beautifully put, and in fact almost mesmerizing, but not the sort of solution that can stand the test of time. Still, as the pronouncement to end a whole era in historical Jesus studies, it is hard to imagine a more fitting and eloquent requiem.

The Period of No Quest (1906–1953)

One of the legacies of Schweitzer's work was to bring to a close, for the time being, the quest for the historical Jesus. The quest was called off partly because his account was so convincing, and partly because it was so depressing. For all of his own personal faith and rhetorical flair, Schweitzer's historical Jesus was still a prophet whose main message was the mistaken one that the end is imminent. Aware that his results would be disappointing, Schweitzer said that historians had set out in quest of the historical Jesus, believing that when they found him, they "could bring Him straight into our time as a Teacher and Savior." But, he concluded, "He does not stay; He passes by our time and returns to His own."[34]

Among New Testament scholars there was also widespread skepticism about whether the historical Jesus could be reliably recovered at all. At the turn of the century, most scholars believed in the priority of Mark. Since Mark was the first gospel, many assumed that it must be the most historically reliable gospel. But there was growing skepticism about whether even Mark was historically reliable. William Wrede, in his influential *The Messianic Secret* (1901), argued that the Gospel of Mark, rather than a historically accurate account of Jesus, was as motivated by theological concerns as any of the later gospels. In particular, Wrede argued that Jesus never claimed to be the Messiah. In Wrede's view, it was only after Jesus' death that the disciples decided that Jesus was the Messiah, and then they proceeded to read the idea back into his life. Wrede concluded that Mark "belongs to the history of dogma" rather than to the history of Jesus.[35]

Also important at this time was the growing conviction that historical inquiry, whatever its results, could not provide a proper foundation for faith. Prior to Schweitzer's work, the theologian Martin Kähler accepted Strauss's idea that the Gospels were never intended by their authors to be read as history, and in a famous paper published in 1896 he advanced the revolutionary suggestion that for the purposes of Christian faith it does not matter that the Gospels are not historically reliable. In his view, what makes Jesus significant for Christians is not the life of the historical Jesus but his death and resurrection. Echoing ideas that had been expressed earlier by the Danish philosopher Søren Kierkegaard (1813–1855), Kähler argued that the quest for the historical Jesus was a misguided attempt to minimize the riskiness of faith by supporting its claims with historical evidence. In his view, a faith that needs support from historical evidence is not genuine faith, but rather a flight from it. Claiming that "Christian faith and a history of Jesus repel each other like oil and water," he concluded that for Christians the quest for the historical

Jesus is at best irrelevant and at worst a perversion of authentic spirituality.[36]

Additional discouragement to engage in the quest came from Karl Barth and Rudolf Bultmann, the two most influential Protestant theologians of the first half of the twentieth century. Barth held that the meaning of Jesus, including the meaning of his life, is found only in his death. Whatever Jesus did and whatever happened to him prior to his death, Barth claimed, is not only theologically irrelevant but a distraction as well. He thus, in effect, called for the cessation of the quest. Bultmann's general view was that the recovery of Jesus' life is both historically impossible and theologically irrelevant. In *Jesus and the Word* (1934) he wrote that "we can know almost nothing concerning the life and personality of Jesus, since the early Christian sources show no interest in either, are moreover fragmentary and often legendary; and other sources do not exist."[37] In his view, all we can really know about Jesus is that he existed and died on a cross. But, Bultmann concluded optimistically, that is all we need to know. God uses this minimal knowledge to call us to live authentically, which, Bultmann said, is what the Christian proclamation, the *kerygma,* is all about. He claimed that to preserve the significance of the kerygma for modern people, it has to be "demythologized." Once this is accomplished, he argued, drawing heavily on the work of Heidegger, one can see that the heart of the Gospels is an existential call to authentic existence, that is, that it directs people to the fact that "God stands before" them, and thus into their present as the time "of decision for God."[38]

So far as his historical methods were concerned, Bultmann developed literary "form critical" techniques for analyzing the Synoptics. He claimed that what the application of form criticism showed is that most of what is in the Synoptics about Jesus originated not in the life of Jesus, but in the early church. For present purposes, more important than his literary methods was that Bultmann was so unabashedly naturalistic. In an essay entitled "Is Exegesis Without Presuppositions Possible?" he argued that while scholars should not presuppose their results, there is nevertheless "one presupposition that cannot be dismissed"—that "history is a unity in the sense of a closed continuum of effects." Bultmann explained that "this closedness means that the continuum of historical happenings cannot be rent by the interference of supernatural, transcendent powers and that therefore there is no 'miracle' in this sense of the word."[39]

The Second Quest (1953–1970s)

In 1953 Ernst Käsemann, who had been one of Bultmann's students and was at the time a professor at Göttingen, delivered a lecture to other former students of Bultmann that is generally thought to have launched a new quest for the historical Jesus. Käsemann did not object either to Bultmann's naturalism or to other aspects of his historical methodology. Rather Käsemann objected to Bultmann's skepticism, which Käsemann was afraid would lead to a "docetic christology," that is, to a view of Christ that divested him of his humanity. Käsemann claimed that "the fact of historical contingency must be recognized," elaborating that "the problem of the historical Jesus," rather than something that historians have invented, "is the riddle with which Jesus himself confronts us."[40] He then selected certain of Jesus' sayings that he regarded as unquestionably authentic and asked what impression, on their basis, we can form of the proclamation and character of Jesus. Other historian-theologians soon joined the project.[41] The hunt was on again for the historical Jesus, spurred this time by "redaction criticism," a new critical method. Whereas "form criticism" had sought to uncover the oral traditions that preceded the Gospels, redaction criticism focused on the Gospel authors' own literary and theological tendencies and how these influenced their writing.[42] Contributions during this period included G. Bornkamm's *Jesus of Nazareth* (1960), the Lutheran scholar J. Jeremias's *Jesus' Promise to the Nations* (1958) and *The Proclamation of Jesus* (1971), and the Dutch Dominican E. Schillebeeckx's massive *Jesus: An Experiment in Christology* (1979).

Bornkamm prefaced his attempt to recover the historical Jesus with the admission that writing "a life of Jesus" is impossible. Nevertheless, he was confident that certain strands of pre-Easter history can be recovered from the Gospel traditions. His Jesus performed no miracles, had no special foreknowledge of events to come, and did not think of himself as the Messiah. He did, though, speak of an eschatological fulfillment in the present, as opposed to the future. Jeremias sought a middle ground between the imminent apocalyptic eschatology of Schweitzer (the end is near) and the realized eschatology of others (the kingdom is already present in Jesus' ministry), settling in the end on the notion of "eschatology in the process of being realized." Schillebeeckx, in his long study, took the novel view that the resurrection appearances are stories from Jesus' own lifetime read forward into the post-Easter period.[43] In spite of such imaginative contributions, by the 1970s the quest for the historical Jesus had again subsided. But it did not subside for long.

The Current Quest

Throughout the 1980s and 1990s there has been an extraordinary new burst of scholarly energy in historical Jesus studies, which has resulted in a great increase in the number and variety of methodologies being employed and of portraits of Jesus being sketched. There is also much more confusion on the part of commentators about how many different quests are currently under way, how they should be characterized, and which historians belong in which camps.[44] Perhaps this is a good sign, showing that older scholarly alliances and structures are breaking up and new ones being formed.

Although there are many factors responsible for the revitalization of the quest for the historical Jesus, a common dominator is growing confidence among virtually all of the scholars involved that more can be known about the historical Jesus than had previously been thought. This new confidence is due in large part to the development of interdisciplinary methodologies. Whereas previous generations of scholars had relied almost exclusively on literary evidence, with some help from archaeology, today scholars are making important use of work that has been done in the social sciences, especially sociology, linguistics, and anthropology. This work has enabled historical Jesus scholars to develop new interpretive contexts in which even the old literary evidence can be seen in a new light. In addition, among liberal historians important use is now being made of new literary evidence, especially the Gospel of Thomas. And among conservative historians as well as some liberals there has been a greater tendency to relax the prohibition against mixing theology and history. Another dramatic change from earlier quests is that for the first time since Schweitzer's study, serious academic accounts of Jesus have begun to appear in books that are widely read by the general public. But beyond these meager generalizations, the current quest is too diverse to characterize. The best way to find out about it is to examine a representative sample of the most important contributions to it. To that task, we now turn.

Part Two

HISTORICAL JESUS STUDIES TODAY

4

TWO CONSERVATIVES

E. P. Sanders
and John Meier

IN THIS CHAPTER I DESCRIBE the interpretations of Jesus of two conservative historians. By *conservative* I do not mean fundamentalists or evangelicals but simply secular historians who arrive at traditional results. And by *traditional* results I mean portraits of Jesus that will be immediately recognizable to readers of the New Testament and that emphasize apocalyptic eschatology as central to Jesus' message.[1] As we shall see in the next chapter, the portraits of Jesus by liberals are far removed from this familiar picture.

Not surprisingly, whether a historian turns out to be conservative or liberal tends to depend importantly on what dates of origin he or she assigns to certain crucial literary evidence. Liberal historians tend to assign relatively early dates to some literary evidence that is outside of the New Testament, and relatively late dates to much that is within it. That is largely why they end up portraying Jesus in unfamiliar ways. Elisabeth Schüssler Fiorenza and J. D. Crossan, for instance, whose views we shall consider in the next chapter, judge that parts of the Gnostic Gospel of Thomas, of which they make important uses, are based on sources that are independent of any of the New Testament Gospels and that originated at least as early as the earliest material from the New Testament Gospels. Marcus J. Borg, whose views we shall consider in Chapter 7, agrees with this assessment of Thomas. The conservative historians E. P. Sanders and John Meier, on the other hand, whose views we shall consider in the present chapter, all regard material (except for Josephus) that is outside of the New Testament and that plays a crucial role in the interpretations of most liberal historians as originating later than, and also as being dependent upon, material that is in the New Testament. So does James D. G. Dunn, whose views we shall consider in Chapter 6, and N. T. Wright, whose views we shall consider in Chapter 7. As we shall see, the assignment of dates of origin to literary evidence can be an exceedingly complex and delicate task; it is not surprising that in assigning dates of origin historians sometimes arrive at different results.

One might have thought that the difference between conservative and liberal historical Jesus scholars would stem from liberals' being more committed to naturalism than are conservatives. Surprisingly, this is not so. The conservatives whose views will be discussed in this chapter as well as the liberals whose views will be discussed in the next share a common commitment to methodological naturalism. In Chapter 7 I discuss the work of two more historians, one a liberal and one a conservative, both of whom qualify their commitments to methodological naturalism in order to open the door to more expanded approaches. In sum, there are two divisions that should interest anyone who wants to understand historical Jesus studies today. One is between conservatives and liberals, the other between naturalists and those with more expanded approaches. In this chapter and the next, we will consider this first division. In the following two chapters we will consider the second.

E. P. Sanders's Jesus:
An Eschatological Prophet

Sanders has been a professor of exegesis at Oxford University and has twice won a National Religious Book Award. His portrait of Jesus appears primarily in two books: *Jesus and Judaism* (1985) and *The Historical Figure of Jesus* (1993).[2] John Koenig, himself a prominent New Testament scholar, said in a *New York Times* review that he "would be surprised if *Jesus and Judaism* does not turn out to be the most significant book of the decade in its field."[3]

Methods

Sanders says that he starts with what he takes to be the most secure information, builds on that the main outlines of an interpretation, and then proceeds slowly to what is the next most secure information, and so on, elaborating his interpretation as he goes. Most follow the same strategy. What distinguishes Sanders is that he regards certain information about Jesus' *actions* as being far more secure than *any* information about his *sayings*. Hence he downplays sayings material on the grounds that it is perennially and, in his view, deservedly under dispute. In his account, sayings material enters late and only in a supporting role.[4]

Sanders assigns great importance to *context*. He says that "if we want to know what Jesus was up to, what he had in mind, what sort of relations he worried about, at what level he addressed other people—national, local, or familial—we need to know the context as well as the words."[5] He concedes that we do not know much about any of the specific contexts in which Jesus acted and spoke. Hence after first discussing the political setting and then Judaism, he stresses especially the importance of two more general contexts: the theological context—salvation history—and the context of Jesus' own career.

Sanders's discussion of the political setting is useful but unexceptionable. His characterization of Judaism is unusually sympathetic. He bristles at what he takes to be the fact that New Testament scholars "often attack" first-century Jews for observing a plethora of commandments, such as those governing sacrifice and food. In his view, these criticisms amount only to saying that ancient Jews were not modern Protestant Christians or secular humanists, a point that he says could be made "with less animosity and self-righteousness." He stresses that not just first-century Jews, but more or less everyone, had divinely mandated laws and customs. What distinguished the Jews was the all-inclusiveness of their laws and customs. It was because of this, he says, that Jews who lived among Gentiles did not assimilate.[6]

Sanders says that in Judaism, although anyone who knew the law could be a religious leader, there were two groups of acknowledged experts: priests and Pharisees. He concedes that the cleansing of the Temple scene in the Gospels (Mark 11:15–19, and parallels), in which Jesus calls the Temple a "den of robbers," has led many to think that the priesthood was "venal and corrupt." Sanders says that it was neither. Whatever dishonesty and abuse may have been present, he says, was in stark contrast to the general rule. The priests believed in God, served faithfully in the Temple, and tried to set a good example by adhering strictly to divine law. The same is true, he says, of the Pharisees, who he claims were respected and liked by most Jews because of their devotion and precision.[7]

For Sanders, the theological context is all-important. According to salvation history, God called Abraham and his descendants, gave them the law, established Israel as a kingdom, and punished Israel for disobedience. But God also promised someday to raise his people again, if necessary by defeating their oppressors in war. According to Sanders, the reason all of this is so important is that the authors of the New Testament Gospels present Jesus as early Christians saw him, "as having a major place—in fact the ultimate place—in the context of Jewish salvation history."[8]

Sanders says that New Testament authors, in characterizing Jesus as fulfilling biblical statements and prophesies, were inventive, but not dishonest. He thinks that there were some genuine parallels between Jesus and characters or prophesies in Hebrew scripture and that Jesus did what he could to strengthen these parallels, such as riding into Jerusalem on an ass, thus consciously recalling a prophesy in Zechariah. Sanders says that this made it "very easy" for early Christians to invent more parallels, and that there is no doubt that the authors of Matthew, Mark, and Luke did this, citing the birth narratives as prime examples. He says that Matthew structured his birth narrative in order to portray Jesus as being a second Moses, and Luke structured his to portray Jesus as being the promised son of David.[9]

The second context that Sanders stresses is that of Jesus' own career, including events that immediately preceded and followed his public ministry and were closely connected to it. The most important of the preceding events was Jesus' relationship with John the Baptist. Sanders says that John warned people to repent in view of the coming wrath. He accepts, as more or less everyone does, that Jesus was baptized by John, since the early Christians would not have made up the story. Sanders thinks that Jesus' baptism by John implies that Jesus agreed with John's message.[10]

For the period shortly after Jesus' execution, Sanders says that our surest information is provided by the letters of Paul, who thought that in his own lifetime history was about to reach its climax and that Jesus would return. Apparently, Sanders says, other Christians agreed. He thinks that "the only reasonable explanation" of the early Christian conviction that history was about to reach its climax is that during his lifetime Jesus had led his followers to expect a new kingdom to be established soon. However, Sanders thinks that it was only after Jesus' death and the resurrection appearances that Christians became persuaded that Jesus himself would return to establish the kingdom. In a claim that is standardly repeated by conservatives and disputed by liberals, Sanders says that the fact that both John the Baptist at the beginning of Jesus' ministry and Jesus' followers shortly after its end thought that the climax of history was at hand provides us "with a secure basic conclusion: Jesus thought that God would soon bring about a decisive change in the world." Sanders says that this conviction on the part of Jesus provides the basic framework of his overall mission. Matthew, Mark, and Luke, he concludes, "were right on target" in setting Jesus in the framework of Jewish salvation history. That history, Sanders says, is the lens through which Jesus saw both himself and the world.[11]

Sanders makes almost no use of apocrypha, including the Gospel of Thomas, saying that he shares "the general scholarly view" that "very, very little" in the apocryphal gospels could "conceivably go back to the time of Jesus," and that of all the apocryphal material, only some of the sayings in the Gospel of Thomas are even worth consideration.[12] Having said that, in neither of his two books does he ever consider them.

Sanders, who is notable among Jesus scholars for his clarity and precision, writes in an academic style. He is reluctant to portray Jesus as a whole person. Compared to some other scholars whose views we shall consider, he tends to hold back, often hedging his bets. He compares himself to a reconstructive surgeon, but one who has no picture of the previously whole person that he can use to guide his task. He says that although he will do what he can to fill in gaps and make coherent sense of bits and pieces of information, the results will be "partial at best," and that a "true title" of his project would be "basic information about Jesus: important aspects of what he did, what he thought, and what others thought of him."[13]

Sanders is a methodological naturalist, that is, he thinks of the world as a closed causal system that is not subject to any "other-worldly" interferences. On the question of miracles, for instance, he says that he fully shares Cicero's view that there are none.[14] The modern historian, he says, wants to know such things as the circumstances in which Jesus worked, why his efforts sometimes succeeded and sometimes failed, and why the Christian movement developed as it did, and the Gospels answer by saying that God, through Jesus, is culminating a process of salvation that God started with the call of Abraham. Sanders says that the plan of God is "difficult" for the historian to study. Though historians have to take into account that the Gospel writers had theological views, the further question of whether those views are true is "essentially beyond the scope of historical inquiry" and hence one with which "we cannot deal."[15] But in saying this, Sanders leaves a basic question unanswered. By "cannot deal," does he mean that he cannot decide one way or the other whether these theological views are true, or that he will assume that the views are false? We have already seen, in his attitude toward miracles, evidence that he closes some theological questions. We shall return to this question in Chapter 6.

Results

Sanders begins both of his books by listing what he regards as "almost indisputable facts." In the earlier book, which is more austere, only eight items make this list: Jesus was baptized by John the Baptist; he was a Galilean who preached and healed; he never left Israel; he called disciples and spoke of there being twelve; he engaged in a controversy about the Temple; he was crucified outside Jerusalem by the Roman authorities; after his death, his followers continued as an identifiable movement; some Jews persecuted parts of this new movement, at least until near the end of Paul's career.[16] But in his later book Sanders supplements a slightly expanded list of "indisputable facts" about Jesus with a brief narrative, which is worth characterizing if only to illustrate how familiar to readers of the New Testament his account will be and hence why in my classificatory scheme, Sanders qualifies as conservative.

According to Sanders, as a child and a young man, Jesus lived with his parents in Nazareth, a village in Galilee, which for almost all of Jesus' life was ruled by Antipas, the son of Herod the Great.

When Jesus was a young man, probably in his twenties, John the Baptist was preaching in or near Galilee. John proclaimed the urgent need to repent in view of the coming judgment. Jesus heard John and felt called to accept his baptism. Antipas later arrested John either because John had criticized his marriage to Herodias or because Antipas feared that John's preaching would lead to insurrection, or both. About that time, Jesus began his public ministry. He went from village to village, but avoided cities, and usually preached on the Sabbath in synagogues. He called a small number of people to be his disciples; they joined him in his travels, which were mainly to villages and towns on the sea. Except for the last few weeks of his life, Jesus remained in Galilee. In contrast to John, Jesus not only preached but also healed the sick. As Jesus' reputation grew, more and more people came to see him. Because of the crowds he had to preach in open areas.

In all, Sanders thinks, Jesus taught for one or possibly two years, after which he went with his disciples and some other followers to Jerusalem for Passover. He rode into the city on an ass. Some people hailed him as "son of David." He then went to the Temple, where he attacked the money changers and dove sellers. The high priest and his advisers determined that Jesus was dangerous and had to die. After the Passover meal with his disciples, Jesus went off by himself to pray. Helped by one of Jesus' followers who betrayed him, the high priest's guards arrested Jesus, who was then tried, after a fashion, and delivered to the Roman prefect with the recommendation that he be executed. After a brief hearing, the prefect ordered his execution. He was crucified as an insurgent, along with two others. He died after a relatively brief period of suffering. A few of his followers placed him in a tomb. Subsequently, some of his followers had "resurrection experiences" that convinced them that in Jesus' life and death God had acted to save humanity and that Jesus would return. They gave Jesus various titles and began to persuade others to put their faith in him. As the decades passed, Jesus' disciples and their converts developed various views of Jesus' relation to God and of his significance in God's plan. When the New Testament Gospels were written, the separation of Christianity from Judaism was not yet complete. Theological explanations of Jesus were at an early stage. Eventually the Christian movement separated from Judaism and became the Christian church.[17]

Like almost all other New Testament historians, Sanders believes that the birth narratives in Matthew and Luke are among the clearest examples of material that the authors of the New Testament Gospels invented. He says that when the authors of Matthew and Luke write that Jesus was born in Bethlehem but grew up in Nazareth, this probably reflects the fact that whereas Jesus was from Nazareth, according to "salvation history," the redeemer of Israel was supposed to have been born in Bethlehem, which was David's city. According to Matthew, Jesus' family home was originally in Bethlehem, whereas according to Luke it was in Nazareth. Sanders says that these two gospels have "completely different and irreconcilable ways of moving Jesus and his family from one place to the other." In Sanders's view, Luke's device for doing this is "fantastic."[18]

In Luke (3:23–38), although David had lived a full *forty-two generations* earlier, Mary's husband, Joseph, still was required to register in David's town. What, Sanders asks, could Augustus have been thinking of in issuing such a decree, which would have caused chaos throughout the Roman Empire? And how would people know where to go to register? No one could trace his or her genealogy through forty-two generations (Sanders says that after twelve generations, people have more than a million ancestors). Further, David may well have had "tens of thousands of descendants who were alive at the time." Did they all know they were descendants of David? If they did, how were all of them going to register in a little village?

Sanders concedes that one can reinterpret Luke's account to make it less fantastic. For instance, perhaps what Luke meant is that only those males who considered themselves to be descended from royalty had to register. But such a revision would cause problems of its own. For one thing, Herod's royal family was in power in Palestine at the time. Augustus, who supported Herod, would not have asked the descendants of a Davidic royal family that had been out of power for over 500 years, and that had been superseded by both the Hasmonaean and the Herodian dynasties, to register in their hometowns. That might have revived hopes of a Davidic kingdom and thereby created social tension.[19] Sanders says that Matthew's story, though more likely, is also unbelievable. He concludes that Matthew and Luke had little information about Jesus' birth and hence created their respective birth narratives "to place Jesus in salvation history."[20]

According to Sanders, the center of Jesus' work was Capernaum. Virtually all towns and villages, he says, had synagogues, and in them visitors were welcome and free to speak. He thinks that Mark's report (Mark 1:21) that Jesus went into Capernaum and on the Sabbath entered the synagogue and taught is "quite believable."[21] On the basis of a few clues, Sanders says, we can guess what Jesus' life was like: He was essentially homeless; he traveled, without much money, with his disciples, some of the time including more than just "the twelve." As a consequence of his having some supporters of means, especially women, sometimes he was able to eat and sleep in comfort.[22]

Sanders says that the story of Jesus' temptation in the desert is symbolic and mythological, but that probably Jesus did fast and pray before he began his ministry and probably he was subject to temptation. He says that the New Testament Gospel story regarding the call of the disciples is basically reliable: The earliest disciples were Galilean fishermen, and among them were Peter, Andrew, James, and John, who left their nets to follow Jesus. Sanders thinks that probably Jesus himself used the term "twelve" symbolically and that it was remembered by the Gospel writers as a symbolic number. But the actual group of followers, he says, may have been more or less than twelve. He thinks that during Jesus' lifetime his close disciples "were neither as uncomprehending as Mark usually depicts them nor as lacking in faith." He also thinks that some of them were women.[23]

Sanders distinguishes between miracle workers and magicians. He says that people could seek miracles from God or the gods directly, or from especially pious or gifted individuals. Many believed that these gifted individuals, *charismatics,* had special spiritual powers to influence God. Magicians, he says, may be thought of as constituting a "guild of miracle-workers." They were not charismatic and autonomous, that is, they did not perform miracles because of their special relationship to a god, using techniques of their own invention. Rather, following rules, magicians physically manipulated items and spoke the right words, thereby *making* the higher deities act as the magicians wished. Also magicians were for hire. Sanders concedes that in some of Jesus' healings there are "techniques that call to mind magic," but he denies that Jesus was a magician.[24]

If Jesus was a miracle worker, why weren't people at the time more impressed by his miracles? Possibly, Sanders says, because the New Testament Gospels exaggerate Jesus' miracles, but more probably because in Jesus' day, miracles did not generally lead people to commit to the miracle worker. He notes that neither the miracles attributed to Jesus nor the public responses to them were greatly different from those attributed to other miracle workers in the same general period, such as Honi and Hanina. Thus, although people did not doubt that Jesus worked miracles, this did not motivate them to become his followers or to conclude that he was God's final spokesman. Rather, most who knew about Jesus probably concluded that he was on intimate terms with God, though his enemies probably concluded that he was on intimate terms with the devil.[25] What about Jesus himself? Sanders thinks that probably Jesus concluded, along with the authors of the New Testament Gospels, that his miracles were signs of the beginning of God's final victory over the forces of evil.[26] He regards *prophet* as the best label for Jesus. He stresses, though, that Jesus was not just a teacher or a moralist but also a healer, and especially an exorcist.[27]

In Sanders's view, the heart of Jesus' message was the coming of the kingdom. But what does that mean? He says that if we were to decide on the basis of the arguably most authentic sayings "what Jesus *really* thought," we would "conclude that he thought that in the very near future God would dramatically intervene in history by sending the Son of Man." Probably, Sanders adds, he also thought that when God sent the Son of Man there would be a great judgment, with the result that some people went to heaven and some to Gehenna (hell). He concedes that Jesus could "conceivably" have called a *present* power "the kingdom," and thus had a primarily this-worldly message, but he thinks our best evidence favors the view that Jesus expected that in the context of the movement that began with John the Baptist, God would very soon intervene in human history, after which God (or His representative) would reign supreme, without opposition.[28]

Sanders thinks that since New Testament authors favored the mission to the Gentiles, they would have included pro-Gentile material, and so we cannot be sure what Jesus' own view was about Gentiles. He says that on general grounds, he is inclined to think that Jesus expected at least some Gentiles to acknowledge the God of Israel and participate in the coming kingdom. These grounds are that quite a few Jews expected this to happen, and that Jesus was a kind and generous man. Sanders says that if Jesus had not looked forward to the conversion of Gentiles, then he must have expected them all to be destroyed, and it is unlikely that he expected this.[29] He says that

Jesus was not judgmental, and that a fair number of his teachings consist of the assurance that God loves each person, no matter what the person's shortcomings. He says that Jesus urged people to regard God as a loving father, to accept his love, and to respond in trust.[30]

Sanders says that since much of Jesus' teaching is summed up in the Lord's Prayer, we are entitled to assume that it is a prayer that he used and taught his disciples.[31] As for ethical teachings, Sanders says that Jesus was concerned with how people behaved toward others, but not with their inner thoughts. "Like any good Jewish teacher," Jesus thought that people should examine their relations to others, doing whatever is necessary to put these in good order. Jesus himself did not live strictly or sternly. For instance, he sought out the company of sinners, and associated with them while they were still sinners. Jesus was not puritanical but compassionate, lenient, and celebratory. Yet he was also an ethical perfectionist. He urged people to be perfect as God is perfect, meaning that they should be merciful as God is merciful. And he displayed this quality himself. The "overall tenor" of his teachings, says Sanders, "is compassion towards human frailty."[32]

In Sanders's view, when we consider Jesus' message it is hard to understand how he came to such a bad end. The clearest and perhaps most important point to keep in mind, Sanders says, is that Jesus regarded himself as having full authority to speak and act on behalf of God. In the views of Jesus and his followers, his authority was not mediated either by any human organization or by scripture. Jesus, acting as a charismatic and autonomous prophet, said, in effect, "Give up everything you have and follow me, because I am God's agent."[33]

Sanders notes that New Testament scholars often claim that Jesus opposed the law or at least parts of it, most commonly suggesting that he upheld the moral law but opposed the ritual law. In Sanders's view, Jesus did not oppose the ritual law. Had Jesus done so, Sanders says, "there would have been an enormous outcry." Yet Jesus was an "absolutist." He required those few who actually followed him to give up everything, but promised others the kingdom without stipulating many conditions.[34]

Sanders concedes that Jesus told tax collectors that God loved them and told other people that tax collectors would enter the kingdom of God before righteous people did. So, in effect, Jesus said to people that if they followed him, "even though they had not repented and reformed in the way the law requires (repayment, 20 percent fine, guilt offering)," God would include them in the kingdom. Sanders says that what would have been most offensive in this behavior, since it would have reduced the importance of the law, is Jesus' assertion of his own authority and the significance of his mission.[35]

In Sanders's view, Jesus probably did not think of himself as the Messiah. After Jesus' death, Sanders says, his disciples decided to give him that title. However, Sanders thinks that in a very general sense the title corresponded to Jesus' own view of himself.[36] Jesus believed that the twelve disciples both represented and would judge the tribes of Israel. Yet Jesus was above the disciples, and hence above the judges of Israel. He considered his mission as having overriding importance, and he thought that how people responded to him was more important than their other duties. He thought that he was God's last emissary and that God was about to initiate his kingdom. He rode into Jerusalem on an ass, recalling a prophesy about the king riding on an ass. He was executed for claiming to be "king of the Jews." Sanders says that Jesus must have thought, therefore, that in some sense he was "king." Sanders's own favorite term for Jesus' conception of himself is "viceroy," which means that although God is king, Jesus represents him and will continue to represent him in the coming kingdom.[37]

Why was Jesus crucified? Sanders thinks that it was because he was perceived as having made some kind of threat to the Temple. His best guess is that Jesus predicted its destruction in a way that made people think that he was threatening it. Sanders says that Jesus' symbolic action of overthrowing tables in the Temple was understood in connection with a saying about destruction, and that in the view of the authorities the action and the saying together were "a prophetic threat." In any case, prophets were considered to be dangerous because they might arouse a crowd, which could easily get out of hand (especially at Passover). In the view of some, prophets were also dangerous because God might listen to them. In sum, Jesus was a potential troublemaker.[38]

So far as Jesus' arrest and trial are concerned, Sanders thinks that "it was Jesus' self-assertion, especially in the Temple, but also in his teaching and in his entry to the city," that motivated the high priest, Caiaphas, to act against him. Once Caiaphas did act, Sanders thinks that he probably made only one decision, not out of theological disagreement, but because of his responsibility to preserve the peace, which was to arrest *and* execute Jesus. Pontius Pilate just "went along." Jesus was then executed almost immediately, with no further witnesses and no trial procedure. Sanders thinks that the stories of Pilate's reluctance and weakness of will are Christian propaganda, the purpose of which was to excuse Pilate, thereby reducing the tension between the Christian movement and Roman authority.[39]

Sanders basically accepts the crucifixion scene as depicted in the Gospels. For instance, he accepts that Jesus cried out, and that his cry was his own reminiscence of the psalm, not just a motif inserted by the early Christians. It is possible, Sanders speculates, that when Jesus drank his last cup of wine and predicted that he would drink it again in the kingdom, he thought that the kingdom would arrive immediately, and that after he had been on the cross for a few hours he despaired and cried out that he had been forsaken. But we do not know, Sanders says, what Jesus thought as he hung in agony on the cross. What we do know is that after a relatively brief period of suffering, he died and some of his sympathizers hastily buried him.[40] Sanders says that since Jesus himself thought—and had convinced his disciples to think—that the kingdom of God was at hand, he "may have died disappointed." In any case, his followers were disappointed. That, Sanders says, is the end of the story of the historical Jesus.

Sanders gives the resurrection stories short shrift, partly because he thinks the Gospel accounts are confusing and confused. He says, for instance, that faced with "sharply diverging stories of where and to whom Jesus appeared, lack of agreement and clarity on what he was like (except agreement on negatives)," he does not pretend to know who saw what, or what they saw. Sanders invites readers who think that it is "perfectly clear" that "the physical, historical Jesus got up and walked around" to "study Luke and Paul more carefully." He concludes that in this case the problem of historical reconstruction is "intractable." The followers of Jesus were sure that he was raised from the dead, but they did not agree on who had seen him. Sanders thinks that some of Jesus' followers (and later Paul) did have "resurrection experiences," but Sanders confesses that he has no idea what gave rise to these experiences.[41]

John Meier's Jesus: A Marginal Jew

Meier, a Catholic priest, is a professor of New Testament at the Catholic University of America and an editor of the *Catholic Biblical*

Quarterly. His portrait of Jesus appears in *A Marginal Jew*, which thus far runs to two volumes (1991 and 1994), the first of which is concerned mainly with sources and methods, and the second, with Jesus' words and deeds.[42] Meier projects a third volume in which he will consider how various individuals and groups—Jesus' disciples, other Jews favorably disposed toward Jesus, Pharisees, Sadducees, toll collectors, sinners, and so on—were affected by and responded to Jesus. On the basis of Meier's first two volumes, one reviewer said that future scholars are certain to judge Meier's "book as one of the foremost studies ever written on the historical Jesus." Another said that his book "will for generations serve as *the* guide on the quest for the historical Jesus."[43] Meier says that his entire study is animated by a single question: Who did Jesus think he was?[44]

Methods

Meier's point of departure is to ask us to imagine that a Catholic, a Protestant, a Jew, and an agnostic, all honest, competent historians of first-century religious movements, were locked up together "in the bowels of the Harvard Divinity School library" and "not allowed to emerge until they had hammered out a consensus document on who Jesus of Nazareth was and what he intended in his own time and place." He says that "an essential requirement of this document would be that it be based on purely historical sources and arguments." His book is what he thinks that document would reveal. In other words, he intends to write a secular history of Jesus, free both of theology and of parochial points of view.[45]

Meier insists on the importance of distinguishing among "the real Jesus," "the historical Jesus," and "the theological Jesus," but it is hard for me to make sense of his distinctions as he draws them.[46] A way of understanding them that would seem to allow him to say what he wants to say is that the *real* Jesus is simply Jesus: whoever he was (or is); the *historical* Jesus is that same Jesus, subject to this constraint: his only properties are those we are justified in attributing to him on the basis of secular historical research alone; and the theological Jesus is that same Jesus, though now his properties are those we are justified in attributing to him on the basis of historical scholarship supplemented by theology.

So far as sources are concerned, Meier's most important decision has to do with his relegation of the Gnostic Gospels to the historical back burner. He concedes that scholars are "fiercely divided" on the nature and sources of Thomas but argues that it is clear that the redactor (editor) of Thomas is motivated by Gnostic objectives and that he intends that the Synoptic-like sayings included in the Gospel be interpreted in secret, Gnostic ways. Meier admits that this leaves open the question of whether, as many specialists have claimed, a source of authentic sayings of Jesus even earlier and more original than those in the Synoptics might be preserved in Thomas. He mentions Helmut Koester, whose view is that Thomas was written possibly as early as the second half of the first century C.E., is independent of the Synoptics, and contains more primitive versions than they do of some of Jesus' sayings.[47] Meier summarizes the argument for accepting Koester's view. Since the issues on which one must make a judgment in evaluating this argument, as well as Meier's reasons for rejecting it, nicely illustrate the gulf in New Testament studies between experts and nonexperts, I shall return to Meier's summary and rebuttal in Chapter 5 (under the heading Difference of Opinion Revisited). Meier concludes that the Synoptic-like sayings of Thomas are dependent on the Synoptics and that the other sayings in Thomas stem from second-century Christian Gnosticism, and hence he does not use them as an independent source. With Thomas and basically all other apocrypha out of the way, Meier is then free to focus almost exclusively on New Testament material and Josephus.[48]

Meier lists the main criteria he will use in assessing the authenticity of sayings material. His four "primary" criteria are *embarrassment* (words or deeds of Jesus that would have embarrassed or created difficulties for the early church); *discontinuity* (words or deeds of Jesus that cannot be derived either from the Judaism of the time or from the early church); *multiple attestation* (words or deeds of Jesus that are attested in more than one independent literary source); and *coherence* (words or deeds of Jesus that fit in well with an initial "database" generated by using the first three criteria). There are no surprises in this list. Virtually all historians use these criteria. In addition, Meier says that he will use *rejection and execution* as a criterion, that is, words or deeds of Jesus that could be used to explain his trial and crucifixion as king of the Jews. He says that Jesus' words and deeds must have alienated people, especially powerful people, and mentions his surprise in reading Sanders's rejection of the authenticity of Jesus' statement that all foods are clean (Mark

7:15) on the grounds that it is "too revolutionary to have been said by Jesus himself." Meier also lists several secondary criteria of authenticity, about all of which he expresses serious reservations. These include *traces of Aramaic, traces of a Palestinian environment* (sayings of Jesus that reflect concrete customs, beliefs, and so on), and *narrational vividness*. Finally, Meier stresses that the use of criteria of authenticity is more an art than a science, requiring sensitivity and not just mechanical implementation.[49]

So far as the sequence of the material in the New Testament Gospels in concerned, Meier cautions that one must always remember the "basic rule" that from Jesus' baptism to the last weeks of his life, "there is no before or after." He elaborates that the authors of each Gospel created their own time frames and plot lines, and that once their frameworks are dissolved by form and redaction criticism, there are in the Jesus tradition very few indicators of temporal order. Hence, he says, the major sayings and deeds of Jesus during his ministry must be studied topically, not chronologically. In other words, since we have no way of knowing the order in which Jesus said almost all of whatever he said, we are not in a position to trace changes and developments in his thought. Instead, we simply have to attend to different topics he discussed and try to make sense out of everything that he said on each topic, even though some of what he said on a given topic may have expressed an earlier thought of his that he subsequently abandoned or modified.[50]

An important respect in which Meier differs from Sanders, as well as from most of the other historians whose views we shall consider, is that he bends over backwards not to step on anyone's toes theologically, particularly with respect to the question of miracles, and particularly the toes of those who, like himself, are believing Christians. It is not that, as a historian, he accepts the miracle stories. Rather, he thinks it is incompatible with his job *as a historian* either to accept *or* reject them. He says that historians should remain uncommitted, that is, simply keep an open mind. In my view, it is hard to quarrel with him about this objective. However, whether he actually succeeds in keeping an open mind is another question, to which I return in Chapter 6.

Finally, on most of the issues that Meier considers, he explains both his own view and the competing views of others before he explains why he thinks his view is superior. That means that his study presents unusually complete data on controversies among New Testament scholars. It also explains why his study is so long. Anyone who wonders what the distinction in New Testament scholarship between expert and nonexpert amounts to can find out by reading volume 2 of Meier's study.

Results

Meier's portrait of Jesus is a lot like Sanders's, except that in addition to highlighting Jesus' Jewishness, Meier also emphasizes Jesus' differences from other Jews of the time. In Meier's view, Jesus was "a *marginal* Jew," for a number of reasons: During the first few centuries C.E., to everyone but Christians, Jesus was not an important figure; Jesus gave up his livelihood and became jobless and itinerant, thereby exposing himself to "shame," in an honor/shame society; Jesus' style of teaching and living was offensive to many Jews; some of Jesus' teaching and practices, such as his total prohibition of divorce, his rejection of voluntary fasting, and his "voluntary celibacy" ran counter to the views and practices of the major Jewish religious groups of the day; and in his "terrifying and disgusting" trial and execution, Jesus had been pushed by both Roman and Jewish authorities to the margins of his own society.[51]

Meier says that Jesus was a prophet and a teacher, but one with these differences: At one and the same time, Jesus acted as "the prophet of the last days, which were soon to come and yet were somehow already present in his ministry"; he was a teacher of general moral truths and also detailed directives concerning the observance of the Mosaic law; he was an exorcist; and he was a healer of illnesses, who was reputed, like Elijah and Elisha, to have raised the dead.[52]

As for details, Meier says that he believes that Jesus underwent a significant experience in connection with his baptism by John, which crystallized two key themes that governed his entire ministry: the loving care of God as Father, and the power of the spirit in his own life. Meier thinks Jesus must have developed these two themes sometime between leaving home and striking out on his own, and that possibly their crystallization in his mind had something to do with his parting company with John. Meier thinks that Jesus' baptism indicates that he acknowledged John's charismatic authority as an eschatological prophet, accepted his message of imminent fiery judgment on a sinful Israel, and that he resolved to change his life and become part of "a purified Israel, on whom God (through some agent?) would pour out the holy spirit on the last day."[53]

Like virtually everyone else, Meier thinks that the heart of Jesus' message was his proclamation of the kingdom of God. He points out that although the symbol of God's rule as king was available and useful to Jesus, since it was only one symbol among many it was not imposed on Jesus. Rather, Jesus' choice of it as a key theme was "a conscious, personal choice." Meier says that the eschatological kingdom Jesus proclaimed involved the reversal of all unjust oppression and suffering, the bestowal of the reward promised to faithful Israelites, and the joyful participation of believers (and even of some Gentiles) in the heavenly banquet with Israel's patriarchs. He says that the fact that the eschatological banquet would be shared with Abraham, Isaac, and Jacob implies life beyond normal bodily death, which Jesus specifically extends to himself in his prophesy (Mark 14:25) that God will save him from death and seat him at the final banquet.[54]

Meier stresses that "this future, transcendent salvation" that Jesus proclaimed was an essential part of his view of the kingdom and that any interpretation of Jesus that "does not do full justice to this eschatological future must be dismissed as hopelessly inadequate." Yet Jesus' triumphal entry into Jerusalem a few days before his death and his cleansing of the Temple would not have made much sense unless he felt that the kingdom whose coming he was announcing—and perhaps even initiating by his prophetic actions—was imminent. How imminent? Meier says that although imminent-future eschatology has its origins in Jesus, the setting of time limits for that eschatology has its origin in the early church. However, by keeping Jesus' imminent eschatology in mind, he thinks that we can begin to see why Jesus was not interested in concrete social and political reforms, either for the world in general or for Israel in particular. He was not interested in reform, because he was not proclaiming that the world was about to become better, but that it was about to end.[55]

Meier thinks that Jesus was not overly concerned about contradicting himself and that he could say without a qualm, and without explaining himself, that the kingdom was both present and future. Nevertheless, he thinks that even though Jesus saw himself and was seen by others as an eschatological prophet who proclaimed the imminent coming of the kingdom of God, Jesus' message was different from that of John the Baptist. Whereas John proclaimed only the future kingdom of God, Jesus also proclaimed the kingdom of God already present in his preaching, his behavior ("his table fellowship offered to all"), and, most strikingly, in his miracles. Meier says that Jesus' message together with his miracles all but inevitably cast him in the role of Elijah, that is, of an eschatological prophet. However, in his proclaiming a kingdom that was both future and yet made present by his miracles, Jesus was unique.[56]

In holding this view, Meier distinguishes himself both from Sanders and from some liberal historians, such as Crossan, whose views we shall consider in later chapters. Contrary to Sanders's view, Meier thinks that some of the authentic sayings of Jesus (e.g., Luke 17:21) clearly proclaim, and some of his actions suggest, that the kingdom is already present in his ministry. Especially significant in this connection, Meier thinks, is a saying in Q in which Jesus interprets his practice of exorcism: "If by the finger of God I cast out demons, then the kingdom of God has come upon you" (Luke 11:20).[57] Contrary to Crossan's view, but in agreement with Sanders's, Meier thinks that Jesus never gave up John's view that God would come in judgment in the near future. Like Sanders, Meier argues that since John the Baptist, immediately prior to Jesus, had a message of future eschatology, and the church, immediately subsequent to Jesus, had a message of future eschatology, it is very doubtful that Jesus did not himself proclaim future eschatology. Meier adds that this contextual consideration poses "a major problem for the whole approach" of liberals, such as Crossan, who "want to do away with the future eschatology in Jesus' preaching."[58]

Meier is no friend of historians who wish to make Jesus "relevant." One of his recurrent themes is that his portrait of Jesus "stands in stark contrast" to the popular portrait of Jesus as "a kindhearted rabbi who preached gentleness and love." He says that the advantage and appeal of this "domesticated Jesus" is obvious: He is "relevant" and "useable" by people with a variety of contemporary programs and ideologies to push. In contrast, Meier says, a first-century Jew who presented himself as the eschatological prophet of the imminent arrival of God's kingdom, which he also makes present and effective by miracles reminiscent of Elijah and Elisha, is not so relevant and useful. Yet, Meier concludes, "for better or for worse, this strange marginal Jew, this eschatological prophet and miracle-worker, *is* the historical Jesus retrievable by modern historical methods applied soberly to the data."[59]

In Meier's view, Jesus both taught his Jewish followers general ethical norms such as love and forgiveness, and instructed them con-
cretely on how to observe the Mosaic law. In contrast to Sanders,
Meier stresses that some of Jesus' concrete directions led to disputes
with other Jewish groups. For instance, although Jesus certainly af-
firmed the law as God's word to Israel, he also sometimes took it
upon himself to rescind or amend some aspects of the law, as in his
pronouncements on divorce, oaths, vows, and perhaps even the
kosher food laws of the Torah. Meier says this dimension of Jesus-
as-teacher "added further spicy ingredients to an already heady
brew." That is, Jesus presented himself not only as eschatological
prophet of the coming kingdom of God, an Elijah-like miracle
worker who made the future kingdom already effective and present
in his ministry, but also as a teacher who could tell Israelites not only
how to observe the Law of Moses but even what they should and
should not observe in the law. Moreover, Meier says, Jesus was a
"true charismatic" in that he found his authority to interpret and
even change the law not in traditional, recognized channels of authority but rather in his own ability to know directly God's will for
Israel in the last days.[60]

As was the case with Sanders, Meier is at pains to distinguish Jesus' miracles from magic. In the ancient world, Meier says, the word
magic often carried a pejorative connotation. But Jesus' religious
miracles were different: The normal context is that of an interper-
sonal relationship of faith, trust, or love between a human being and
a deity (or his agent); the petitioner, a worshiper or disciple rather
than a business client, asks some benefit of God or His envoy; usually Jesus grants the miracle with terse, intelligible words spoken in
his own language, sometimes accompanied by a symbolic gesture
(touching, use of spittle), sometimes not, but "there are no lengthy
incantations, endless lists of esoteric names and unintelligible words,
amulets, charms, or recipes of foodstuffs to be boiled"; the miracle
takes place not through coercion, but usually because the miracle
worker personally responds to the petitioner's urgent request or
some afflicted person's unspoken need; the Gospel miracles are not
simply independent acts of divine power granting benefits to individual petitioners, but are understood as symbols and concrete realiza-
tions of the kingdom of God, who has come, through Jesus' ministry, to save His people in "the end time," that is, at the end of
history; and Jesus' miracles do not punish or hurt anyone. Meier

says that magic is the opposite of all of this.[61] Meier dismisses the so-called nature miracles as an invention of the early church. But he stresses that the fact that Jesus performed extraordinary deeds deemed by himself and others to be miracles is so well-supported that if we were to reject altogether as nonhistorical the miracle tradition from Jesus' public ministry, we would have also to reject all other Gospel traditions about him and thereby simply abandon the quest for the historical Jesus.[62]

Finally, in Meier's view, and in contrast to the views of many historians, including Sanders, there is no significant puzzle about why Jesus was put to death. He says that what moved Caiaphas to action in arresting Jesus included, first, Jesus' proclamation that the definitive kingdom of God was soon to come, ending the present state of affairs and restoring Israel to its glory by reconstituting it as the twelve tribes in the end time; second, his claim to teach God's will authoritatively, even when this seemed to run counter to the Law of Moses; third, his ability to attract a large following, and perhaps his decision to form a stable inner circle of twelve disciples, representing the twelve patriarchs and the twelve tribes of a restored Israel; his practice of a special rite of baptism to admit persons into his group of disciples; and, finally, his "freewheeling personal conduct that expressed itself in table fellowship with toll collectors and sinners." Taken together, Meier says, these words and deeds of Jesus were "disturbing enough." But if one adds to this already "volatile mix" the likelihood that some of Jesus' followers believed him to be the Davidic Messiah expected by pious Jews, and that Jesus sometimes spoke in veiled fashion of his own future role in the eschatological drama, perhaps even using special self-designations or titles, then the mix becomes "positively explosive."[63] Interestingly, in Meier's characterization of the ways in which Jesus was a "marginal Jew," he seems to agree with Crossan and others that Jesus was a definite "nobody." However, in this later part of Meier's account, which contrasts strikingly with Crossan's characterization of Jesus' arrest, execution, and death, Jesus emerges, out of a large sea of nobodies, as a definite somebody.

5

TWO LIBERALS

Elisabeth Schüssler Fiorenza
and J. D. Crossan

HISTORICAL JESUS STUDIES, J. D. Crossan recently remarked, have become "a scholarly bad joke." "There have always been historians," he continued, "who said it could not be done because of historical problems" and "theologians who said it should not be done because of theological objections." And "there were always scholars who said the former when they meant the latter." These, he said, are "negative indignities"; but "what is happening now, the production by competent and even eminent scholars" of widely varied interpre tations of Jesus, is a "positive indignity."[1]

It might seem that Crossan must be right. In the past few decades alone noted scholars have characterized Jesus as a political revolutionary,[2] a magician,[3] a charismatic,[4] a rabbi,[5] a Hillelite or proto-Pharisee,[6] an Essene,[7] a wisdom prophet,[8] a Cynic philosopher,[9] and an eschatological prophet.[10] Quite a varied list. Reciting it evokes a sense of scholarly chaos. Should it be an embarrassment to the discipline of history? I don't think so.

There is not as much difference among scholars in their overall interpretations of Jesus as it may seem from comparing the labels they have affixed to Jesus. The discipline of history, like all academic disciplines, rewards *new* truth. Historians of Jesus announce their new truths by picking different labels to represent their overall characterizations of Jesus. It is in their interests to package their conclusions distinctively. And they do. Yet beneath the labels historians tend to agree about quite a lot. For instance, almost all of them agree that Jesus was a disciple of John the Baptist; that about the time John was put to death, Jesus became a teacher in his own right; that the core of Jesus' message was about the kingdom of God; that Jesus was unusually egalitarian for his time and place, and that this too may have been part of his message; that Jesus sometimes practiced communal eating in which, regardless of societal status, everyone was welcomed as an equal; that Jesus was a healer and that he had a reputation as a miracle worker; that during Passover Jesus got into trouble in Jerusalem with the Roman authorities and was summarily put to death. And there are more agreements. But even this short list is quite a bit for a group of diverse scholars, all of whom are motivated to come up with fresh results, to agree about in connection with a Jewish peasant who lived almost 2,000 years ago, who wrote nothing, and whose evidential tracks are extremely thin and ambiguous. In addition, historical Jesus scholars tend to admit that there is a case to be made for the interpretations they reject (and even for including potential evidence that they dismiss) but simply feel that on balance there is a better case to be made for their own interpretations.

Yet, admittedly, historical Jesus scholars also disagree about quite a lot. Why so much? Part of the answer is that on the basis of evidence that is slender and ambiguous they are expected to come up with interpretations of Jesus that, beyond merely sketching a few of Jesus' actions and traits, actually explain who he was and what he was about. That is, they are expected not only to identify Jesus but also to provide relatively well-rounded portraits of him as a person and to tell us what was central to his teachings and what he hoped to accomplish.[11] Historians place this demand on themselves, and we—the consumers of historical scholarship—put this demand on historians. To provide a relatively well-rounded portrait of Jesus, historians have to engage in a fair amount of educated guessing. There is nothing wrong with their doing this. We do not want historians to guess blindly or to make things up, or to portray their results as being more certain than they actually are. But we also do not want them to hold back and refrain from giving us such a fuller portrait of Jesus just because they are not absolutely sure. In short, we expect results. In the case of historical Jesus studies, the only result about which most of us really care is one that lets us know who

Jesus was and what he taught and hoped to accomplish. If, even with the help of some educated guessing, the evidence cannot sustain any such result, then so be it. We want to be told that. But if, with a little educated guessing, the evidence can sustain it, then we want historians to take their best shot. In my view, that is what secular historians have been doing all along, and are still doing today. It is also what they should be doing.

In a situation in which evidence is slender and ambiguous and scholars are nevertheless expected to come up with full-fledged interpretations, a certain amount of scholarly disagreement is both predictable and harmless. The mere fact that you and I are reading academic historians at all suggests that we are sophisticated enough not to expect any of them to come up with the final truth. We know that to improve our own understanding of who Jesus was and what he was about, we will have to sift through the disagreements among historians by attending sympathetically to the tensions in their competing accounts. If there are many competing accounts, as in fact there are in historical Jesus studies, then we realize that the best we may be able to do is not to discover who Jesus *actually* was but who he *might* have been, that is, the range of plausible options as to who he was. That is simply how the discipline of history works, not only in the case of historical Jesus studies but in general.

In historical studies, typically we do not come away with just one interpretation of what happened. Yet even when there is significant difference of opinion among historians, by reading their accounts we better understand the past. We accomplish this partly by learning more truths about the past and partly by learning what is and is not likely. We also learn what the obstacles are that prevent historians from arriving at more certain results. In my view, given the evidence with which historians of Jesus have had to work and what they are expected to do with it, there is about as much variation in their overall results as should be expected if they are doing their jobs properly. It would be much more an embarrassment to the discipline of history if all or even most historians of Jesus were to have arrived at the same conclusion. Then we would know that something was amiss. As it is, what we know is that *any* historical interpretation of Jesus that tells us who he was and what he was about is bound to be speculative.

In any case, from the point of view of traditional Christians who are trying to understand the challenge that historical Jesus studies pose to their beliefs, there are at present only two divisions among secular historians of Jesus that really matter. The first is between those traditional historians—I've called them *conservatives*—who portray Jesus primarily as an eschatological prophet and those other historians—the *liberals*—who do not. The second division is between those scholars who presuppose methodological naturalism and those who do not. But we are now ahead of our story. Only after we have a fairly good idea of what historians have proposed will we be in a position to consider responsibly how to assess their proposals. In Chapter 4, we reviewed the methods and results of two prominent conservative historians. Now we shall review the methods and results of two prominent liberals.

Elisabeth Schüssler Fiorenza's Jesus: Wisdom Prophet

Schüssler Fiorenza is a professor at Harvard Divinity School. She was the first woman president of the Society of Biblical Literature and is cofounder and coeditor of the *Journal of Feminist Studies in Religion*. Many regard her as the foremost feminist working in historical Jesus studies. Although she has not yet integrated her observations about Jesus into a fully developed interpretation, the main outlines of her emerging view may be found primarily in two of her books: *In Memory of Her* (1984) and *Jesus: Miriam's Child, Sophia's Prophet* (1994).[12] She has also written or edited a number of other books in which she explains and promotes a feminist approach to biblical interpretation.[13]

Methods

Schüssler Fiorenza characterizes her own historical work as "advocacy scholarship." She wants her professional writing to have social and political implications, changing the ways people in general, and particularly scholars, think, talk, and write. Currently, she says, people, including New Testament scholars, tend to think, talk, and write in ways that are based on "relations of domination and exploitation." In place of these, she would have them promote freedom, human rights, dignity, and self-respect. It is hard to argue with these objectives. She says that her approach "is firmly planted within liberation theories and theologies in general, and feminist epistemologies and interpretive practices in particular," and that it draws inspiration from liberation movements around the globe.[14] Not surprisingly, given this activist stance, she rejects value-neutral ideals in historical research. She doubts that historical research ever is value-neutral, and even that it can be. In her view, historical research is inevitably ideological. So she thinks that historians, rather than trying to hide their ideological commitments, may as well reveal them.

Schüssler Fiorenza advocates what she calls a *hermeneutic of suspicion* toward all early Jewish and Christian texts, including the New Testament Gospels. In her view, these texts were written from the perspective of male dominance, and often to promote male dominance; that is, they reflect and often were written to sustain the "androcentric and patriarchal" social world out of which they came.[15] As a consequence, she thinks, these texts often give misleading or even mistaken characterizations of events that do not fit an androcentric and patriarchal mold. New Testament authors in particular, she says, rather than wanting simply to report what Jesus said and did, tried to comprehend the meaning of his life for their own time and communities. As a consequence, they were more concerned "with proclamation and interpretative persuasion" than with literal accuracy. To counter this bias, she argues, historians must learn to "read the silences" in the texts, searching "for clues and allusions that indicate the reality about which the text is silent."[16] In other words, historians have to read between the lines.

Few New Testament scholars would argue with this. What distinguishes Schüssler Fiorenza is her sensitivity to the ways in which New Testament texts may have suppressed and distorted information about women. For instance, in her view, these texts routinely underestimate the agency of women (and the poor and dispossessed in general) and undervalue their experience. But the problem, she argues, goes much deeper. It is not a question of bias only on the part of the authors of ancient texts but also on the part of New Testament scholars, the vast majority of whom are male. She says that "our societal and scientific structures define women as derivative and secondary to men." This, she says, has conditioned the perception both of men and women scholars so as to ensure that women "remain historically marginal."[17]

Some of the problem, Schüssler Fiorenza claims, has to do with the way in which New Testament texts have been translated, notably in the use of masculine language in the translation of forms of expression that originally were being used to address both men and women. For example, she says that often "brothers" has been used when "brothers and sisters" would have been more appropriate. Translators, she claims, often err by being overly literal. Part of the remedy, she says, is for translators to "understand and translate New Testament androcentric language on the whole as inclusive of women until proven otherwise." In response to the anticipated objection that translators should just translate and leave interpretation to someone else, she replies that a *good* translation is a perceptive interpretation.[18]

Schüssler Fiorenza says that passages from the New Testament that directly mention women tend to do so because the women "were exceptional or their actions had become a problem." It would be a mistake, she says, to assume that such texts express all available information on women in early Christianity. For instance, translators and interpreters typically assume that while 1 Corinthians 11:2–16 speaks about women prophets, the rest of chapters 11–14 refer only to male charismatics and male prophets; in fact, she says, the truth is just the opposite: "In 1 Cor 11–14 Paul speaks about the worship of all Christians, men and women, and he singles out women in 11:2–16 only because their behavior constituted a special problem."[19]

The fundamental difficulty, Schüssler Fiorenza continues, is not due to the procedures that translators and interpreters use, but to their minds. She says that because translators and interpreters tend to share in the androcentric-patriarchal mind-set of Western culture it is hard for them to appreciate texts that speak positively about women and then to integrate these texts into their models of early Christian beginnings. She says that New Testament scholars "generally presuppose that men, and not women, developed missionary initiatives and exercised central leadership in early Christianity," and so texts that do not fit this preconception are quickly interpreted so as to make them fit. For example, most modern interpreters assume that Romans 16:7 speaks about two men, one of whom is named Junia, who had become Christians before Paul and who had great authority as apostles. But, she says, there is no reason to assume that *Junia* is a shortened form of the male name *Junianus*, since *Junia* was a "well-known female name," and "even patristic exegesis understood it predominantly as the name of a woman."[20]

Scholars should know better, she claims, since there are many indications in New Testament texts that positive information about women is being suppressed. For instance, although the letters of Paul indicate that women have been apostles, missionaries, patrons, coworkers, prophets, and leaders of communities, Luke does not write of any instance of a woman missionary or leader of a church. Although Luke seems to know that women perform such functions, as his references to Prisca or Lydia indicate, his knowing this does not influence the way he portrays early Christian history. To cite another example, whereas all of the Gospels know that Mary Magdalene was the first resurrection witness, the pre-Pauline tradition of 1 Corinthians 15:3–5 does not mention a single woman as being among the resurrection witnesses. Again, the Gospel of John and its tradition ascribe to a woman a leading role in the mission of Samaria, whereas Acts knows only a Philip as the first missionary of this area.[21]

Schüssler Fiorenza concludes from such examples, and related evidence, that because New Testament authors adhered to male interests and perspectives, the texts they produced do not accurately reflect women's actual leadership and participation in early Christianity. She says that New Testament authors thus have manufactured the idea that in early Christianity women were historically marginal.[22] To correct this bias, she proposes three rules for interpreting androcentric texts. First, never interpret them in isolation, but always in terms of their immediate textual contexts. Second, interpret them in full awareness of their intended social-political function. And third, in the case of texts that are intended to be normative for a community, that is, to give advice on what people should believe or how they should behave, remember that their authors often distort how things used to be in order to bolster their recommendations about how things should be.[23]

In addition to problems such as these, Schüssler Fiorenza says that there are a host of subtler ways in which New Testament scholars have tended to ignore or distort the status of women. For instance, the scholars in their interpretations have allowed women in biblical times "to identify" with general male or neutral categories and groups, such as the poor and the lonely, but not to identify themselves "*as women* in solidarity with other women." As a consequence, she says, poor women, *as women*, have become invisible.[24] For instance, Schüssler Fiorenza says that the final form of the story of the anointing of Jesus by a woman is told by a community that already envisions a worldwide mission; the text says that wherever the gospel is announced, this woman's action will be remembered. What did this woman do? Schüssler Fiorenza says that like the prophets of old who anointed the kings of Israel on the forehead, this woman anointed Jesus and in a prophetic action publicly named him. The woman, who spent a great deal of her own money to perform this action, was "reprimanded sanctimoniously" by Jesus' male disciples, who have "projected their messianic dreams of greatness and dominance on Jesus [and] use 'the poor' as an argument against her." Jesus defends her by reminding them that "you always have the poor with you," and hence can do them good whenever you want to, "but me you do not always have."25

Schüssler Fiorenza says that because Luke does not understand this powerful story as that of a woman prophet, he replaces it with the story of "the repentant sinner." In addition, because he does not understand "the 'solidarity from below' that inspired Jesus and his first followers," he portrays the poor as an object of almsgiving and charity. The eucharistic formula, "in remembrance of me" (1 Cor 11:24–25), is verbally similar to the gospel proclamation, "in remembrance of her." Yet the church has not ritualized this story of the woman prophet but instead has used it to assert as God's will that poverty cannot be eliminated.26

Schüssler Fiorenza draws what she takes to be the proper moral, which is that the "church of the poor" and the "church of women" need to be recovered at the same time if "solidarity from below" is to become a reality for the whole community of Jesus again. Jesus' vision of *basileia*—God's rule—calls all women without exception to wholeness and selfhood as well as to solidarity with women who are impoverished, maimed, and outcasts of society and the church. Jesus' vision thus "enables us not to despair or to relinquish the struggle" in the face of violence, but "empowers us to walk upright, freed from the double oppression of societal and religious sexism and prejudice." By such means "the woman-identified man, Jesus, called forth a discipleship of equals that still needs to be discovered and realized by women and men today."27

In sum, in Schüssler Fiorenza's view, Jesus had a special message of importance to women, to which some women of the time responded. However, his message and the story of women's response to it have become hidden. Her goal is to reveal this message and this story:

"Only when we place the Jesus stories about women into the overall story of Jesus and his movement in Palestine are we able to recognize their subversive character." In "the discipleship of equals," women are not peripheral or trivial but at the center, and thus of utmost importance to the phenomenon of "solidarity from below."[28]

Results

Schüssler Fiorenza claims that to understand Jesus one must attend to two contrasts: that between John the Baptist and Jesus; and that between the movement within Israel, led by Jesus, and the movement within the Greco-Roman world, led by Paul and others. In her view, John was a prophet of apocalyptic judgment *in the near future,* whose message was, "Repent, the end is coming." Jesus, on the other hand, was a prophet of wholeness and healing *now,* whose message was that "eschatological salvation and wholeness" are "already experientially available." She says it is not so much that Jesus rejected John's vision as that he expanded it. That is, although Jesus and his movement shared the belief of all groups in Greco-Roman Palestine that Israel is God's elect people and were united with other groups in the hope of God's intervention on behalf of Israel, "they realized that God's *basileia* was already in their midst." In other words, Jesus "proclaimed the *basileia* of God as future and present, eschatological vision and experiential reality."[29]

In the case of the other contrast, Schüssler Fiorenza says that Jesus led a radically egalitarian, prophetic renewal movement that was opposed to androcentrism, patriarchy, and hierarchy. He saw himself, and is best seen by us, as a prophet of God, whom he viewed not only as Father but also as Sophia, or Wisdom. His initial disciples understood him as Sophia's messenger and later as Sophia herself. And Jesus probably understood himself as the prophet and child of Sophia. The Christian movement in the Greco-Roman world, on the other hand, was deeply committed to androcentrism, patriarchy, and hierarchy, and hence it conveyed a very different message.[30]

In Schüssler Fiorenza's view, Jesus called for a "discipleship of equals." She concedes that this interpretation is "historically plausible" only if feminist impulses "are thinkable within the context of Jewish life and faith." She argues that they are thinkable given that prior to Jesus, Judaism already "had elements of a critical feminist impulse." Rather than imposing these elements on Judaism from outside, she says, Jesus simply brought them to the fore. She concludes that the practices and vision of Jesus and his earliest followers are best understood not as a movement that rejected the values and practices of Judaism but as "an inner-Jewish renewal movement" that presented an *alternative* to the dominant patriarchal structure.[31]

Schüssler Fiorenza says that Jesus did not choose twelve males as his chief disciples and did not support the institution of family. In defending this view, she interprets Mark 12:18–27, in which Jesus says that when men and women rise from the dead they do not marry, to mean that when the kingdom of God arrives fully, patriarchal marriage will be abolished. In Mark 10:2–9, she says, Jesus supports the view that husband and wife are partners. And she claims that since Jesus equates hardness of heart with patriarchy, and since hardness of heart has no place in the kingdom, it follows that patriarchy has no place in the kingdom.[32] In addition, she argues that Jesus did not allow males to assume father roles in his movement and that he rejected the idea that males should be the heads of families. In support of this, she reads texts such as Luke 14:26 and the Q material in Matthew 10:34–6/Luke 12:51–3 as expressions of a radical antifamily ethos in the Jesus movement. In sum, in her view, Jesus opposed patriarchy in any form and, more generally, challenged the powerful to become equal with the powerless.[33]

Schüssler Fiorenza says that the prevailing ethos in the Jewish culture in which Jesus taught is expressed in the image of Israel as a "kingdom of priests and holy nation" and that the culture's central symbols were Temple and Torah. In this world, she says, purity and holiness were understood in the context of a hierarchical patriarchal structure. Jesus challenged this system, practicing inclusive wholeness in a discipleship of equals, and he promulgated this challenge by a social program of festive table-sharing in which all were welcome. She says that the Jesus movement in Palestine did not "totally reject the validity of Temple and Torah as symbols of Israel's election, but offered an alternative interpretation of them by focusing on the people itself as the locus of God's power and presence." In the Jesus movement, "the God of Israel is the creator of all human beings, even the maimed, the unclean, and the sinners," and "human holiness must express human wholeness." In sum, in Schüssler Fiorenza's view, Jesus' central vision was not the holiness of the elect, but "the wholeness *of all*."[34]

J. D. Crossan's Jesus: Cynic Philosopher

Crossan, who received his doctorate from the National University of Ireland, pursued postdoctoral studies at the Pontifical Biblical Institute in Rome and at the Ecole Biblique in Jerusalem. He has been co-chair of the Jesus Seminar and chair of the Historical Jesus Section of the Society of Biblical Literature. From 1969 until his retirement in 1995, he was a professor of religious studies at DePaul University, in Chicago. A gifted writer, he is the author of many books, several of which have been best-sellers. His account of Jesus may be found primarily in *The Historical Jesus* (1992), which many scholars regard as one of the most important twentieth-century contributions to historical Jesus studies, and his shorter and more popular *Jesus: A Revolutionary Biography* (1995).[35] In recent years he has been one of the most influential liberal historians of Jesus.[36] Even a staunch critic of his interpretation of Jesus recently said of him that in addition to being "one of the most brilliant, engaging, learned and quick-witted New Testament scholars alive today," he seems "incapable," in his recent work, "of thinking a boring thought or writing a dull paragraph."[37]

Methods

In two respects, Crossan's approach is distinctive. As compared especially with conservative historians of Jesus, but also with many liberals, his work is unusually interdisciplinary. And as compared with *any* historian of Jesus, he is unusually explicit about what evidence he is using, and why, to support his conclusions.

Crossan says that he follows a "triple triadic process." The first triad involves the "reciprocal interplay" of three sources of information: cross-cultural and cross-temporal anthropology, Greco-Roman and Jewish history, and literature. The anthropology includes whatever scholars have learned about imperial and colonial conflict, elites and peasants, politics and family, taxes and debts, class and gender, trance, possession, healing, magic, exorcism, and so on in ancient Mediterranean culture. The history is primarily the work of the Jewish historian Josephus (ca. 37–100 C.E.). And the literature is ancient texts, including, of course, the New Testament. In a recent essay Crossan mentions Galilean archaeology as a fourth source of evidence.[38] He stresses that these sources of evidence do not stand alone but must work together to form an effective synthesis. He asks us to imagine that they are "transparent overlays laid one upon another so that the one below always shows through and relates to those above, just as they relate to it."[39]

In Crossan's view, the authors of the New Testament Gospels, in their own individual accounts, were in general "unnervingly free" about omission, addition, change, and correction, and nowhere is this more true than in the birth narratives. Crossan begins by noting that both Matthew and Luke agree that Jesus was born in Bethlehem. In the Old Testament, he says, it is written that David was born in Bethlehem, and many Jews imagined that the Messiah for which they waited would be a descendant of David. In addition, in the Old Testament (Micah 5:2) there is a prophesy that suggests that the Messiah will be born in Bethlehem. Matthew (2:6) cites this prophesy to explain why the Messiah would be born in Bethlehem.

Crossan says that whereas Matthew seems to take it for granted that Joseph and Mary had always lived in Bethlehem and that they moved to Nazareth only after the birth of Jesus, Luke starts his story with Joseph and Mary living at Nazareth. Hence, Crossan continues, Luke, who is also aware of the prophesy, needs to have Mary and Joseph go to Bethlehem before Jesus is born. But why would they go? Luke (2:1–7) says that Mary and Joseph went to Bethlehem in response to Augustus' call for a census. But, in Crossan's view, there was no such census under Augustus. He says that while there was a census of Judea, Samaria, and Idumea, it was ten years after the death of Herod the Great, hence decades too early to be the census in question. Moreover, from census and taxation decrees in Roman Egypt, he says that we know that individuals were usually registered where they lived and worked, and it was *there* to which they had to return if they were someplace else at census time. Crossan's source for these points is *history*. Crossan adds that "the idea of everyone going back to their ancestral homes for registration and then returning to their present homes would have been then, as now, a bureaucratic nightmare." What was important then, as now, he says, was to get you registered where you could be taxed.[40] His sources for this point are *anthropology* and *history*.

Finally, Crossan claims, there is no indication in any New Testament text other than Luke that anyone else knows that Jesus was born at Bethlehem. In John 7:41–2, for instance, where a discussion is reported, the issue comes up explicitly, yet no one who is party to the discussion seems to have heard that Jesus was born in Bethlehem. His source for this point is *literature*.

Crossan notes that it was not unusual for authors of the period to make up exalted origins for their heroes. He cites as an example the case of Gaius Octavius, who was born on September 23, 63 B.C.E., and who became the adopted son and heir of Julius Caesar, who was assassinated on March 15, 44 B.C.E. Almost two years later, on January 1, 42 B.C.E., Julius Caesar was deified by the Roman Senate, which made Octavius not only emperor but also the son of a god. Octavius then victoriously ended twenty years of civil strife, after which he became Augustus. A month after his death, on September 17, 14 C.E., the Roman Senate deified him also. Yet, Crossan notes, even though all of these dates and the relationships among Julius's parents, Julius himself, and Octavius were well known, Virgil, in the *Aeneid*, made both Julius Caesar and Octavius heirs to an ancient and divine ancestry. Drawing on the stories in Homer's *Illiad* and *Odyssey*, Virgil imagined that Julius's father had been Aeneas, who was himself the son of a human father and a divine mother. In Virgil's account Aeneas had saved Julius from the destruction of Troy and brought him to Italy as sire of the Julian family. Crossan asks, if Virgil and presumably his audience preferred mythology to history, even when the history was well known, why not also Luke? He concludes that Luke's story about the journey to and from Nazareth for census and tax registration is "pure fiction, a creation of Luke's own imagination, providing a way of getting Jesus' parents to Bethlehem for his birth."[41]

In Crossan's triple-triadic process, his approach to the two New Testament birth narratives serves as an example of his "first triad," which involves an interdisciplinary integration of all sources of evidence. His second triad focuses only on literary evidence and involves four steps:

- The making of an "inventory" that lists all of the texts, both canonical and extracanonical
- A sorting of items in this inventory into four chronologically ordered "strata," or layers:
  - material that dates from 30 C.E. to 60 C.E.
  - material from 60 to 80
  - material from 80 to 120
  - material from 120 to 150

- A sorting by topic of the items in the inventory into "complexes," such as "bread and fish," "who has ears," "against divorce," and so on
- Determining the number of items in each complex that come from *independent* sources

Having completed these four steps, Crossan then assigns two numbers, separated by a slash mark, to each complex. The number to the left of the slash mark is the number of the earliest stratum in which an item in the complex appears. The number to the right is the number of independent sources in the complex. For instance, the complex "against divorce" is assigned "1/4," which means first stratum, four independent sources. In general, the lower the number to the left and the higher the number to the right, the better the complex as evidence.

Crossan's third triad has to do with making use of literary evidence, once it has been properly sorted. Here he follows two rules. First, start with evidence in the first stratum, not going on to the second stratum until the first has been exhausted, and so on. Second, make use of a complex only if it contains more than one independent source. As it happens, he relies exclusively on evidence from his first stratum. He does this because he thinks he can develop a coherent interpretation of Jesus based just on this supposedly more reliable evidence. Thus in his interpretation, for a complex to be used, the number to the left of the slash mark must be 1 and the number to the right higher than 1. Obviously, then, for Crossan's interpretation, it is tremendously important what gets included in his first stratum. So, what does? We do not have to guess. He tells us the numbers for *every* complex of literary evidence that he recognizes—an exhaustive ranking.

Crossan's crucial first stratum includes all and only the following items of literary evidence: first letter of Paul to the Thessalonians; letter of Paul to the Galatians; first letter of Paul to the Corinthians; letter of Paul to the Romans; Gospel of Thomas I; Egerton Gospel; Papyrus Vindobonensis Greek 2325; Papyrus Oxyrhynchus 1224; Gospel of the Hebrews; Sayings Gospel Q; Miracles Collection (derived from Mark and John); Apocalyptic Scenario (from Didache 16 and Matthew 24); and the Cross Gospel (from the Gnostic Gospel of Peter). For many of these items, Crossan lists a reference to a secondary source in which an assignment of a date of origin for the item is justified. For instance, after his listing of the first letter of Paul to the Thessalonians, he cites Helmut Koester's *Introduction to the New Testament,* including the page number.[42] As a consequence of his being so explicit, anyone reading Crossan's book knows the stratum in which he places every item of literary evidence. And any reader who wants to take the trouble to investigate the citations he provides can find out what argument he is relying on to assign a date of origin to almost every item of literary evidence.

Since Crossan confines himself to his first stratum in using literary evidence, it is worth reflecting briefly not only on what is included but also on what fails to make the cut. In stark contrast to Sanders and Meier, at least seven sources that are not in the New Testament are included. And what is cut? Quite a bit, it turns out. Crossan's second stratum includes the Gospel of Mark, Gospel of Thomas II, and Letter to the Colossians, which he says "was written most likely not by Paul himself but posthumously by one of his students, in his name." Crossan's third stratum includes the Gospel of Matthew; Gospel of Luke; and Gospel of John I. And his fourth stratum includes the Gospel of John II, and Acts of the Apostles.[43]

In sum, whereas many historians of Jesus say little about how they are going to proceed, and even less about why, Crossan, by contrast, goes a long way toward revealing both how and why. As a consequence, he has made it easier than any historian of Jesus ever has for ordinary readers to discover what his evidence is for his conclusions. In my view, he deserves a lot of credit for this.

In constructing his account of Jesus, Crossan supposes that what his readers really want to know is not what early believers wrote about Jesus but what they themselves would have seen and heard as neutral observers in the early decades of the first century. That is, he supposes that his readers want "to move behind the screen of creedal interpretation and, without in any way denying or negating the validity of faith, give an accurate but impartial account of the historical Jesus as distinct from the confessional Christ." He says, "That is what the academic or scholarly study of the historical Jesus is about, at least when it is not a disguise for doing theology and calling it history, doing autobiography and calling it biography, doing Christian apologetics and calling it academic scholarship."[44] In Chapter 6 we will reconsider whether Crossan actually does recover his version of the historical Jesus "without *in any way* denying or negating the validity of faith."

Results

In Crossan's view, Jesus was a Cynic sage. Cynicism was a Greek philosophical movement founded by Diogenes, who lived between 400 and 320 B.C.E. Greek Cynics were famous for negating distinctions of rank and privilege and for flouting social conventions. They were also famous for reducing their personal needs to the bare minimum. In a classic story told by Cicero, Alexander the Great once asked Diogenes, who was sunbathing at the time, to name anything he wanted and it would be granted. Diogenes asked Alexander to step to one side, so as not to block the sun.

F. G. Downing in England and Burton Mack in the United States had already advanced the view that Jesus was a Cynic sage by the time Crossan did,[45] and in that respect their views are the same as his. But in other respects their views differ from his. For instance, Mack's Jesus, while neither eschatological nor very Jewish, had little sense of mission or purpose; rather, as a wandering Cynic sage in a thoroughly Hellenized Galilee, he was a clever teacher of world-mocking wisdom who specialized in "outrageous" and often humorous criticism of social pretensions and cultural conventions.[46] In Crossan's view, by contrast, Jesus definitely did have a mission—and one for which he was prepared to risk his life.

Crossan says that although Jesus was a sage, he was not an intellectual; in fact, he was probably illiterate and did not have scribal skills or scribal awareness.[47] Yet, Crossan says, Jesus was quite intelligent. And what he said and did made sense to many of the people—mostly fellow peasants—to whom he delivered his message. What, though, was Jesus' message? In Crossan's view, it can be summed up in one word: equality. And his mission? To destroy distinctions of rank and privilege by bringing into being a society in which all are equal.

Originally, of course, Jesus was a disciple of John the Baptist. As such, says Crossan, Jesus must have accepted John's eschatological message. However, Crossan thinks that around the time that John was executed, Jesus underwent a conversion to something like Cynic philosophy. He argues that Jesus had ample opportunity to learn about Cynic ideas but treads lightly on the questions of just when and how Jesus actually learned about them. He says that we have "no way of knowing for sure what Jesus knew about Cynicism, or whether he knew about it at all." Perhaps, he concedes, Jesus "had never even heard of the Cynics and was just reinventing the Cynic wheel all by himself." But whether Jesus knew about Cynicism, he says, "is not really the point." The point, rather, is that Jesus is usefully compared with Cynic sages, with whom he is strikingly similar: Both Jesus and the Cynics were populists, who appealed to ordinary people; both were lifestyle preachers, who taught by deeds as well as by words; and both symbolized their message in the way they dressed. Crossan emphasizes that there were differences too: Jesus was rural, the Cynics urban; Jesus organized a communal movement, the Cynics were individualists; Jesus' symbolism required no knapsack and no staff, the Cynics' required them. "Maybe," Crossan suggests, "Jesus is what peasant *Jewish* Cynicism looked like."[48]

In Crossan's account, Jesus' medium was his message; that is, Jesus taught as much by his actions as by his words. And Jesus' medium was *magic* (healing) and *meals*. In contrast to Sanders and Meier, Crossan prefers to call Jesus a *magician,* rather than a healer, because Jesus was operating outside of the system of established social practices and in a way that challenged established religious authority. He says that Jesus' low social status is primarily what makes it appropriate to characterize him as a magician. "Magic," Crossan says, is "a term that upper-class religion uses to denigrate its lower-class counterpart." A magician "is somebody else's healer." Crossan says that he does not use the word *magician* pejoratively but rather to describe "one who can make divine power present *directly through personal miracle* rather than *indirectly through communal ritual.*" But although Crossan says "*divine* power," he does not really mean it. He distinguishes between doctors who "cure disease"— the organic, physical ailment—and others who "heal illness"—the diseases' effect on patient, family, and community. In his view, Jesus did not cure disease, he healed illness.[49]

What about those alleged miracles of Jesus that involve more than just healing illnesses—say, his raising of Lazarus from the dead? Crossan says, "I do not think that anyone, anywhere, at any time brings dead people back to life." Then, taking his cue from Strauss, he adds that while he does not think the raising of Lazarus ever did or could happen, he thinks the story of Jesus' raising of Lazarus "is absolutely true," in that it symbolizes what Jesus was about: "life out of death." Crossan claims that life out of death is how peasants all over Lower Galilee would have understood Jesus' talk of the kingdom of God, in which they would begin to take back control over their lives.[50]

Equally central in Crossan's portrait is that Jesus encouraged "open commensality," that is, eating with others without regard to social boundaries. This practice, he says, was the heart of Jesus' program, and it was subversive in that it embodied a "religious and economic egalitarianism" that called into question "the hierarchical underpinnings of Jewish religion and Roman power: the distinctions between rich and poor, patron and client, honor and shame, pure and impure, male and female, slave and free."[51]

In direct opposition to conservative historians, Crossan denies that Jesus preached a doctrine of apocalyptic eschatology.[52] In his view, Jesus understood the kingdom of God not as a divine intervention into worldly affairs at the end of ordinary human history but as a humanly accessible way of life. The kingdom of God was not for the future, not even the near future, but for the immediate present. In this respect, he says, Jesus differed from John, with whom Jesus originally agreed.

To support his view about the change in Jesus' attitude toward John's message, Crossan appeals to three pairs of sayings. Each of the first two pairs includes one from the Gospel of Thomas and one from the Q Gospel in Matthew and Luke. The two sayings in the first pair exalt John above Antipas. Those in the second pair exalt anyone "who becomes a child" above John. Those in the third pair are from friends or enemies of Jesus, who point out that whereas John fasts, Jesus feasts. In direct contradiction of Meier's "basic rule" that from Jesus' baptism to the last weeks of his life, "there is no before or after" (see Chapter 4), Crossan says that the sayings in the first two pairs, which "derive from the historical Jesus," leave "only one conclusion": Between the first pair of sayings and the second Jesus changed his mind about John's mission and message. When Jesus made the first pair of remarks he had accepted John's vision of awaiting the apocalyptic God. By the time he made the second pair of remarks he had decided that it is not enough to await a future kingdom; rather "one must enter a present one here and now." Crossan says that the third pair of sayings support the view that Jesus broke from John's vision and partially indicate how.[53]

Crossan admits that in the New Testament Gospels, Jesus often speaks apocalyptically of the coming "Son of Man," but he denies the authenticity of these sayings. In all of the Son of Man sayings put together, he says, there is only one case in which two independent sources have the expression "Son of Man" in more than a single version, and in that one case Jesus used the expression generically, to mean *human being*.[54]

Crossan also differs sharply from conservative historians in his view of Jesus' last days. Except for the Temple incident, he dismisses as later Christian invention most of the New Testament account of Jesus' passion, death, and resurrection. In connection with the Last Supper, for instance, as recounted in Mark 14:22–5, Crossan asks whether before his death Jesus instituted "a new Passover meal in which his martyrdom with its separation of body and blood was symbolized by the meal with its separation of bread and wine." He concedes that Paul knew about such an institution. But he points out that in John 13–17, Jesus and his disciples have a last supper that is neither the Passover meal nor any type of institutionalized symbolic commemoration of his death, and that neither the Gospel of Thomas, nor the Q Gospel, nor Didache 9–10 exhibits any awareness of a Last Supper tradition. He says that he "cannot believe" that the authors of those documents knew about the tradition and studiously avoided mentioning it. Hence he concludes that the tradition was "not there for everyone from the beginning—that is, from solemn, formal, and final institution by Jesus himself." In Crossan's view, what Jesus began and left behind was a tradition of open commensality, and after his death some Christian groups invented the idea of the Last Supper to combine ritualistically remembrance of commensality from Jesus' life with commemoration of his death. Crossan thus concludes that the Last Supper never happened, and so it cannot be used to explain anything about Jesus' death.[55]

Crossan distinguishes three stages in the development of the New Testament stories of Jesus' trial, crucifixion, death, and burial. The first stage is the *historical passion*—what actually happened. He says that the fact that Jesus was crucified "is as sure as anything historical can ever be." However, since, in Crossan's view, it is unlikely that Jesus' followers knew much about the details of his arrest, crucifixion, death, or burial, he reconstructs an account of what probably happened that is based on what we know in general about how cases like Jesus' were handled by the Roman authorities and what we know in particular about Pilate's normal practices. On the basis of such information, Crossan doubts that Jesus had a trial. What probably happened, he thinks, is that Jesus was arrested during the Passover festival, and that when that happened, those closest to him fled for their own safety. In Crossan's view, the Roman authorities must have viewed Jesus not just as a "nobody" but also as a potential troublemaker. Such a person would have been put to death summarily, by crucifixion, without any fuss. There would have been no consultations between Caiaphas or Pilate about or with Jesus. Crossan concedes that it may be hard for us to imagine "the casual brutality" with which Jesus was probably taken and executed. Nevertheless, he concludes, what we may have so much difficulty in imagining is almost surely what actually happened.[56]

Crossan also doubts that Jesus was buried, by his followers or anyone else. In general, he says, those with influence were not crucified, and those who were crucified did not have enough influence to obtain a burial. Without either influence or bribery, he says, it would have been impossible to obtain the corpse of someone who had been crucified. Moreover, it would have been dangerous to request it. Normally, Crossan says, soldiers guarded the crucified person until he was dead, and then his body "was left for carrion crow, scavenger dog, or other wild beasts to finish the brutal job." He says that it is possible that as part of their job the soldiers themselves may have buried Jesus in a shallow grave. But either way, he concludes, "the dogs were waiting." And Jesus' followers, who had fled, would know what that meant.[57]

What happened next, Crossan thinks, is what he calls the *prophetic passion*—the search by scribally learned followers of Jesus to find a basis or justification in the Hebrew Scriptures for Jesus' shocking fate. Since he thinks it is so likely that Jesus' followers would have looked for such a scriptural basis, he explains what they would have found. And then he explains how they might have made the transition from what they found to each element in the New Testament passion accounts. He concludes that what we have now in those detailed New Testament passion accounts "is not *history remembered* but *prophecy historicized*," that is, an after-the-fact fictional account of Jesus' passion specifically constructed so that the elements in the story fulfilled prophesies from the Hebrew Scriptures.[58]

The final stage is what Crossan calls the *narrative passion*—the weaving together by the New Testament authors of elements in the tradition (the prophesy historicized) into as plausible a historical reconstruction of what happened as they could muster. Moreover, these reconstructions were tailored to fit into each author's unique theological and liturgical agenda.

What about the resurrection? In Crossan's view, the New Testament accounts of it are pure fiction, based perhaps on after-the-fact apparitions of Paul and some other followers of Jesus. The resurrection stories were constructed in order to serve a practical, political function having to do with the distribution of authority, power, and leadership in the emerging Christian community. Crossan supports his view that such political issues were important concerns by giving careful textual analyses of texts such as 1 Corinthians 15:1–11. He suggests that other stories in the Gospels from before the execution of Jesus, the so-called nature miracles, serve the same political function. In his view, such stories are "not about Jesus' miraculous physical power over the world but about the apostles' political power over the community."[59]

Difference of Opinion Revisited

At this point let us return briefly to the topic of disagreement among historians with which this chapter began. Earlier I quoted Crossan's view to the effect that there is so much disagreement among historians about who Jesus was and what he was about that it is a professional embarrassment; he called it "a scholarly bad joke." I suggested, contrary to his view, that New Testament historians should not regard their disagreements as an embarrassment. I have now summarized some of the sorts of differences that there are among historians, both in their *methods* and in their *results*. But before we leave the topic of disagreement, it should be noted that historians also often disagree about the *evidence* on which they base their results.

One example of a conservative/liberal disagreement about evidence that is rather telling, and also uncomfortably typical, is that between Sanders and the Jesus Seminar on the authenticity of Jesus' alleged prohibition against divorce. Sanders calls the prohibition of divorce "the best-attested tradition in the gospels." He says that it "appears a total of four times in the synoptics and once in Paul" and that it is one of two themes in the New Testament that have "the strongest possible support" (in his view, the other is the Last Supper). Sanders says that at least two of Jesus' alleged sayings on divorce, the

so-called long and short forms, seem to have been "transmitted independently for some time," a fact that he says enhances the likelihood
that they are authentic, as also does the fact that the authors of the
Gospels and Paul evidently found the prohibition against divorce a
hard saying. Sanders concludes that we may be "certain" that the
prohibition against divorce on the grounds that remarriage is
adultery goes back to Jesus. He then proceeds to use this "fact" as
evidence that there was a kind of "ideal-perfectionism" in Jesus'
ethical message.[60]

When we turn to *The Five Gospels,* published by the Jesus Seminar, we get a different story. There the passages on divorce, which
Sanders found to be so unquestionably authentic, show up, on what
is reported to be a close vote, in the next to least authentic (gray)
grouping of the Seminar's four-tier rating system.[61] Here is a summary of the reasons behind the Fellows' verdict:

> The arguments in favor of authenticity are: remarks on the subject by
> Jesus are preserved in two or more independent sources and in two or
> more different contexts; an injunction difficult for the early commu-
> nity to practice is evidence of a more original version; Jesus' response
> is in the form of an aphorism that undercuts social and religious con-
> vention. Further, the Markan version implies a more elevated view of
> the status of women than was generally accorded them in the patriar-
> chal society of the time, which coheres with other evidence that Jesus
> took a more liberal view of women.
>
> The arguments against authenticity are: the Markan version reflects
> the situation of the early community; the variations in the tradition
> suggest that the community struggled to adapt some teaching to its
> own context; the appeal to scripture in vv. 6–7 is not characteristic of
> Jesus but reflects the Christian use of the Greek Bible; familiarity with
> Roman rather than Israelite marriage law in vv. 11–12 indicates a later,
> gentile context. Further, the roles of Jesus and the Pharisees seem re-
> versed: here the Pharisees view the Mosaic law as permitting divorce,
> whereas Jesus cites the scripture in support of a more stringent view.

Since these arguments tend to cancel each other out, the Fellows of
the Jesus Seminar were almost evenly divided on the question of authenticity.[62]

The experts disagree on this question about the authenticity of
these sayings. What are we, the nonexperts, supposed to think?
What can we responsibly think? In my view, it would be arbitrary
for us to choose to side with one group of experts over the other. Af-

ter all, they are the experts, not us. As nonexperts, we lack the knowledge and skill necessary to arbitrate disputes such as this one among the experts. Hence unless we have some special reason to think that the experts are biased, if we want to form a view about Jesus based on historical evidence alone, from which as nonexperts we are admittedly one step removed, we have to suspend judgment.

Consider a second example. This one is a dispute between Meier and various liberals, led by Helmut Koester, on the authenticity of certain sayings in the Gospel of Thomas. Meier summarizes Koester's argument that the sayings are authentic as follows:

- in *Thomas*, sayings and parables are generally shorter and more streamlined; they lack the theological concerns, narrative framework, allegory, and other redactional "fingerprints" of the four evangelists;
- the editor of *Thomas* would have lacked a motive to reduce so drastically sayings or parables from the Synoptics;
- often the parables in *Thomas* coincide remarkably well with hypothetical original forms reconstructed from the Synoptics by twentieth-century form critics;
- many of the sayings are easily retroverted into Aramaic; many show the rhetoric and rhythm scholars often associate with authentic sayings of Jesus; and
- if *Thomas* were dependent on the Synoptics, then the order of the sayings in at least one of the Synoptics should be apparent, especially since Thomas has no overarching redactional order of his own; yet, in the opinion of some scholars no Synoptic order is apparent.[63]

Meier's counterarguments are patient and complicated—too complicated to review in their entirety here, especially since our purpose is not to settle this dispute but to illustrate the sort of considerations on which it is based.[64] However, I shall mention one of the main considerations on which Meier relies.

Meier says that when comparing the Synoptics and the Gospel of Thomas it is necessary to remember "the controlling hermeneutical principle" that is stated at the beginning of Thomas: "These are the obscure [or 'hidden' or 'secret'] sayings that the living Jesus uttered. . . . Whosoever finds the meaning [or 'interpretation'] of these sayings will not taste death." Meier concludes that the redactor of Thomas did not intend the sayings of Jesus to be readily intelligible to every reader. Instead the sayings are presented as esoteric teachings, intelligible only to the initiated, that is, those who can use their understanding of Gnosticism to illuminate the hidden significance of Jesus' words. As a consequence, Meier says, the redactor of Thomas "will purposely drop from the tradition anything that makes Jesus' sayings too clear or univocal, or anything that employs the general saying to highlight one specific (often moral or ecclesial) application." Thus the redactor will try to undo what the four canonical evangelists struggled so hard to do, which is, by allegory, other redactional additions, and reformulations, to "explain the meaning of Jesus' statements or apply them to concrete issues in the Church."[65]

On the basis of this and other considerations, Meier rejects the view favored by Koester and Crossan and thereby dismisses the Gospel of Thomas as an independent source for the historical Jesus.[66] In our survey of the views of different historians, it should be obvious by now that this dismissal of Thomas is no small matter. Whether Thomas is accepted or dismissed makes a huge difference in the subsequent interpretations of scholars. With Thomas and basically all other apocrypha out of the way, conservatives like Sanders, Meier, and Wright are free to focus almost exclusively on the canonical material, plus Josephus. With Thomas and some of the other apocrypha in play, it is a different game entirely.

What should we, the nonexperts, think about who is right? In my view, it is easy to see from the merest glance at the dynamics of this exchange that most of us have no business even having an opinion. Do the sayings under discussion in Thomas "lack the theological concerns, narrative framework, allegory, and other redactional 'fingerprints' of the four evangelists"? And if they do, is this because they are earlier and independent, or because the redactor of Thomas intentionally pared down the sayings to make them esoteric? I, for one, have no idea. Probably you do not either. This, like so much else, is a question for the experts to decide. And the experts disagree. Clearly, insofar as we nonexperts plan to base our view about Jesus on historical evidence alone, we should suspend judgment.

This sort of dispute over sources nicely illustrates what I have been saying about the importance of the distinction between experts and nonexperts. New Testament scholars, such as the four whose views we have considered, are certainly competent to make a judgment about the independence of sources such as Thomas. Since the issues underlying such judgments are complicated and the evidence meager and ambiguous, we expect their verdicts to vary—and they do vary. However, the ultimate shape of the interpretations they favor depends crucially on their differing verdicts. Those of us who are not New Testament scholars—presumably you and certainly me—are not competent to make a judgment about the independence of sources such as Thomas. For that and a host of related reasons, in most cases we are also not competent to decide which of the competing interpretations of the historical Jesus is most likely to be reliable. The evidence New Testament scholars use in making up their minds consists, for the most part, in original sources. The evidence you and I have to use consists, for the most part, not in these same sources but in the interpretations of New Testament scholars. That is, while the experts rely on primary evidence, we amateurs have to rely mostly on secondary evidence: the opinions of the experts. When the experts agree, we are entitled to accept their interpretations. When they disagree, usually we have no basis on scholarly grounds alone to pick and choose among them.

Part Three

FAITH AND REASON

6

HISTORY AND
THEOLOGY

SINCE THE SEVENTEENTH CENTURY scholars have aspired to write objective histories of Jesus. It has been hard for them to do. One major obstacle, even in accounts that have achieved the status of standard texts, has been overcoming ordinary bias. W. Boussett, the author of a widely used text that was published originally in 1913 and reprinted as recently as 1966, is a case in point. He contrasted Jesus and Judaism as follows:

> On the one hand was the artificiality of a hair-splitting and barren erudition, on the other the fresh directness of the layman and the son of the people; here was the product of long generations of misrepresentation and distortion, there was simplicity, plainness, and freedom; here a clinging to the petty and the insignificant, a burrowing in the dust, there a constant dwelling upon the essential and a great inward sense of reality; here the refinement of casuistry, formula- and phrase-mongering, there the straightforwardness, severity, and pitilessness of the preacher of repentance; here a language which was scarcely to be understood, there the inborn power of the mighty orator; there the letter of the law and here the living God."[1]

E. P. Sanders has called Boussett's comparison "a fairy tale" that was dictated primarily by theology and has little to do with historical scholarship.[2]

Understandably, contemporary academic historians, such as Sanders, have wanted to distance themselves not only from such apologetics but from theology altogether. Many of them, especially recently, believe that they have done so. Sanders too, as we shall see, believes that he has done so. But on the plausible assumption that the denial of a theological claim itself involves a theological commitment, Sanders is mistaken. And so are the others mistaken.

The question at issue has implications that go well beyond the history of Jesus per se or, for that matter, even beyond religious history. It has implications, for instance, for such fields as the history of magic and the anthropology of shamanism. And since nonacademic history is such a ubiquitous part of our lives, it also has implications for the deeply existential issue, as we try to understand ourselves and the world, of how open we can be or should be to the possibility that we have been influenced in "non-natural" or at least exotic ways (by voodoo or angels, for instance). Can we be open-minded without being empty-minded? That is, if we do not believe in exotic sources of influence on our lives, can we suspend that disbelief without abandoning our critical standards? And even if we can, should we? These are large, unruly questions. For the time being, then, I want to return to our consideration of the quest for the historical Jesus, but without forgetting that what we decide in this limited domain has broader implications.

J. D. Crossan

In the two books by Crossan that we considered, he follows the same supposedly secular approach. In the later book, as we have seen, he asks you, the reader, to suppose that you wanted to know not what early Christians wrote about Jesus but what you would have seen and heard if you had been there as a more or less neutral observer of Jesus. He asks, What if you wanted "to move behind the screen of creedal interpretation and, without in any way denying or negating the validity of faith, give an accurate but impartial account of the historical Jesus as distinct from the confessional Christ?" Doing that, he says, is his goal.[3]

Has Crossan succeeded in writing about Jesus "without in any way denying or negating the validity of faith"? In *Jesus: A Revolutionary Biography,* he makes the following remarks:

- "I understand the virginal conception of Jesus to be a confessional statement about Jesus' status and not a biological statement about Mary's body."[4]
- "Since between 95 and 97 percent of the Jewish state was illiterate at the time of Jesus, it must be presumed that Jesus also was illiterate."[5]
- "The divine origins of Jesus are, to be sure, just as fictional or mythological as those of Octavius."[6]
- "I presume that Jesus, who did not and could not cure that disease or any other one, healed the poor man's illness by refusing to accept the disease's ritual uncleanness and social ostracization."[7]
- "I propose that other [miracle] stories in the gospels" are "not about Jesus' physical power over the world but about the apostles' spiritual power over the community."[8]

In my view, in assuming that Jesus could not have been born of a virgin, was probably illiterate, and could not have performed miracles, Crossan, in effect, has assumed that Jesus was neither God—by which I mean a being whose knowledge and power are unlimited—nor divinely empowered. If Jesus had been God or divinely empowered, then he might have been able to do the things that Crossan assumes he could not do. If I am right about this, then the question is whether in Crossan's assuming that Jesus could not do any of these things, and thus was neither God nor divinely empowered, he has in *any* way denied or negated the validity of faith.

How one answers will depend on what one means by *denying or negating the validity of faith*. I assume that if a person of faith, because of his or her faith, assumes, asserts, or implies one thing—say, that Jesus was God or divinely empowered—and someone else either by assumption, assertion, or implication denies that very same thing, then the person who does the denying has in some way denied or negated the validity of the other's faith. Granted, the denier may have denied or negated the other's faith only temporarily and/or methodologically, say, for the purpose of composing a secular history of Jesus. Even so, the antifaith person has *in some way,* and it would seem in a fairly important way, denied or negated the validity of the other's faith. Thus Crossan has not succeeded in doing what he set out to do.[9]

Assume, for the sake of argument, that some historian has denied or negated the validity of someone's faith only temporarily
and methodologically, for the purpose of composing a secular
history of Jesus, and that the historian leaves open the option
of letting that person's faith back in later. This seems to be
what Crossan wants to do. For instance, in his remarks on the
uses to which he thinks Christians should put secular histories
of Jesus, including his own history, which come as addenda at
the very end of each of his two books, he says, in brief, that Christian belief is "an act of faith in the historical Jesus as the man-
ifestation of God."[10] He assumes that there will always be divergent accounts of the historical Jesus and that there will always be
divergent Christs built upon these accounts. But, he says, "the
structure of Christianity will always be: this is how we see Jesus-
then as Christ-now," and that each generation of Christians must
"make its best historical judgment about who Jesus was then and,
on that basis, decide what that reconstruction means as Christ
now."[11]

The key words in these remarks are "on that basis." Crossan's
view is, first, that whatever ideas the best secular historians have
about who Jesus *was* as a historical person should be the point of
departure for Christians' views about who Jesus *is* as Christ and,
second, that the transition from Jesus to Christ is the work of faith,
which he allows may be perfectly valid. But these sentiments, which
seem meant to be conciliatory, leave a crucial question unanswered:
What role, if any, should the secular quest for the historical Jesus
play in determining Christians' views about the historical Jesus—
that is, about Jesus-then? Crossan suggests that secular historians
should produce candidate portraits of Jesus-then, and that these
should then exercise some sort of *constraint* on what sort of Christ-
now Christians make out of Jesus-then. But it is not obvious that
Christians should go to secular historians for their portraits of Jesus-
then or, even if they do, that these should *constrain* them in any way
in their elaborating a Christ as the focus of their religious belief. I
am not saying that Crossan is wrong in his apparent view about how
Christians ought to proceed, but merely that it is not obvious that he
is right. And while he may be right, he has not given us any reason
to think that he is right. That is, he has not argued for his view, but
merely asserted it.[12]

E. P. Sanders

In a book that Sanders wrote with Margaret Davies on how to study the Synoptic Gospels, he stresses that secular historians study the New Testament not to proclaim or denounce the Christian faith, and not for purposes of worship, but objectively. They aim "at *disinterested* inquiry," he says, where "disinterested" means "not [being] committed to conclusions in advance of the study of the evidence," and hence they cannot aim "to establish the truth of Christianity" or to establish "the truth of one version of it over another," but "must study with open minds."[13]

What I want to suggest, of course, is that Sanders is in fact committed to conclusions in advance of the study of the evidence. I say this not as a criticism, but merely because it is a fact, and one that needs to be taken into account in assessing the relative merits of secular and religious histories of Jesus. Secular historians, like all historians, bring to their study of the historical evidence a certain framework of real possibilities. It is only within this framework, if anywhere, that they are genuinely open-minded. What lies outside this framework has already been excluded from serious consideration.

As we have seen, in the later of the two history books by Sanders that we considered, he says that "the plan of God is difficult for a historian to study" and that consequently he "cannot deal with the question" of whether the theological views of New Testament authors are true.[14] Presumably by this he means that he intends to leave the question open. But does he leave it open? One of the theological views of the authors of the New Testament Gospels was the conviction that Jesus was God or divinely empowered. Does Sanders leave open the question of whether that conviction is true?

In my view, he does not—at least for the purposes of his historical study, he does not. Instead, he denies that Jesus was God or divinely empowered, as, for instance, in the following remarks:

- "The view that Jesus died for grace thus ends with sheer invention about what would constitute an issue in first-century Judaism. . . . [It] is basically opposed to seeing Jesus as a first-century Jew, who thought like others, spoke their language, was concerned about things which concerned them, and got into trouble over first-century issues. It is thus bad history. Though I am no theologian I suspect that it is bad theology."[15]

- "Jesus did not expect the end of the world in the sense of destruction of the cosmos. He expected a divine, transforming miracle. As a devout Jew, he thought that God had previously intervened in the world in order to save and protect Israel."[16]

- "These partial overlaps between Jesus and other Jews of his time . . . help us understand Jesus."[17]

- "Everyone, including Jesus and his followers, believed that God gave the law to Moses and that he had inspired the other scriptures as well."[18]

- "My own assumption about such [miracle] stories is that many of the 'incredible' ones are based on wishful thinking, others on exaggeration, and only a very few on the conscious wish to deceive."[19]

Obviously, Sanders has assumed, in the absence of evidence to the contrary, that Jesus believed whatever most other Jews in his time and circumstances believed. And he has assumed that the miracle stories are false. But if Sanders had left open the real possibility that Jesus was either God or divinely empowered, there would be no nontheological reason to make such assumptions. Hence Sanders must have assumed that Jesus was neither God nor divinely empowered.

Is any scholar bothered by the fact that many secular historians interpret Jesus on the basis of what I am calling *methodological naturalism*? The answer is, yes, some are bothered, and understandably so. Ben Witherington, for instance, a religiously conservative historian, is a case in point. He says that he finds the discussion of miracles in Sanders's and Crossan's books "rather frustrating":

[Sanders] argues that some of the claimed miracles are based on exaggeration (a psychosomatic illness is seen as something more, and thus the cure is seen as miraculous), some on wishful thinking, and a few, but only a few, on the conscious wish to deceive. He also argues that those "miracles" that actually happened are things that we cannot yet explain because of ignorance of the range of natural causes, because of lack of scientific knowledge. Presumably, then, in Sanders' view those actual miracles that Jesus performed were simply manipulations of presently unknown natural causes.

Witherington continues:

> These explanations may work for some of the exorcisms, or some of the unverifiable illnesses (a person with an internal problem), but they certainly do not explain things like the healing of the blind, or of the deformed, or of those with impurities of the skin and the like, and it certainly does not explain the raising of the dead, which is one of the best and most frequently attested motifs in the Gospels. If Jesus did not really heal these people, then when they went to report to the authorities it would surely have been obvious to them that the person was not well. If on the other hand he did heal them, are we to attribute to Jesus a scientific knowledge of cures and natural healing principles that have escaped other doctors in the last two thousand years? Is it not easier to believe that perhaps God does intervene in human lives in ways we would call miraculous? In view of how little we know about our universe, do we really know that nothing can happen without a "natural" cause?[20]

For better or for worse, there seems to be no room in Sanders's approach for admitting that, for all we know, sometimes Jesus did cure people miraculously.

John Meier

As we have seen, in questions of theology in general and of miracles in particular, Meier bends over backwards not to step on anyone's toes:

- "[I]t is not my intention here or elsewhere in this book to make the theological claim that Jesus actually worked miracles. It is sufficient for the historian to know that Jesus performed deeds that many people, both friends and foes, considered miracles."[21]
- "My major point is that a decision such as 'God has worked a miracle in this particular healing' is actually a theological, not a historical, judgment. A historian may examine claims about miracles, reject those for which there are obvious natural explanations, and record instances where the historian can find no natural explanation. Beyond that, a purely historical judgment cannot go."[22]

- "Just as a historian must reject credulity, so a historian must reject an a priori affirmation that miracles do not or cannot happen. That is, strictly speaking, a philosophical or theological proposition, not a historical one."[23]

Hence, in Meier's view, the historian must leave it an open question whether Jesus performed miracles. He thinks that in deciding this question *either* way, one ceases to be a historian pure and simple and becomes a part-time theologian. Clearly Meier does not want to mix these roles. But can he avoid mixing them?[24]

Consider, first, Meier's hope to know what Jesus' baptism by John meant to Jesus. He says that it surely meant that Jesus saw himself as a part of the people of Israel. Further, in Jesus' accepting John's baptism as a "divinely appointed means of passage from this sinful Israel to a group of Israelites promised salvation on the day of judgment," Jesus was accepting an unofficial, charismatic ritual. Meier says, "Indeed, Jesus would have been a very strange 1st-century Jew if he had rejected all religious ritual."[25] The clear implication is that Jesus was not a very strange first-century Jew. But, of course, if Jesus were God or divinely empowered—even if Jesus in some other way had *genuinely* miraculous powers—then he would have been a very strange first-century Jew. Similarly, Meier says that "there is every reason to suppose" that Jesus thought that certain religious texts, such as the Five Books of Moses and the Prophets, were "authoritative" since "the divine authority of the core of the canon was a given for devout Jews [and, hence, for Jesus] by the time of Jesus."[26] And Meier says that it was "quite natural" for Jesus as a first-century Jew to understand that he was performing exorcisms, which "simply underscores the obvious: Jesus was a man and a Jew of his times."[27] But obviously God or one who was divinely empowered would not necessarily be a man or a Jew of Jesus' times.

The inescapable conclusion is that in composing his historical account, Meier did in fact take what by his own admission is a theological stand. He assumed that Jesus was neither God nor divinely empowered—or, more precisely, he assumed at least that if Jesus was God or divinely empowered, his being exceptional in either of these ways did not extend to the cases considered. But if Jesus was neither God nor divinely empowered, then it would seem that the odds decline rather sharply that Jesus was a genuine miracle worker, that he could, say, actually walk on water or raise the dead.

Methodological Naturalism

We have seen that even with the best of intentions it is difficult for historians of Jesus to avoid being methodological *naturalists* (which implies that they are methodological *atheists* as well). Why is it so difficult? Other secular scientists, it may seem, can be theologically neutral. Why must only secular historians be closet methodological atheists? The answer is that other scientists also are closet atheists.

If this is not obvious, think back to the earliest beginnings of scientific philosophy in the West. Consider the first steps that were taken toward what today we would call a *scientific approach*. One of the very first such steps was taken by the Greek philosopher Heraclitus (ca. 540–470 B.C.E.) when he began using the Greek word *kosmos* in a new way. He was followed in this by the *physiologoi*, who were sixth- and fifth-century B.C.E. philosophers from Greece and Asia Minor.[28] Previously *kosmos* had meant an arranged, beauty-enhancing order. Heraclitus, and then the physiologoi, used it to mean a natural system that is closed to supernatural interference. Along with other thinkers of the time, they believed that the *physis* of a thing, that is, its stable characteristics, set limits both on what it can do and on what can happen to it. Whereas these other thinkers made an exception in the case of supernatural intervention, Heraclitus and the physiologoi refused to make this exception. That is, they made the world into a cosmos by retaining in their conception of the world the physis of things and eliminating everything else. Historians of science often characterize that decision, which was crucial to the origins of science, in heroic terms. Gregory Vlastos, for instance, said of it that "for the first time in history man had achieved a perception of a rational universe" in which the destiny of everything is determined solely by its physis. On this point, he continued, the physiologoi stood united, "a handful of intellectuals against the world."[29]

No doubt it did not occur to the physiologoi to adopt their secular point of view only methodologically. Surely they also adopted it substantively. That is, in all likelihood, they did not just adopt it for the purpose of studying the world but also believed that only what is revealed from such a naturalistic perspective is actually real. Admittedly, their having adopted a secular point of view, even if only methodologically, was a major advance toward natural science. Even so, as a substantive thesis, their postulate went well beyond anything they could prove. There were many things the physiologoi could not explain. For all they knew, some of these unexplained happenings resulted from "supernatural" intervention. As a matter of *secular faith,* they believed that none of them did. But that was something they merely believed, not something they had good reason to think was actually true. The physiologoi were thus the first authors of a kind of secular, antitheological faith—the first, but, as we have seen, not the last. Ever since, scientists and scientifically minded historians, at least for the purpose of doing science and history, have excluded supernatural intervention from the world. The question I want to consider is whether this is the only responsible way for scientists in general and scientifically minded historians in particular to proceed.

Many feel strongly that it is the only responsible way for scientists and historians to proceed.[30] Yet even though today we know a great deal more than the physiologoi knew about the natural world, we are not even close to being able to explain everything. The merest glance at any of countless controversies in the sciences or in historical studies will quickly confirm this. Thus, as a substantive thesis, the view that everything can be explained naturalistically still goes well beyond anything we can prove, even today.[31] Some might argue that our success in explaining naturalistically so much of what previously was unexplained gives us good inductive grounds for claiming that everything *can* be explained naturalistically. But such arguments always depend on the assumption that everything we cannot explain is analogous in all relevant respects to what we can explain. There is no non-question-begging reason I can think of to make this assumption.

Consider, for instance, faith healings. At the shrine of Lourdes in France, teams of doctors of various theological and secular views have conducted before-and-after examinations of scores of people, many of whom claim that they were suddenly cured by divine power. In many cases, these doctors have determined to their own satisfaction that people who claimed to have been cured were once seriously ill and, for reasons that currently cannot be explained scientifically, have suddenly overcome their illnesses.[32] Or, to take another example, consider interactions with "the spirit world" that are regularly reported to have occurred in the context of Native American spiritual rituals. Allegedly neutral and scientifically trained observers have reported that bizarre things for which we currently have no "natural" explanation have happened there also.[33] One can and, I think, should admit that a great many, perhaps most, stories both of faith healings and of interactions with the spirit world are based on incidents that have a natural explanation, whether or not anyone will ever discover what it is. But do we have reason to believe that the incidents reported in *all* such stories can be explained naturalistically? Methodologically, for the purpose of doing history and anthropology, we may be entitled to act as if they all have natural explanations. Substantively, too, we may be entitled to believe that the incidents reported all have natural explanations. But, substantively, do we have so much reason to believe that they all have natural explanations that it would not *also* be rationally *permissible* for someone to leave the matter open? If we do, I cannot imagine what that reason might be.

Suppose we were all to agree that, as a substantive thesis, one is rationally entitled to leave it an open question whether everything that occurs can be explained naturalistically. Even so, we might still doubt whether, methodologically, for the purpose of doing science, and in particular for the purpose of doing "scientific" histories of Jesus, one can or should leave it an open question. Many, probably most, academic historians believe that historians cannot leave this question open. For instance, according to Morton Smith, a renowned New Testament historian, whether "supernatural beings exist is a question for metaphysics." But, he said, even if they do exist "and exercise some regular influence on the world," with consequences that "are taken to be a part of the normal course of natural events," the historian requires "a world in which these normal phenomena are not interfered with by arbitrary and ad hoc divine interventions to produce abnormal events with special historical consequences." Smith said that "this is not a matter of personal preference, but of professional necessity." In his view, the historian's job "is to calculate the most probable explanation of the preserved evidence." "The minds of the gods are inscrutable and their actions, consequently, incalculable." Hence, Smith concluded, unless the possibility of their special intervention is ruled out, there "would always be an unknown probability that a deity might have intervened." And so long as there is that unknown probability, "there can be no calculation of most probable causes."[34]

Smith was mistaken in that conclusion. Historians do not have to assume that God does not (or the gods do not) intervene ad hoc in the human world. They can get along with weaker assumptions. Before explaining how, I want to show that the problem under consideration is not just one for historians such as Crossan and Sanders who would write the history of Jesus in a purely secular way, but also one for some of their most intelligent and well-meaning critics, who advocate that the history of Jesus should be written on the basis of theological presuppositions.

C. Stephen Evans

Evans is a philosophically sophisticated and well-informed critic of secular historical Jesus studies. As a religiously conservative Christian, he has tried to answer the challenge that such studies pose for Christian beliefs. In his view, a basic problem with all such studies is that their authors are closet philosophers. It is that, he seems to think, rather than slim and ambiguous evidence and the demand for full-fledged interpretations of Jesus, that explains disagreement in historical Jesus studies.

Evans imagines someone—he calls him "James"—who, by hypothesis, lacks the professional expertise of trained historians. In Evans's view, since a good deal of disagreement among secular historians of Jesus is rooted in assumptions ("philosophical, theological, and literary") they have made about which they "may not have any special expertise either," then, with respect to views so rooted, "James may be competent to evaluate the views of the scholars."[35] One such philosophical assumption is a prejudice that Evans says many secular historians have against the miraculous and, in general, against any supernatural intervention into the natural world, including prophesy.[36] In his view, one "cannot begin by ruling out as impossible any supernatural knowledge or insight on the part of Jesus, if one wishes fairly to test the claim that God was at work in Jesus in a special way, or that Jesus was actually God incarnate."[37] But then Evans says almost nothing about how an enlightened historian is supposed to deal with the possibility that Jesus may have had foreknowledge.

This silence on Evans's part causes problems. For instance, he endorses enthusiastically an interpretation offered by the philosopher Eleanor Stump of the story of the raising of Lazarus. According to Evans's presentation of Stump's interpretation, in this story "Jesus may be seen as delaying his coming partly so as to reward the faith of the sisters with a glorious miracle." However, "when he arrives, the distress of the sisters reveals that his plans have not proceeded precisely as he wished and expected."[38] Thus, in the interpretation that Evans endorses, in this instance Jesus expected one thing and something else happened. What, then, of Jesus' supposed divine foreknowledge? Does it come and go? Does it come into play only on certain kinds of issues? Is it normally reliable but simply failed him this time? The closest Evans comes even to raising such questions, let alone answering them, is to say that "it is thus quite coherent with the story to see Jesus as empowered with supernatural insight at times."[39] True enough, but even conceding that it is coherent, we are still left with a huge question about how, as historians, we should proceed.

J.D.G. Dunn

Dunn is professor of divinity at the University of Durham, in England, and the author of several books on the history of early Christianity.[40] In one of these, *The Evidence for Jesus* (1985), he addresses the quest for the historical Jesus. Dunn makes no bones about his being a believing Christian. And he admits that he wrote this particular book to quiet the fears of other Christians about historical Jesus studies. Like Evans, he makes the point that Christians have "nothing to fear from scholarship." However, unlike Evans, he makes this point not by trying to put historians down but by arguing that Christians "should welcome the critically inquiring and investigative skills of scholars." He thinks that Christians should welcome them partly because he thinks that eventually scholars will arrive at results that are congenial to Christians, but also partly for theological reasons: "Liberty of opinion, genuine respect for those who differ and a reverent agnosticism in many matters of secondary importance is a wholly proper and indeed essential response of faith"; "since we walk by faith and not by light, our confidence should be in the God and Father of our Lord Jesus Christ, rather than in what we can see and handle and control. 'Let him who boasts, boast of the Lord!'"[41]

Needless to say, Dunn's methods differ sharply from those of Crossan and Sanders. They are closer to those of Meier. But whereas Meier thinks that it is no part of the historian's task to assess the plausibility of claims that God intervened in the natural world,

Dunn thinks that it is part of the historian's task. He agrees with other New Testament scholars that the authors of the New Testament Gospels were often inventive. But he trusts the New Testament authors to reveal what really happened *much* more often than do liberal historians, and he puts a different spin than do liberal historians on those passages of the New Testament that he admits are inventive. For instance, in response to the question, "Has New Testament scholarship undermined the ordinary Christian's belief that the Gospels are historically trustworthy and accurate in what they tell about Jesus?" he answers, "Yes and No." Yes, in that New Testament scholars agree that the authors of the Gospels did not just report, but also interpreted. *"No, in that when the Gospel writers intended to provide historical information, that information can be trusted as reliable."* [42] In explaining what he means, Dunn never mentions the birth narratives, focusing instead only on examples from New Testament accounts of Jesus' public career and his resurrection.

In the case of the resurrection, Dunn says that the claim that God raised Jesus from the dead is of "fundamental importance to Christian faith" and that if this claim is false, or only vaguely true, many basic Christian doctrines would have to be revised, including Christian understandings of who Jesus was and is and of the significance of his death, and the hopes that Christians entertain for themselves and others. He says that the question of whether modern scholarship has "disproved the resurrection of Jesus, or even made belief in his resurrection more difficult," is as important for Christians "as any question can be." [43]

Dunn begins his account of the resurrection by saying that we should start by recognizing that we cannot get back directly to the resurrection itself since it belongs to "the irretrievable pastness of history." [44] Even so, he continues, we have five sorts of historical evidence that it actually occurred: reports of Jesus' tomb being found empty; reported "sightings" of Jesus after his death; the transformation of the first disciples and the subsequent initial spread of the new faith; the very high regard in which Christians soon came to hold Jesus; and claims of believers since the beginning of Christianity to encounter Jesus alive here and now. [45]

Dunn says that many Christians want to include as basic data the testimony of believers today. He concedes that "in a full-scale evaluation of the evidence such testimonies would have to be examined with care" and that their potential value, "as 'eye'-witness reports," is considerable. He says, however, that he will pass over this evidence, since such testimonies "almost always depend to an important extent on the [witnesser's] prior beliefs." In other words, he explains, it is because Christians already believe that Jesus rose from the dead that they can recognize their experience in prayer or devotion as an encounter with Jesus.[46] Dunn says that the same is true of the previous two sorts of evidence that he listed: the transformation of the disciples and the high opinion that early Christians had of Jesus.

Dunn's reason for dismissing reports in our own times of people having seen Jesus is curious. Surely many contemporary "experiences of Jesus" are had by people who are not already Christians. In our own times, there must be hundreds of reported cases of people who in the throes of a *conversion* experience to Christianity came to believe that Jesus is alive. Are *their* experiences evidence that Jesus is alive, or not? If they are, then why don't they count importantly in favor of the New Testament reports that Jesus rose from the dead? I shall return to these questions later.

Dunn rests his case for the veracity of the resurrection reports on his first two sorts of evidence: reports of the empty tomb, and early "sightings" of Jesus.[47] So far as the empty tomb reports are concerned, he says there are two kinds of evidence that the reports are not reliable. One is that the various reports conflict, and the other is that Paul, in 1 Corinthians 15, does not say anything about an empty tomb. Counterbalancing these negative considerations, he claims, are four sources of evidence in favor of the reliability of the empty tomb reports: All four Gospels attribute the discovery of the empty tomb to women; the confusion between the different accounts of the resurrection in the Gospels; archaeological evidence; and the lack of any indications that Christians regarded the place where Jesus had been buried as having any special significance.

Regarding the first of these positive considerations, Dunn says that in first-century Judea, since women did not have much status, they "were probably regarded as unreliable witnesses." Hence the fact that they were reported to be the primary witnesses is evidence that the reports are factual, since, in his view, the only good reason for attributing the empty tomb reports to women is that this is how it was remembered as having actually happened. Regarding the confusion between different accounts, Dunn says that it is "a mark of the sincerity of those from whom the testimony was derived" and shows that "we cannot plausibly regard [the reports] as deriving from a single source." In particular, he adds, "the fact that the earliest Gospel (Mark) ends without any record of a 'resurrection appearance' [Dunn accepts that the original version of Mark ended at 16:8] has to be matched with the fact that the earliest account of 'resurrection appearances' (I Cor. 15) has no reference to the tomb being empty." Dunn says that there is nothing to indicate that one was contrived to bolster the other, and that this "speaks favourably for the value of each."

The archeological evidence, Dunn says, shows "that at the time of Jesus, a popular understanding of resurrection in Palestine would have involved some 're-use' of the dead body." Thus "a claim made in Jerusalem within a few weeks of [Jesus'] crucifixion, that God had raised Jesus—that is, the body of Jesus—from death, would not have gained much credence had his tomb been undisturbed or the fate of his body known to be otherwise. The absence of any such counterclaim in any available literature of the period, Christian or Jewish, is important." Finally, there is no evidence that the first Christians regarded the place where Jesus had been laid as having any special significance. This "strange silence," which Dunn says was exceptional in view of the religious practice of the time, "has only one obvious explanation": the first Christians did not regard Jesus' grave as having any special significance because it was empty. Dunn concludes that on the whole the evidence points firmly to the conclusion that Jesus' tomb was found empty and that its emptiness was a factor in the first Christians' belief in the resurrection of Jesus.[48]

Dunn's account of the "resurrection appearances," while shorter, follows a similar pattern. As evidence against the veracity of the reports, he mentions again conflicts in the New Testament accounts. As evidence in favor, he mentions the testimony of 1 Corinthians 15:3–8, which Dunn says "goes back to within two or three years of the events described." The prominence of women in the records of the first sightings and the absence of any indication that the reports are contrived are also significant, he claims. In his view, the most plausible alternative explanation is that "the witnesses were deluded"—"not deceitful, but deceived"—in which case, the "resurrection appearances" would simply be hallucinations, perhaps born of frustrated hopes, "visions begotten of hysteria." It counts against this alternative explanation, he says, that the experiences reported by the early Christians were unexpected and that their reports differ from other life-after-death visions from the same period. In no other case, he says, did the person who saw the vision conclude, "This man has been raised from the dead."[49]

Dunn cautions that while historians have good evidence that the resurrection took place, they do not know in what it consisted. Not only do we have no record that anyone actually witnessed it, but also we cannot be sure that it could be witnessed. However, he says, we can say that by "resurrection" these earliest Christian witnesses meant that something had happened to Jesus and not just themselves. God had raised *him,* not merely reassured *them.* "He was alive again, made alive again with the life which is the climax of God's purpose for humankind, not merely retrieved from the jaws of death, but conqueror over death, 'exalted to God's right hand.'" Dunn says, "It was this glowing conviction that lay at the heart of the chain reaction which began Christianity."[50]

Clearly Dunn, unlike Meier, thinks that it is professionally appropriate for a historian to conclude that God intervened in the natural world. Even more clearly, he does not, as Crossan and Sanders did, rule out *in advance* divine intervention as a possible explanation. Still, it is hard to believe that his assessment of the plausibility of competing accounts of the evidence is not influenced by his extrahistorical conviction that Jesus did rise from the dead. For instance, does the lack of "evidence that the first Christians regarded the place where Jesus had been laid as having any special significance" have as the "only obvious explanation" that Jesus' tomb was empty? For the early Christians, wouldn't the fact that Jesus rose from the dead *out of that tomb* have itself given the tomb quite a bit of special significance? If in fact Dunn's assessment of the evidence is influenced by his extrahistorical conviction that Jesus rose from the dead, then he joins Crossan and Sanders, in that all of them are interpreting the historical evidence against the backdrop of controversial and perhaps even question-begging extrahistorical convictions. In the cases of Crossan and Sanders, these background convictions rule out the miraculous. In the case of Dunn, they seem to make it more likely, at least in connection with Jesus. Also, Dunn's refusal to consider contemporary reports of "experiences of Jesus" suggests that, like Meier, he recognizes that certain issues fall beyond the purview of the historian, even though he and Meier have different ideas about which issues those are.

Earlier, when we considered Evans's view, it turned out that what we needed to know from him—or someone—is how to determine which circumstances are those in which we are entitled to assume that Jesus had foreknowledge. Evans did not tell us, and in fact he did not even raise the question. His not raising it left open the possibility that the kind of historical research that he endorses is a game without rules. I have the same worry about Dunn's account, though admittedly others may feel differently about it. The assumptions of Crossan and Sanders that non-natural intervention into the natural world is out of the question may be high-handed and arbitrary, but at least we know the basis on which they are going to proceed. In my view, one cannot say the same about either Evans or Dunn. Should we conclude, then, that Morton Smith was right after all, and that historians must assume that God does not intervene ad hoc into human affairs? I don't think so. Rather, what we should conclude is that historical research must proceed under the rubric of some rules *or other.* What leads to methodological chaos is to proceed without *any* appropriate rules, rather than not proceeding under the particular rules favored by Crossan, Sanders, and Smith. Methodological naturalism is only one among a large number of possible ways for historians to generate appropriate rules for interpreting evidence.

Faith-History

What I am suggesting, in effect, is that there is unexplored middle ground between Smith's overly restrictive approach to historical research and Evans's and Dunn's overly permissive approaches. Put simply, it consists in three steps: First, except in certain kinds of circumstances, proceed on the basis of ordinary secular historical methodology, that is, on the basis of methodological naturalism; second, specify which kinds of circumstances are to be considered exceptions; and, third, explain which alternative methodology is going to be followed in these kinds of circumstances. I call the product of following these rules a *faith-history.*

So far as I know, in writing a faith-history, no historian has ever been explicit about which methodological rules he or she has followed (but I have not surveyed all of the attempts). Typically, what would-be faith-historians do is either to throw ordinary historical methodology to the winds or, as in the cases of Evans and of Farrar (Chapter 3), use ordinary historical methodology and then drop it, willy-nilly, without explaining the basis for their doing so or even addressing the possibility that they may be proceeding arbitrarily.

Sometimes historians who are at least trying to make room for exceptions to naturalism proceed more consistently, as Dunn and Meier surely have, but still without ever being explicit about which background assumptions are guiding their historical accounts or how these assumptions are affecting their assessments of the relative merits of competing interpretations. Hence, to the best of my knowledge, faith-historians (to whatever degree) have not done particularly well at explaining what they are doing.[51] Even so, faith-history is clearly a possible option.

How should faith-historians proceed? I would suggest that the basic task of faith-historians is to explain, presumably on theological grounds, the ways in which some historical figures, such as Jesus, are more than human or have more than ordinary human powers. And they have to do this in a way that makes non-natural influences in the natural world the exception rather than the rule, so that for the most part historians can proceed on the assumption that what happens can be explained naturalistically. How might the faith-historians do this? Consider, first, a limiting case, so far as the quest for the historical Jesus is concerned. It is a way in which Jesus might have been more than human that would not make any difference at all to historical methodology.

Suppose that a theologically oriented historian believes that although God has intervened in the natural world, He did so only once, by manifesting as Jesus. That would secure the doctrine of the incarnation, which, for Christians, is no small matter theologically. Suppose our historian also believes that, in manifesting as Jesus, God manifested as a human being subject to *all* of the limitations of ordinary human beings. In that case—except for the incarnation, which may have involved just a miraculous intervention in the physiological processes that led to Jesus' conception, a matter about which historians rarely comment anyway—the task of such a theologically oriented historian would be the same as that of wholly secular historians. Hence Smith is wrong: Without unleashing methodological chaos, one can believe that God has intervened in the natural world, even that God has intervened miraculously.

What about historians of Jesus who take a more robust view of God's interventions? How should they proceed? One way would be to start from the limiting case scenario just sketched and then to make exceptions to it. For instance, it might be the historian's view that God, in manifesting as Jesus, manifested as a human being subject to all of the limitations of ordinary human beings except one, namely, that whereas in the case of ordinary human beings biological death ends all of their activity on Earth, in the case of Jesus it did not; rather, without Jesus' having the slightest idea in advance that it would happen, he rose from the dead in some sort of "human" form and subsequently had augmented powers. Thus, in the pre-Easter part of such a historian's study, his or her methodology would be the same as that of wholly secular historians. In the post-Easter part, it would be different. To be methodologically transparent, the historian would have to specify the scope and limits of these differences, which would involve specifying the scope and limits of Jesus' post-Easter augmented powers. Put to one side, for the moment, the question of how a faith-historian might do this. There is no reason that I know of to think that it could not be done. And, if it were done successfully, the faith-historian would then have made quite a bit of room for Christian theology. He would have made room for the incarnation and also for the claim that Jesus rose from the dead with augmented human powers. And he would have made this room for Christian theology without having unleashed methodological chaos, at least in the pre-Easter part of the story.

Finally, how are historians of Jesus who take an even more robust view about God's interventions to proceed in a way that allows them to continue to do history? The answer, I think, is that it all depends. Clearly, however, one could continue, step by step, in the way I have just illustrated, without necessarily being methodologically irresponsible, to enrich dramatically the scope of one's taking into account what one assumes to be God's interventions in the world. Equally clearly, at some point in such a step-by-step progression, if one kept going, eventually one would have gone too far. Even if one proceeded in small steps, and just kept going, methodological chaos probably would creep back in gradually, in a variety of ways. There is no point in trying to enumerate them. That theology can undermine secular historical methodology is not controversial. The controversial question is whether theology, if it were allowed to exert its influence on an otherwise secular historical inquiry, would *necessarily* undermine it. Many, perhaps most, secular historians believe that it would. I have argued that they are wrong.

It may seem that in opting for the procedure I have sketched, faith-historians are stuck with an impossibly daunting task—that of describing their alternative historical methodologies. But they would not have to describe their alternative methodologies in any more detail than secular historians (who, as I have been arguing, are really faith-historians of a different stripe) describe their secular historical methodologies, which is not in much detail at all. So the faith-historian's task may not be so daunting after all. Still, the task is not an easy one, either. And until some faith-historian tries to perform it, the rest of us are stuck with an unpleasant choice: either the so-called secular history, with its methodological naturalism, or theologically inspired history, played without rules, or at least by unspoken rules.

7

CROSSING LINES

Marcus J. Borg and
N. T. Wright

BOTH BORG AND WRIGHT PROFESS to be devout Christians, actively involved in church life. Both wrote their doctoral dissertations at Oxford University, just a few years apart, under the direction of the same man, George Caird. And both are extremely influential. Yet, as historical Jesus scholars, they differ in important ways: Borg is a liberal, Wright a conservative; Borg a member of the Jesus Seminar, Wright a severe critic of the Jesus Seminar; Borg a prominent critic of apocalyptic interpretations of Jesus, Wright a prominent defender of apocalyptic interpretations.[1]

What is of most interest for present purposes is that both Borg and Wright, as historical Jesus scholars, cross the line between historian and theologian that has been so important, from Reimarus to the present day, in the self-definition of virtually all of the major players in historical Jesus studies. Borg crosses the line by invoking mysticism, Wright by invoking theology and philosophy.[2] As a consequence both of them emerge, in different ways, as faith-historians of a sort—though it might come as a shock to Borg to have his work characterized as faith-history. In any case, the purpose of the present chapter is to explore the consequences, so far as historical methodology goes, of a historian's crossing the line between history and theology.

Marcus J. Borg

Borg, a professor of religion and culture at Oregon State University, has been chair of the Historical Jesus Section of the Society of Biblical Literature. His major book, *Jesus, A New Vision* (1987), has been quite influential. He has written several other widely read books, including his more recent *Jesus in Contemporary Scholarship* (1994) and *Meeting Jesus Again for the First Time* (1994).[3] I shall draw on all of these sources. Since my concern in this chapter is primarily with questions of method, I will reverse the order of exposition that I followed in the previous chapters, sketching for each author first his results, and then his methods.

Results

Borg's Jesus was Jewish, and remained Jewish all of his life. He did not intend to found a new religion but to bring about a change within Judaism. All of his early followers were Jewish. In Borg's view, we do not have any historically reliable *stories* about Jesus before he was about thirty years old, but we do have some historically reliable *information*. We know that he was born shortly before 4 B.C.E., that his parents, Joseph and Mary, were Jewish, that he had four brothers and some sisters, that he grew up in Nazareth, and that Joseph probably died before Jesus began his public ministry.[4] We also know that Jesus' family would have had very low social status—less than that of subsistence farmers—and that the environment in which Jesus grew up, though rural, was remarkably "cosmopolitan." For instance, many Jews in Jesus' environment spoke both Aramaic and Greek.[5]

At some point, Borg says, Jesus must have become a religious seeker and embarked on a quest. Otherwise it is hard to explain his having become a follower of John the Baptist. In Borg's view, probably Jesus underwent a "conversion experience" or "internal transformation," as a consequence of which "religious impulses and energies" became central to his life, and probably this transformation had something to do with John the Baptist. In any case, soon after Jesus began associating with John, Jesus began his public ministry, perhaps stepping in to carry on when John was arrested.

Borg stresses that Jesus probably did not think of himself as the Messiah or as the Son of God in some special sense. Contrary to the impression one gets from reading the New Testament, Jesus' message was neither eschatological nor about himself and the importance of believing in him. Rather, his message was about God.[6] Borg says that Jesus was a teacher of wisdom, a social prophet, a movement founder, and, most important, a "person of Spirit." In characterizing Jesus as a person of Spirit, Borg means that Jesus had "an experiential awareness of the reality of God" and of "other dimensions of reality," which were foundational to everything else he was.[7]

Borg explains that persons of Spirit are found in every religious tradition, and that their exotic experiences take different forms: visions; journeys into other dimensions of reality; strong impressions that another reality has descended upon them; experiences of natural objects "momentarily transfigured by 'the sacred,'" such as a bush that burns without being consumed; and so on. Common to all of these forms, Borg says, is that the special experiences of such persons are vivid and revealing, making ordinary perceptions of the world seem like "blindness."[8] As a consequence, persons of Spirit "become funnels or conduits for the power or wisdom of God to enter into this world," and often they are mediators who connect their communities to other dimensions of reality.[9] These other dimensions of reality, Borg says, are nonmaterial, yet "charged with energy and power." They are not "somewhere else" but in us and we in them. Borg says that whereas the modern, naturalistic worldview is "one-dimensional," the worldview of persons of Spirit is "multidimensional."[10]

According to Borg, in Jesus' view, our goal in life should be to live in imitation of God, who Jesus believed is compassionate. Jesus' main message was, "Be compassionate, as God is compassionate." His view and orientation, though not dominant in the Jewish tradition from which he sprang, were nevertheless rooted in that tradition. The dominant view was, "Be holy, as God is holy." Jesus, in effect, proposed that holiness, as an ideal, be replaced by compassion. Borg says that "for Jesus, compassion was more than a quality of God and an individual virtue: it was a social paradigm, the core value for life in community." Thus Jesus advocated a "politics of compassion." This brought him into conflict with the prevailing purity system, at the center of which were the temple and the priesthood. Jesus challenged this purity system by word and deed, including by his practice of open and inclusive table fellowship.[11]

Borg says that Jesus was a teacher of wisdom, or a sage, in that he explained to people how to live in accordance with reality. But Jesus was the type of sage who teaches "subversive" rather than "conventional" wisdom, which he conveyed primarily in parables and aphorisms, often one-liners that were meant to be "striking, enigmatic and evocative." Borg suggests, for instance, that Jesus' saying, "Leave the dead to bury the dead" was intended to wake people up by drawing attention to a way of living "that amounts to living in the land of the dead." Borg thinks that although Jesus probably believed in an afterlife, his message was not about how to get there or about the threat of hell, but about the danger of living unconnected to Spirit. Whereas conventional wisdom is preoccupied with requirements, Jesus' subversive wisdom emphasized "the graciousness of God."

In Borg's view, the gospel of the historical Jesus—the good news of his own message—is that there is a way to live that moves beyond both secular and religious conventional wisdom and beyond a life of requirements and measuring up, with its attendant anxiety and the bondage of self-preoccupation. This way to live moves toward a God-relationship, with its ensuing peace and trust, and the freedom of self-forgetfulness. In sum, Jesus' message was that it is both possible and desirable to move from a "life centered in culture" to a "life centered in God."

Methods

Borg says that when he initially went to seminary it had not occurred to him that the Jesus of history might be different from the Christ of faith. At seminary, however, he soon learned that although the Christ of faith is spoken of as divine, of one substance with God, the second person of the Trinity, and so on, the Jesus of history would not have known any of this about himself. Borg says that this came to him as quite a shock. Previously, he had assumed that Jesus talked about himself as he does in John. In seminary, he learned that the contrast between John and the Synoptics is so great that one of them—and it had to be John—must be nonhistorical. Borg says that this made him so angry that he would have been happy to have seen John excised from the New Testament. He also learned then of two further views that were dominant at the time in Jesus scholarship. One was that we cannot know much about the Jesus of history, not even from the accounts in the Synoptics; and the other was that the little we can know is not attractive. For instance, Borg learned that Jesus was an eschatological prophet who expected and proclaimed the end of the present world and the coming of the kingdom of God in the very near future, and that this false expectation—not his own identity or the importance of believing in him—was the heart of Jesus' message and the basis of his urgent call to repent.[12] Borg says that his dissatisfaction at finding this out was not much relieved by the received view that since the historical Jesus is theologically irrelevant, our not being able to know much about him, except for a few unattractive tidbits, does not really matter.[13] Borg says that this new "knowledge," together with the tension that he had already been feeling between his image of God and his otherwise modern image of reality, quickly propelled him from "closet agnostic" to "closet atheist." Increasingly, he says, he began to see not only Christianity but all religions as cultural products: "The notion that we made it all up was somewhat alarming, but also increasingly compelling."[14]

Borg says that his skepticism about God caused him to concentrate his historical research on Jesus' involvement with social and political issues, especially his challenge to the prevailing Jewish purity system. His main conclusion then was that in a social world dominated by the politics of purity, Jesus advocated a politics of compassion.[15] Then, when he was in his thirties, Borg had several experiences that were "moments of transformed perception in which the earth is seen as 'filled with the glory of God,' shining with a radiant presence." These experiences led him to a "rediscovery of mystery," not as "an intellectual paradox," but as an experiential confrontation with the sacred. As a consequence, he came to understand God differently. Instead of as a supernatural being "out there," God became "the sacred at the center of existence, the holy mystery that is all around us and within us"—the "non-material ground and source and presence," in which "we live and move and have our being." Gradually it became obvious to him "that God—the sacred, the holy, the numinous was 'real,'" and no longer merely a concept or an article of belief, but "an element of experience."[16]

Borg's new understanding of God soon transformed his old understanding of the historical Jesus. He says that he was now able to see the centrality of God (or "Spirit") in Jesus' own life. This perception became for Borg "the vantage point" for what he now regards as "the key truth about Jesus": that Jesus was both deeply involved in the world of everyday social issues and deeply grounded in the world of Spirit, and that Jesus' grounding in Spirit was "the source of everything that he was."[17]

As a consequence, Borg says that he now understood why the Christian community out of which John's gospel came falsely portrayed the *pre-Easter* Jesus as saying such things about himself as, "I am the light of the world," "I am the bread of life," "I am the way, the truth, and the life," and so on. They portrayed Jesus in such ways because that is how they experienced the *post-Easter* Jesus.[18] Borg concluded that "John's gospel is 'true'" even though it is not, by and large, historically accurate. And whereas before, Borg had seen Christian life as being primarily about believing, now he sees it as being primarily about entering into a relationship with that to which the Christian tradition points, which, he says, is no more the property of the Christian tradition than it is of other religious traditions.

Analysis

For present purposes, two things are initially intriguing about Borg's autobiographical revelations: first, that he put a realist theological interpretation on his "mystical" experiences; and, second, that these experiences, so interpreted, profoundly affected his interpretation of Jesus. What I mean by saying that Borg put a realist theological interpretation on his experiences is that he took (and still takes) his experiences to have revealed truths about "God" and "dimensions of reality" that are unavailable to scientific investigation. In other words, he does not merely think that he and others have had exotic experiences that they have *believed* or that they now *believe* to be experiences of God and other dimensions of reality. Instead of merely making such a psychological claim about beliefs, Borg claims that he and others have had experiences that *actually were* experiences of God and other dimensions of reality. Thus his claim is not merely about human beliefs but about transcendent realities. Moreover, it is about transcendent realities that, currently and for the foreseeable future, are beyond the reach of any conceivable sort of scientific test.[19]

It is clear from Borg's autobiographical remarks that his "mystical" experiences, as he interpreted them, profoundly affected his interpretation of Jesus. By his own account, he interpreted the evidence regarding Jesus in one way before he had his mystical experiences. Then, after his experiences and at least partly because of them, he interpreted the evidence in a different way. Although Borg does not put it this way, the unmistakable implication of his remarks is that in having these mystical experiences, he became (at least to some extent) a person of Spirit himself and thereby was enabled to see that Jesus also had been a person of Spirit. In short, Borg's mystical experiences, interpreted in the theologically realistic way that he interpreted and interprets them, affected his assessment of the historical evidence, not just marginally but in a central way.

Another intriguing thing about Borg's autobiographical revelations is that in his self-understanding of his work as an academic historian, he seems to think that he has been able to proceed without being influenced by extra-academic religious convictions.[20] Yet, by his own account, in interpreting Jesus, his acceptance of the view that persons of Spirit experience God and other dimensions of reality affected his evaluation of the historical evidence. Hence if the question is, did Borg allow his acceptance of a particular view about God and dimensions of reality to which science has no access to affect his evaluation of evidence, the answer is clearly yes. In this sense, Borg interpreted his experiences in ways that had definite theological content, and these experiences, so interpreted, affected his evaluation of the evidence.

Yet, in my view, in doing this Borg did not violate any reasonable norm having to do with secular scientific methodology. The main reason he did not is that the theological dimension of his interpretation is easily excised, leaving a naturalistic thesis intact. What I mean by this is that even though Borg interpreted Jesus' experiences as genuine experiences of God and of "other dimensions of reality," all that he really needed for his interpretation of Jesus as a person of Spirit is to have said that Jesus (and some of his followers) *believed* that his (and their) experiences were genuinely of God and/or of other dimensions of reality. Quite apart from whether mystics actually experience God or other dimensions of reality, anyone can recognize that some people do have mystical experiences and that these may profoundly affect their lives. Thus, so far as historical methodology is concerned, at least the core of Borg's theology and also its influence on his interpretation of Jesus are completely innocuous.

In one respect, however, it may seem that Borg's "theology" is not innocuous, namely, in his handling of the miracle stories. In short,

Borg is "soft" on miracles. Like Meier, but perhaps for different reasons, he wants to leave it an open question whether Jesus did things that more naturalistic thinkers would regard as genuine miracles. For instance, after accounting for Jesus' exorcisms and healings in ways that more naturalistically inclined historians could also accept, Borg turned to the harder cases: resuscitations of dead people, the stilling of storms, walking on water, and so on. Borg asked whether these stories should be taken seriously. He replied that, for two reasons, "it is very difficult to know." The first is that Jesus was a "charismatic mediator," and "we simply do not know" what the limits are to the powers of a charismatic mediator. The second is that "symbolic elements" abound in these miracle stories, which suggests that those who wrote them may have had a motive for writing them other than that of telling the literal truth about what actually happened. In the end, Borg concludes that so far as the literal truth of these miracle stories is concerned, "a clear historical judgment is impossible."[21]

Here again I think that Borg is innocent of any inappropriate mixing of theology and secular historical studies. In my view, in saying that we do not know the limits of what is possible in such cases and hence are not in a position to rule out the possibility that Jesus actually did perform some of the miracles that are attributed to him, Borg is simply telling the truth. I think a better case could be made for saying that Crossan and Sanders, in summarily brushing aside the possibility that any of the miracles stories might be true, are relying inappropriately on a kind of "antitheology theology." They, more than Borg, are pretending to know something that it seems to me no one actually knows.[22]

In my view, Borg's approach also contrasts favorably with the approach taken by Meier, who reaches a similar conclusion—agnosticism—about the miracle stories. As you will recall, Meier refrains from making a judgment about the reliability of the miracle stories because he does not think that it is part of his job *as a secular historian* to make such judgments. But who determines "the job requirements" for secular historians? And whoever determines the job requirements, who gave *them* the right to set the limits? Meier does not address such questions. Perhaps he should have. In my view, Borg's approach is better: Historians cannot say whether any of the miracle stories are true not because it is not their job as historians to say, but because they do not know. Yet Borg's admirable willingness to accept responsibility for his own interpretation comes at a price.

The price is that Borg should be more forthcoming than he is about how he knows that certain other incidents that he regards as nonhistorical merit that judgment. For instance, he says that "the image of the historical Jesus as a divine or semi-divine being, who saw himself as the divine savior whose purpose was to die for the sins of the world, and whose message consisted of proclaiming that, is simply not historically true." This image, he claims, "is the product of a blend produced by the early church—a blending of the church's memory of Jesus with the church's beliefs about the risen Christ." In other words, in Borg's view, the early church remembered through a lens that was colored by its beliefs about the risen Christ, that is, through a lens "of faith."[23] But how does Borg know this? If we should leave it an open question whether the historical Jesus could perform miracles, such as bringing the dead back to life, shouldn't we also leave it an open question whether the historical Jesus saw himself as a "divine savior"? After all, he would not even have had to perform a miracle to have done that.

N. T. Wright

Wright, Dean of Lichfield, has taught New Testament studies at Oxford, Cambridge, and McGill Universities and has written many books that in one way or another are related to the question of interpreting Jesus.[24] Most of these books are histories, with some theology mixed in, but some are primarily devotional. His latest and most fully developed contribution to historical Jesus studies may be found primarily in his (projected) four-volume Christian Origins and the Question of God, two volumes of which have been published: The New Testament and the People of God (1992) and Jesus and the Victory of God (1996). Both of these volumes, while quite readable, are massive works of staggering erudition. Like Meier, though not with as much attention to arguments, Wright tends to survey the views of other historians before presenting his own, and so these volumes, like Meier's, can be used to get an overview of the current state of historical Jesus studies. Wright has also written a shorter, more popular book, Who Was Jesus? (1992), the purpose of which is primarily to refute the interpretations of Barbara Theiring, A. N. Wilson, and Bishop John Spong.

Results

Wright, whose views on the historical Jesus are unusually elaborate and finely nuanced, rejects altogether the idea that history should be kept separate from theology. Sometimes he seems even to reject the very distinction between history and theology. This adds to the excitement and interest of his work, but it also makes it harder to summarize. A good place to start, though, is with his answers to four questions that he says all historians of Jesus need to address.

How Does Jesus Fit into Judaism?   Wright says that many historians have erred in regarding Jesus as either too typically Jewish or not Jewish enough. For instance, he thinks that Geza Vermes, who portrayed Jesus as a wandering Hasid (Jewish holy man), and S.G.F. Brandon, who portrayed Jesus as a common sort of Jewish revolutionary, erred by making Jesus too Jewish, and that Bultmann, in portraying Jesus as a teacher of timeless truths, and J. Downing, Burton Mack, and Crossan, in portraying Jesus as a Cynic sage, failed to make Jesus Jewish enough. Wright also categorically rejects what he calls the "well-worn" traditional Christian position of distinguishing Jesus from his Jewish background by portraying first-century Judaism as a morass of legalism and formalism and Jesus as the teacher of an interior, spiritual religion.[25] Wright says that first-century Jews were hungry for God to act *within* history, and that if Jesus had been primarily a teacher of abstract, interior truths, he would have been "incomprehensible" and "irrelevant."[26]

Imagine, Wright suggests, that you had been a Galilean peasant, working on your small parcel of land, and that you had heard that a prophet named Jesus was announcing that God was now at last becoming king. This could only mean, Wright says, that Jesus was announcing that Israel was at long last going to be rescued from oppression. He says that when people set down their tools and trudged up a hillside to hear Jesus talk, they were not going to hear someone tell them to be nice to each other or that if they behaved themselves or acquired the right beliefs, a rosy future would await them in heaven. Nor were they going to hear someone tell them that God had decided at long last to do something about forgiving them for their sins. Wright says that first-century Jews already knew that they ought to be nice to each other, and to whatever extent they thought about life after death, they also knew that God would look after them, eventually giving them new physical bodies in a renewed world. Neither were they gloomily wandering around wondering how their sins were ever going to be forgiven. For that, they had the temple and the sacrificial system. In other words, according to Wright, if Jesus had said what a lot of commentators seem to think he said, he would have put his audiences to sleep, whereas what he actually said woke them up.[27]

In Wright's view, Jesus was very Jewish, and first-century Judaism can be understood only within the context of "intense eschatological expectation." However, like some others (he mentions Borg as an example), Wright thinks that Jesus must have confronted Judaism by reinterpreting a key part of its heritage.[28] In particular, he says, Jesus' warnings about imminent judgment must have been about social and political events, "*seen as the climactic moment in Israel's history* and, in consequence, as a summons to *national* repentance." Wright says that Jesus must have appeared to be "a successor to Jeremiah and his like." But part of Jesus' warning was that since Israel's history was drawing to a close, he was not merely one more in a long line of prophets, but the last in the line. The rest of his warning to Israel was that business as usual would bring "political disaster," as "the judgment of Israel's own god."[29] Finally, Jesus proclaimed that Israel's God was going to establish his kingdom through his (Jesus') own work. Wright says that this way of viewing Jesus not only makes him intelligible as a product of his culture but also explains how he got into so much trouble: "To tell all sides that their vision for the nation is wrong, and to act as if one has glimpsed, and is implementing, a different vision, is to invite trouble."[30]

What Were Jesus' Aims? Wright says that the traditional, pre-critical Christian view is that Jesus was born on Earth to die for the sins of the world and to found a church. In contrast to this view, the first critical historians claimed that Jesus was essentially a teacher, primarily of ethical truths. And in the twentieth century, historians have supposed that Jesus' aims had to do with the kingdom. But beyond that, Wright says, interpretations are varied: Brandon and others, for instance, claim that Jesus was trying to foment revolution of one sort or another; M. Hengel and Borg, that Jesus was against revolution; Sanders, that Jesus intended to initiate a "restoration eschatology" involving the destruction and rebuilding of the Temple; and so on. However, one thing about which previous historians in this century have agreed is that it is "outlandish" to suggest that Jesus intended to found a church.[31]

In Wright's view, Jesus intended to found a "church." He agrees with other historians that Jesus never intended to found an institution that would have the career that the Christian church has taken. But, he says, if instead we "see Jesus' aim as the restoration, in some sense, of Israel, beginning with the highly symbolic call of twelve disciples," then the seemingly outlandish "idea of Jesus 'founding' a community designed to outlast his death gives way to a more nuanced, and perfectly credible, first-century Jewish one: that of Jesus restoring the people of God," in some sense "around himself." Wright says that an advantage of supposing that Jesus may have had this intention is that it raises the question of whether Jesus thought that he himself was to have a special role in the kingdom that he was proclaiming. In Wright's view, Jesus did think so. After all, Wright says, Jesus welcomed sinners and outcasts into a kingdom that he calmly and quietly implied was being redefined around himself, in and through his own work.[32]

Wright says that what Jesus grasped—which so many others, both among his contemporaries and modern readers, missed—was that Israel's destiny was moving swiftly toward its climax and that if Israel did not watch out, "she would fall to her doom." Wright says that it did not take prophetic insight for Jesus to know that Israel might be in for trouble. Anyone could see that the Romans would tolerate only so much provocation before smashing Jerusalem and the nation "into little bits." "Where Jesus' prophetic insight came into play was in the awesome realization that *when this happened, it would be the judgment of Israel's God on his wayward people.*" In other words, "Jesus saw the judgment coming, and realized that it was not just from Rome, but from God."[33] In sum, Jesus' first aim was to deliver the message that if Israel failed to repent, disaster would swiftly follow.

Jesus also had a second aim, one that even 2,000 years later, Wright says, "still sends shivers down the spine." It was that he would go out ahead, in place of Israel, and meet the terrible judgment alone. Jesus drew on ancient Jewish beliefs to predict a time of bitter, harsh suffering and testing for the people of God. But he believed that "if he went out to meet it, to take it upon himself, then he might bear it on behalf of his people, so that they would not need to bear it."[34] Wright says that whereas "the Jewish hope was that when

Israel's strange destiny reached its fulfillment, the world would be saved," Jesus' variation on this theme was his belief that all of this would happen "through his own life, death, and resurrection," which he foresaw.[35]

Why Did Jesus Die?   Wright says that even if one were to take the view that Jesus intended to die, and that he invested his death in advance with a theological interpretation, there would still be unanswered questions, such as what the Romans thought they were doing in crucifying Jesus. What we need in the first instance, Wright says, is not a theology of the cross—such as that Jesus died for the sins of the world or to save people from eternal death—but a history of the cross. This history would then reveal what the various people involved were trying to accomplish, thereby explaining why Jesus was crucified.

In Wright's view, to explain Jesus' death in the manner in which he died, one has to suppose that he offended either official Israel or official Rome or both. "Someone, or more likely some group," Wright says, "wanted Jesus out of the way." But why? Wright says that the Romans had a political motive for Jesus' death, in that they were convinced, or persuaded, that he was some sort of a troublemaker. But who convinced or persuaded them? Wright says that there are two mainstream answers: the Pharisees, and the Temple hierarchy. He agrees with Sanders that it is not historically plausible that the Pharisees were as petty as they are depicted of being in the New Testament. In any case, he says, there is no evidence whatsoever that they were linked directly to Jesus' death. That leaves the Temple hierarchy.

Why would the Temple hierarchy want Jesus out of the way? Wright thinks, as does Sanders, that it is because Jesus threatened the Temple.[36] In other situations, Wright says, Jesus acted with deliberate scriptural overtones. Hence the most plausible interpretation of the Temple incident—Wright says it is "irresistible"—is that Jesus intended that his actions in the Temple be taken to symbolize its imminent destruction. Jesus intended this to express his view that Israel's god was in the process of judging and redeeming his people, as the culmination of Israel's history, and that God's judgment would involve the destruction of the Temple by the Romans, who would be acting as the agents of God's wrath. Ultimately, in Wright's view, that is why Jesus was sentenced to die.[37]

How and Why Did the Early Church Begin? Wright notes that many historical Jesus scholars regard this question as extending beyond the scope of their inquiries. But he says that interpretations of Jesus that have to postulate a large gap between Jesus and the early church are weaker than those that do not. For his part, he aims to show that there are continuities as well as discontinuities between Jesus and the early church.[38] He begins by saying that he agrees with Sanders that but for the resurrection, Jesus' disciples probably would not have endured any longer than did John the Baptist's. But, he asks, what content do we then need to give to the resurrection? Wright again approvingly quotes Sanders, who says that Jesus' followers, by carrying through the logic of Jesus' position *"in a transformed situation,"* created a movement that would grow and continue to alter. But Wright asks, transformed how? His answer is that whereas first-century Jews looked forward to a public event in and through which "their god would reveal to all the world that he was not just a local, tribal deity, but the creator and sovereign of all," the early Christians "looked back to an event in and through which, they claimed, Israel's god had done exactly that."[39]

Methods

Among prominent historians of Jesus, Wright is far and away the most sophisticated and articulate philosopher of historical methodology. In fact, among historians in general, whatever their field, he would get high marks in this respect. Foundational to his approach is his denial that it is either possible or desirable for historians, in their work as historians, to insulate their interpretations from their larger worldviews. In the case of historians of Jesus, he thinks that these larger worldviews all but invariably include either theologies or antitheologies. Moreover, he recognizes, as few seem to, that appropriately integrating one's historical views and one's larger worldview is not merely a challenge for Christians, or even for historians of Jesus, but should be an issue for every thinking person. What we all need to do, he says, but especially in connection with our consideration of historical Jesus studies, is to rethink our worldviews in light of the internal collapse of the one that has been predominant in the West for the past two centuries; and we need to be cognizant while rethinking them that it was due to this collapsing worldview that we came in the first place to believe "that 'history' and 'theology' belong in separate compartments." He says that this task is one that "faces modern Western culture in its entirety."[40]

A continuing theme in Wright's philosophy of historical methodology is that there is no such thing as an uninterpreted fact or an objective history. More explicitly than anyone else whose views we have considered except for Schüssler Fiorenza, he questions what he takes to be an outmoded concept of objectivity that he says was born during the Enlightenment and has outlived whatever usefulness it may once have had. But whereas Schüssler Fiorenza questioned this conception of objectivity mainly on the grounds that historical studies are always at least covertly ideological, Wright questions it also on the grounds that historians necessarily interpret against the backdrop of a larger worldview, and hence are not as "neutral," even in a scientific way, as many of them present themselves as being. Wright thinks that discarding the prevailing concept of objectivity has implications not only for how historians should conduct historical Jesus studies but also for how Christians should respond to these studies. He says, for instance, that "all sensible readers see at once" that the Gospels "are written from a position of Christian faith" but then asks, "So what?" Only when we have abandoned "the myth of neutrality," he says, whether our own or that of any single source, can we "start engaging in real history," after which "we will discover that the gospels make remarkably good historical sense."[41]

In Wright's view, it will not do to try to keep history and theology in separate compartments. He says that Jesus "is either the flesh-and-blood individual who walked and talked, and lived and died, in first-century Palestine, or he is merely a creature of our own imagination, able to be manipulated this way and that." He adds that to this extent he totally agrees with skeptical historians of Jesus, from Reimarus to the present, who have claimed that the church has distorted the real Jesus. Wright says that while the church "needs to repent of this and rediscover who its Lord actually is," this does not mean that the church has been totally mistaken in what it has said about Jesus, but that "only real no-holds-barred history can tell us whether that is so." In his view, the problem with skeptical historians is *not* that they have portrayed Jesus in ways that the church must resist in order to protect "its cherished traditional faith," but that they have offered us a Jesus of their own invention, which anyone interested in serious history ought to resist. Wright cautions, however, that serious history will challenge some Christians, who, he says, are as prone to "muddles and misconceptions" as anyone else. But he thinks that Christianity will emerge from its confrontation with historical inquiry "more solid and robust." Instead of bad portraits of Jesus, he says, Christians need good ones.[42]

Such is Wright's case that theology ought to take history seriously. But should theology also influence how history is actually done? His answer is a qualified yes. It's a *yes* because he thinks that one's theology (or antitheology) cannot help but influence the results of one's historical work. It's a *qualified* yes because he thinks that the influence of theology on history has to be mediated by some sort of "public" justification of results, which, for Wright, means by more or less ordinary historical evidence. He says that "history, like magic, has got to get the details right," and that in historical Jesus studies one determines whether this has happened in the same way that one determines it in any other area of history.[43]

How does Wright's philosophy of historical methodology work out in practice, particularly in connection with those parts of the New Testament accounts that are most offensive to secular rationality—the virgin birth, the miracle stories, and the resurrection? Wright says that the attraction of Christianity for some Christians is basically that it is *supernatural*. He says that it is not so much that these Christians first believe in Jesus and then find that they have to stretch their worldviews in order to make room for things they had not counted on. Rather, their basic commitment is to there being a supernatural dimension to life, and "they find this conveniently confirmed by Jesus." In response to the observation that this sort of supernaturalism has been under attack for the past 200 years, he replies, "Frankly, it deserved it."[44]

Wright derides those who think that being Christian commits one to believing in "miracles," in the sense of "irrational suspensions of the normal laws of nature." But it is not so clear what he would put in the place of such beliefs. In part, he thinks that God works miracles "by being *within* his creation, within 'instinct' and hidden motivations."[45] But Wright emphasizes that Christianity makes claims not just at the level of isolated occurrences, such as the virgin birth and miracles, but also at the level of worldviews. In his opinion, a central worldview claim of Christianity, one that is based on the resurrection of Jesus as seen in the context of the whole Jewish tradition, is that "the creator God was active in and as Jesus to redeem Israel and the world."

On the assumption that this is what the early Christians believed, Wright says that it is less surprising than it might otherwise be to find them saying that Jesus' mother remained a virgin at the time of his conception. In other words, whereas from the perspective of a strictly naturalistic worldview, the claim of a virgin birth is not only surprising but outrageous, Wright thinks that from an early Christian perspective, the claim fits.[46] But then, in the midst of explaining why the early Christians might have believed what they did about God's activity in the world, Wright shifts to talk that now includes the theological question of what God's activity actually was. He says that the doctrine of the virgin birth "is precisely the sort of strange truth which creeps up on you unawares, which takes you by surprise, but which then makes itself at home." He adds that although no one could prove to the satisfaction of post-Enlightenment skepticism that the virgin birth occurred, "in the light of the resurrection we are called to be sceptical about scepticism itself."[47]

It is the resurrection, Wright claims, rather than the virgin birth or other supposed miracles, that is the key to understanding the early Christians as well as the truth about Jesus. He points out that for Jews of the period resurrection was not resuscitation, that is, a matter of returning to the same sort of life, and it did not imply immortality, or the transmigration of a disembodied soul or spirit. Rather, it was a matter of going through death into a new world, in which the resurrected person has some sort of physical body. In addition, he claims, first-century Jews were not expecting people to be resurrected one at a time, on an individual basis. Rather, they thought that resurrection was something that would happen to all dead Jews, and perhaps to all dead human beings, on the great future occasion when God finally brought history around its last great corner "into the new day that was about to dawn." For Jews of the period, Wright says, resurrection "was about God's restoration of his whole people, about his coming Kingdom, about the great reversal of fortune for Israel and the world," about "the birth of a whole new world order."[48]

In light of this, Wright continues, there is a crucial question that must be addressed: Why did the early Christians, who had these Jewish beliefs about resurrection, say that Jesus, as a single individual, was resurrected? Obviously, he says, they did not think that Israel had suddenly become ruler of the world. And it hardly suffices to say, as many have, "that the disciples had a wonderful inner experience and sense of the love and grace and forgiveness of God." He notes that without introducing talk of resurrection, the Jews had well-developed ways of talking about their experiences of God's love, grace, and forgiveness. Nor is it plausible, he adds, to say that Jesus' disciples were so shocked by his death and unable to come to terms with it that they "invented the idea of Jesus' 'resurrection' as a way of coping with a cruelly broken dream." Whatever the apparent psychological plausibility of this suggestion, Wright says, it is not serious first-century history, since we know of many other messianic and similar movements in the Jewish world roughly contemporaneous with Jesus, many of whose leaders died violently at the hands of the authorities, yet we never hear of the disappointed followers claiming that their leader had been raised from the dead. Wright says, "They knew better." For first-century Jews, resurrection involved human bodies and empty tombs. According to Wright, a Jewish revolutionary whose leader had been executed by the authorities and who managed himself to escape could either give up the revolution or find another leader, and we have evidence of revolutionaries doing both. But claiming that the original leader was alive again was simply not an option. "Unless, of course, he was."[49]

Wright makes even stronger claims about the case to be made for the resurrection. He says that as historians we are "forced" to take "very seriously" the Christian claim that "Jesus of Nazareth was raised from the dead three days after his execution," and he says that "the alternative explanation, when examined, turns out to be remarkably lame." Presumably, by "the alternative explanation," Wright means *any* competing explanation of how the early Christians came to believe that Jesus was raised from the dead.[50] But while one might agree with Wright that as historical explanations go, even the best of the competing explanations are "pretty lame" in the sense that they are speculative, it is less obvious that they are also pretty lame in comparison to Wright's preferred explanation. I shall return to this issue.

Wright of course recognizes that if we accept his preferred explanation of the resurrection, then we are forced to throw naturalism to the winds. The resurrection, he says, "breaks open all other worldviews and demands that the closed systems with which humans try to make sense of their world must be held open to allow for the God who, having created the world, has never for a moment abandoned it." But he cautions that "this does *not* mean that the resurrection throws open the door, after all, to a miscellaneous 'appeal to the supernatural.'" Rather, he says, the resurrection opens the door to two different beliefs: that "the creator," who "never abandoned his world, called Israel to be the spearhead of his redeeming purposes for it; and that the creator "has now, in Jesus, drawn together the threads of Israel's long destiny, in order to deal with evil in the world and to begin, dramatically, the creation of a new world." This new world, Wright says, is not superimposed on the old one, but "grows out of its very womb in a great act of new creation, like the oak from the acorn."[51]

Analysis

The first thing to notice, I think, is that from the point of view of historical methodology, there is nothing particularly pernicious about introducing a theological perspective, especially if one argues for it, as Wright does, by trying to show the difficulties with naturalistic alternatives. One of the reasons for this, as we saw also in the case of Borg, is that usually it is relatively easy for naturalists to excise the theological part so that the resulting interpretation is compatible with naturalism. Consider, for instance, Wright's discussion of the resurrection, which is pivotal for his interpretation of Jesus. As we have just seen, he argues, first, that for first-century Jews, resurrection was not a private event but one that involved human bodies, so there would have to be an empty tomb somewhere; and, second, that a Jewish revolutionary whose leader had been executed by the authorities could give up the revolution or find a new leader, but not claim that the original leader was alive again, unless he was. But, of course, all that really follows from this line of reasoning is that the revolutionary could not claim that the original leader was alive again, unless he *sincerely believed* that he was.

Assume, then, that early Christians *sincerely believed* that Jesus was resurrected from the dead, in the sense in which Wright claims that first-century Jews understood the notion of resurrection. In that case, the secular historian is left with the burden of explaining how, presumably (though not necessarily) in the absence of an empty tomb, early Christians could have sincerely believed that Jesus had been resurrected. One possibility, of course, is that they may have believed this as a consequence of visions that some of them had. If I understand Borg correctly, this is how he explains the seminal early

Christian beliefs in a resurrected Jesus. Of course Borg may regard the post-Easter visions of Jesus not as hallucinatory but as glimpses into other dimensions of reality that are just as real as (or perhaps even more real than) the only one to which most people have experiential access. But, as we have seen, such extranaturalistic embellishments can be excised from Borg's view too. The point is that to answer Wright's argument, all a historian has to do is to suggest that the early Christians may have sincerely believed that Jesus rose from the dead as a consequence of visions that they had, leaving the metaphysical status of these visions an open question.

What about the empty tomb? According to Wright, if Jesus really rose from the dead, then there would have to have been an empty tomb somewhere, a detail, presumably, that could easily be checked. But, as Crossan has argued, there may have been no tomb for Jesus, empty or not. And even if there had been a tomb that at one point had Jesus' body in it, at some point before the claim was made about Jesus' being resurrected, the body could have been removed—not necessarily to deceive people into thinking that Jesus had risen from the dead, but for some other reason. And so on.

Wright unquestionably interprets the history of Jesus in a way that is more congenial to traditional Christians than the interpretations of most purely secular historical Jesus scholars. He claims that since history of whatever sort involves interpretation, there is no reason why one should rule out in advance *theological* interpretations, such as the one he advances. Whether such an interpretation is true has to be judged, he says, on its ability to explain the evidence. Well and good. But then Wright seems to want to draw the line at the sort of theological interpretation for which he has labored to make room and exclude other extranaturalistic contenders. And, for me, there's the rub. For instance, Wright derides Christians who believe in "miracles" as "irrational suspensions of the normal laws of nature." But calling these alleged suspensions of the laws of nature, or the belief that they occurred, "irrational" simply begs the question. Why should miracles as *exceptions* to the normal laws of nature be ruled out of court? Meier wants to leave the door open to this possibility. And even without insisting on some sort of sharp boundary between the natural and the supernatural, there is always the option of a view like Borg's, according to which persons of Spirit—among whom Borg is willing to include not just Jesus but also some Zen masters, shamans, and the like—may have extraordinary powers that normal people lack. More generally, but in the same vein, Wright claims that the resurrection challenges not only all views of the world, and of history, that insist on reducing everything to "materialistic analysis" but also those that explain things by appeal to "pagan superstition or magic." But why if we are going to let Israel's god into the picture should we be in such a hurry to kick pagan gods out of it? If YHWH can work wonders, why not also Dionysus?

I'm not sure how Wright would answer these questions. The only answer that I have been able to find in his long, insightful discussion of historical methodology is his view that "the proof of the pudding is in the eating." By this, of course, he means that the proof of the interpretation is in its ability to make coherent sense of the data. But this is not nearly enough of an answer. On the face of it, it seems very likely that radically different sorts of interpretations are going to make coherent sense of the data to different sorts of people. To Sanders and Crossan, for instance, one or another naturalistic interpretation is bound to make more coherent sense of the data than any interpretation that involves theological or other sorts of exotic commitments. To Borg, an interpretation that allows for there being individuals who have special access to other dimensions of reality is bound to make more coherent sense than any that closes the door on that possibility. And for Wright, as we have seen, only an interpretation that is based on his version of Jesus' appropriation of Jewish eschatological expectations and that includes Jesus' resurrection is going to make the most coherent sense. So if, as he says, the proof of the pudding is in the eating, then we need to take a very careful look not only at the pudding but also at who is doing the eating.

Part Four

RESPONSES

8

ONLY FAITH

What has Athens to do with Jerusalem?

—*Tertullian (ca. 200 C.E.)*

*The more the church has sought to ground itself in some-
thing other than the transforming work of the Spirit . . .
[the more] it has missed the point of its existence. . . . [The
church's discourse] should not be the same as the academy's, nor should it be subject to the same rules or the
same criteria of validity. It is time for a return from the
academic captivity of the church.*

—*Luke Johnson,* The Real Jesus, *1996*

THE SECULAR QUEST for the historical Jesus has challenged many
thoughtful Christians. How should they respond? In my view, there
are just three basic responses, which I call the *Only Faith* response, the
Faith Seeking Understanding response, and the *Only Reason* response. However, rather than neatly defined categories of responses,
these three should be understood as points on a spectrum, at one end
of which—Only Faith—is the view that Christians should be totally
*dis*missive *of* even the expert opinions of secular historians, and at the
other end of which—Only Reason—is the view that Christians should
be totally *sub*missive *to* the expert opinions of secular historians.[1]

Midway between these two extremes is the Faith Seeking Understanding response, according to which Christians should arrive at some sort of *harmonious integration* of what they think they know about Jesus by faith and what historians claim to know about Jesus on the basis of evidence. The first two of these responses are alike in that both refuse any compromises. The Faith Seeking Understanding response is usually chosen only by those who think that compromise is not only possible but essential.

Christians who respond to the challenge to their beliefs posed by historical Jesus studies, rather than neatly fitting into any of these categories of response, tend to lean toward one or another of them. For instance, even those who are drawn to the Only Faith response generally concede that there are a variety of limited roles that may be assigned legitimately to historical evidence, such as allowing it to be used to fill in small gaps in, or even to correct in minor ways, beliefs that are arrived at through faith. Thus a person who is drawn to the Only Faith response might leave it to the historians to determine, say, how many siblings Jesus had or what languages he spoke, but not whether he worked miracles or rose from the dead.

Few Christians who defend their religious beliefs against the challenge from historical studies explain where they draw the line between what is determined by faith and what is left to the historians, or on what grounds they draw it. Most are intent on making the more fundamental point that Christians do not have to knuckle under to secular historians, at least not across the board or on any important point. For present purposes, I am going to suppose that Christians who draw the line between what faith contributes and what secular scholarship contributes to their beliefs, in such a way that only crumbs are left to scholarship, subscribe to the Only Faith response, even though they may not be pure instances of that type. Christians who, while insisting on the importance of faith, nevertheless envisage a more genuine engagement with scholarship are more usefully regarded as Faith Seeking Understanding types. And Christians who basically accept the results of secular scholarship, leaving only crumbs to faith, are more usefully regarded as Only Reason types.

It is natural to suppose that the current conflict between faith and secular historical scholarship is a child of the Enlightenment, recently grown to maturity. In a way, that supposition is right. However, the underlying issues at stake in the conflict between faith and historical scholarship have to do not so much with anything that is peculiar to *historical* scholarship per se as they do with the deliverances of *secular rationality* more generally, whether these come from historical scholarship, science, philosophy, or just plain thinking. And in that more general form in which the conflict is not between faith and secular historical scholarship but between faith and secular rationality, the conflict is as old as Christianity. In the second and third centuries C.E., the conflict in this more general form arose within the emerging Christian community when some church fathers, including Origen, Clement, and Gregory of Nyssa, tried to integrate what they believed on the basis of Christian scripture with what they had learned from Greek philosophy (in effect, the "science" of the day), while others, such as Tertullian, argued that their attempt to integrate the sacred and the profane was a big mistake.

Tertullian, then, represents an earlier advocate of the Only Faith response. In his day, the center of Greek philosophy was Athens, and the center of Christianity, Jerusalem. Hence in asking, "What has Athens to do with Jerusalem?" he posed the crucial question. In his more conservative moments, his answer was "Nothing." This is the answer that I am calling the Only Faith response. Characteristic of those who take this extreme view, Tertullian was not always consistent. Sometimes he too tried to integrate faith and "science"; for instance, he accepted from the Stoics—a school of Greek philosophy established in Athens about 300 B.C.E.—that the soul is corporeal, and then tried on that basis to explain immortality.

Tertullian is one of the few Christian *intellectuals* who have sided with the Only Faith response. Almost all of them have adopted the Faith Seeking Understanding response. Of course intellectuals' preference for the Faith Seeking Understanding response is partly due to their being intellectuals in the first place. On the face of it, the Only Faith response is an anti-intellectual response. This is not to say that it is an unintelligent response. It may in fact be a Christian's best response to the challenges posed by secular rationality. However, those whom we know about historically who have embraced the Only Faith response tend not to be philosophers and theologians.

There are exceptions. Pierre Bayle, whose views we considered briefly in Chapter 2, may have been an exception. He suggested that one should give the back of one's hand to rationality and blindly follow faith. However, no one has been able to figure out whether in making this suggestion he was serious. In any case, historically the

most interesting and influential exception to the rule that those ad-
vocating the Only Faith response tend not to be philosophers or
theologians is the nineteenth-century Danish philosopher Søren
Kierkegaard. He not only thought that faith should override reason
when the two conflict, but that faith is more valuable when it does
override reason. In his view, the value of someone's believing something on faith is directly proportional to how improbable the belief
is when it is assessed on the basis of secular rationality. Tertullian is
famous for having said, "I *believe* because it is absurd." Kierkegaard
might have expressed his own point of view by saying, "My belief is
spiritually authentic to whatever degree it is absurd."[2] And, as we
saw in Chapter 3, in a famous paper published in 1896 the theologian Martin Kähler, echoing Kierkegaard, argued that a faith that
needs support from historical evidence is inauthentic.

Today, among educated people who are neither theologians nor
philosophers, it is difficult to find pure cases of the Only Faith response. The Enlightenment has taken its toll. One of the "lessons"
of European intellectual culture that is widely accepted among educated people is that one has to be something of a yahoo to give reason (and ordinary procedures for gathering evidence) the back of
one's hand.[3] Yet one does not have to be a yahoo to think that a
Christian's best response to the challenge posed by secular historical
scholarship is the Only Faith response. There are thoughtful and articulate advocates of this response—not many, but some. In the
United States today the most highly visible of these thoughtful re-
spondents is Luke Johnson, a theologian at Emory University. In a
series of articles and now in a book, *The Real Jesus* (1996), Johnson
defends the Only Faith response.[4] As we shall see, like Tertullian,
Johnson does not defend the Only Faith response in a way that is
wholly consistent. Often he wavers and makes concessions to the
opposition that make his view as a whole hard to understand. In the
final analysis, it may be that even he endorses the Faith Seeking Understanding response. But this more moderate side of Johnson is not
the side that one notices first, or the side that has made him a darling
of theological conservatives. And it is not the side that has made him
so highly visible.

In the main part of what Johnson has to say, he defends the Only
Faith response, and it is this part that I want to consider first, after
which I'll explain how he qualifies his commitment to this view. The
reason for not bothering now with his concessions and qualifications

is that my goal is not primarily to explain *his* views but to consider the best case that can be made for the Only Faith response, so that we can assess *its* strengths and weaknesses. Johnson has defended the Only Faith response in a way that has better expressed how a lot of conservative Christians feel about the challenge posed to Christian belief by secular historical scholarship than has anyone else with whom I am familiar. That is why we are considering his views.

Johnson begins his defense of the Only Faith response by criticizing a number of contributions to the secular quest for the historical Jesus on the grounds that they are sensational, speculative, and sloppy. In this part of his defense, Robert Funk and the Jesus Seminar come in for special criticism. However, Johnson thinks better of the work of a few secular historians. He says, for instance, of John Meier's account that it is "carried out with the utmost sobriety and seriousness" and "is as solid and moderate and pious" as a secular history of Jesus is ever likely to be.[5] Yet, in Johnson's view, even Meier's account is too limited to be useful.

Johnson says that the main problem with Meier's account and with secular histories of Jesus generally is that historians begin their work by dismantling the narrative structures of the canonical Gospels. They do this to determine what in the Gospels is historically reliable. But in Johnson's view, once historians have taken this initial step, they are left only with a pile of fragments, and they have no responsible way to reconstruct the fragments into a meaningful whole. Hence the secular historians' project is merely destructive, lacking the resources also to be constructive. In the case of Meier, for instance, Johnson concedes that he identifies those pieces of the Gospel narratives that our best evidence suggests reach back to Jesus himself, or to traditions very close to Jesus. But, Johnson says, "we are not *on that account* allowed to make inferences from such a *collection of facts* to the frequency, connectedness between, sequence, proportion, relative importance, and above all, the meaning of these facts."[6] In Johnson's view, secular historians are, in effect, spiritual terrorists. In one fell swoop, he suggests, they reduce a beautiful, deeply meaningful structure—the New Testament Gospel narratives—to a pile of useless, ugly rubble.

But are secular historians guilty of leaving everything in shambles? As we saw in Chapter 4, Meier does in fact reassemble the "pieces" of the New Testament that he regards as authentic into what seems to be a meaningful whole. In his view, Jesus emerges as a marginally

Jewish, (perhaps) miracle-working, eschatological prophet. And it is not just Meier who reconstructs the pieces into a meaningful whole—virtually all high-visibility secular historians of Jesus do that as well, though they do not all do it in the same way. Even in the case of someone as revisionist as Schüssler Fiorenza, the Jesus that emerges from her studies is in fact deeply meaningful to many contemporary feminists. So what's the problem?

The problem, in Johnson's view, is not so much with Meier's reconstruction per se—and, by implication, with the reconstructions of other historians—as it is with what he sees as the fact that Meier is not *entitled* to his reconstruction. Johnson says that "the synthetic picture of Jesus' ministry" that Meier advances, "however true it might be," is "not strictly derivable from the methods that he himself has employed, and owes more than a little to the contribution made by the Gospel narratives that the method began by excluding."[7] In other words, Johnson's complaint is that the destructive parts of historians' attempts to ferret out the real Jesus are more scientifically reputable than the constructive parts. But if in constructing an alternative portrait of Jesus one is going to go beyond where one is entitled to go strictly on evidential grounds, then why not simply stick with the traditional New Testament portrait of Jesus? The only reason for criticizing the New Testament portrait in the first place was that on evidential grounds one is not entitled to believe it. So where is the gain?

There is some truth in Johnson's criticism. As we discussed in Chapter 5, not just Meier but virtually all high-visibility secular historians of Jesus go well beyond their evidence in proposing their positive accounts of who Jesus was and what he was about. Their positive accounts are based on their best educated *guesses,* not on their secure, evidentially grounded *conclusions.* In my view, that is largely why there is so much disagreement among historians of Jesus. But historians might well respond as follows: If what we've done—solely on the basis of historical evidence—is the best that anyone can do, what's the matter with it? The most reasonable answer, in my view, is that if what the secular historians have done is the best that anyone can do solely on the basis of historical evidence, then for the purpose of promoting the objectives that animate the secular historical project, nothing is the matter with it. After all, it is not their fault that there is not more and better evidence.

Johnson would not agree. In his view, and presumably in the views of many Christians, plenty is wrong with what the secular historians have done. The secular historians, he is saying, are destroyers. Even when, like Meier, they rebuild in an attractive way, they are not rebuilding on firm foundations. Hence in Johnson's view, traditional Christians are ill advised to follow them, especially when Christians already have a beautiful, accommodating structure, resting securely on the rock-solid foundation of faith. Why wrench themselves out of the security and comfort of that structure to inhabit another that is less beautiful and accommodating and rests precariously on the speculative pretensions of secular historians? Still, there is something ironic about Johnson's singling out Meier for criticism. In almost everyone's opinion who has an opinion about secular historians of Jesus (the only exceptions would be some liberal historians), Meier stands at the top of his field. One may not agree with his results, but it is hard not to admire his erudition, skill, thoroughness, and even his evenhanded way of dealing with historians who have opposing views. One might have expected someone like Johnson to criticize Meier for being too skeptical. Ironically, Johnson criticizes Meier for not being skeptical enough!

It is tempting to suppose—and this is merely supposition—that Meier comes in for special criticism from Johnson precisely because he is *both* so respectable *and* reassembles the pieces of his puzzle in a way that is fairly close to what many Christians already believe about Jesus. To conservative Christians, Crossan and Schüssler Fiorenza will look like the enemy. Meier, by contrast, can look like a friend. That may be why Meier, rather than more liberal historians, emerges in Johnson's view as the biggest threat. It is as if Johnson does not want Christians to get to choose between faith by itself and faith informed by, and possibly integrated with, the account of someone like Meier. Rather, he wants them to face a starker choice: either offensively liberal histories, such as those of Crossan and Schüssler Fiorenza, who presumably represent the abyss, or the familiar and, to conservative Christians, profoundly more meaningful New Testament Gospel narratives.

Johnson does not conclude that there should be no secular histories of Jesus, however. He concedes that for secular historians and their students "it is obviously important to study Christian origins historically" and that "in such historical inquiry faith commitments should play no role." His point, rather, is that this secular project has virtually nothing to do with what Christians should believe. One of his reasons, as we have seen, is that the evidence is too slender and ambiguous "to enable a truly comprehensive reconstruction of Christian origins."[8] Another is that secular accounts—merely because they are secular, and regardless of how well they might be done on their own terms—do not proceed from "the perspective of faith." It is not clear whether Johnson thinks there can be more than one perspective of faith. He gives no indication that there may be different perspectives of faith. In any case, in his opinion, "the perspective of faith" is the only perspective from which results can emanate that should influence the beliefs of Christians. He says that "the most destructive effect" of the secular quest for the historical Jesus "has been the perpetuation of the notion that history somehow determines faith," that is, that for faith in what happened historically "to be correct, the historical accounts that gave rise to it have to be verifiable."[9] In his view, it is on the basis of faith, not secular scholarship, that Christians should make up their minds about what Jesus said and did during the first century C.E.

But *how* should faith determine what one believes—does "anything go" so long as one believes it on faith, or are there constraints? Philosophically, this is the crucial question. Johnson gives three answers to it. Perhaps his answers might somehow be unified into one coherent answer, but he does not unify them and it is not obvious how to do so. For present purposes, which have to do with understanding the strengths and weaknesses of the Only Faith response, I am going to treat his "three" answers as if they really are three, with an acknowledgment that this may not be fair to Johnson.

The question, recall, is how, in Johnson's view, faith should determine what one believes. In what I am going to call his *religious experience answer,* he writes, somewhat Gnostic-like, that each Christian's own personal experience of Jesus, and that alone, should be the standard for his or her interpretation. Thus, in this answer, there seem to be no limits—none certainly imposed by historical evidence—on what one can believe about Jesus. The only constraint is that one's beliefs must accord with one's own personal experience, and Johnson puts no limits on the conditions under which one has those experiences or on how thoughtful and circumspect one is in interpreting the experiences, or on what one learns about Jesus as a consequence of having had experiences, and so on. In short, his view seems to be that so long as one's own experience sustains one's faith, anything goes.

An obvious problem with this view is that it would sanction believing some pretty weird things. You may recall that many of the disciples of David Koresh in Waco, Texas, who in 1993 met a fiery end at the hands of the FBI, accepted on faith that he was Jesus. Presumably many of his disciples felt that this belief was confirmed by their own experience. Assume, for the sake of argument, that they felt this. Assume also that most of the rest of us, had we been in the place of these disciples of Koresh, would have interpreted our experiences of him not as proving that he was Jesus, but as proving that he was a fake. Nevertheless, in Johnson's view, what Koresh's disciples believed on faith is perfectly acceptable.

Naturally Koresh's disciples have a right to believe whatever they want, including that he was Jesus. I am not questioning that. The question, rather, is whether in basing their faith as they did on their experiences of Koresh, they might have made some sort of interpretive mistake, say, by interpreting their experiences in a way that was incorrect, or at least less than ideal. In the part of what Johnson has to say that we are examining, he does not try to answer any question of this sort. He does not even acknowledge, as it seems he should, that some question of this sort might need to be answered.

Had Johnson tried to respond to the possibility that many of Koresh's disciples may have interpreted their experiences in a way that is less than ideal, there are only two sorts of answers that he might have given. First, he might have said that what Koresh's disciples believed about Koresh was perfectly acceptable, regardless of what experiences formed the basis for their beliefs, so long as their beliefs really were based on their experiences. In other words, he might, as Tertullian and Kierkegaard did, have bitten the bullet and taken the view that when it comes to faith, anything goes. Or, instead of that, he might have said that in order for what Koresh's disciples believed about Koresh to be acceptable, it is not enough that their beliefs were based on their experiences, but some further constraint also had to be satisfied. But, of course, if some further constraint had to be satisfied, then the question arises as to whether this constraint, or any part of it, has anything to do with historical evidence. Apparently Johnson's answer to this latter question would be no.

Johnson says that "Christians direct their faith not to the historical figure of Jesus but to the living Lord Jesus." He concedes that Christians "assert continuity" between the historical Jesus and the living Lord Jesus, but insists that "their faith is confirmed" not by evidence regarding the past but by "the reality of Christ's power in the present." He says that if Christian faith were "directed to a human construction about the past, that would be a form of idolatry." Instead, authentic Christian faith is directed to "the living God, whom Christians declare is powerfully at work among them through the resurrected Jesus."[10] In other words, it is only the present that matters. The past is irrelevant. Or, more modestly, present experiences, not ordinary historical evidence, should determine one's view of the past. According to Johnson, to allow ordinary historical evidence to determine one's view of the past would be to direct one's feeling about what one takes to be those past events not to the past events themselves but to "human constructions" of those past events.

But Johnson's accusation of idolatry cannot be right. If someone were to be informed by some secular historian's interpretation of Jesus and, as a consequence, conceived of Jesus somewhat differently than before, there is no reason to suppose that his or her faith in Jesus would be directed "to a human construction about the past." The Christian presumably would still be directing his or her faith at Jesus—the same Jesus Johnson says should be the focus of any Christian's faith, and the same Jesus that the secular histories purport to be about. This should be clear in the following analogy:

Suppose that I dislike President Clinton because of some things I think he did as president. And suppose it is because of what I've read and heard in news reports that I think he did these things. Even so, in disliking Clinton, I do not dislike the news reports, each of which, admittedly, is "a human construction about the past"; rather, I dislike Clinton. If the news reports are incorrect or misleading, I may dislike Clinton for mistaken reasons. But that would not change the fact that it is still Clinton whom I dislike. The same thing would be true, of course, if on the basis of news reports, I liked (rather than disliked) President Clinton. The general moral is that what we appeal to in order to form beliefs about someone is one thing, and what (or whom) the beliefs are about is another. I may appeal to my current experience, to my memory of what I experienced in the past, to historical evidence, or whatever, to form a belief about some past person. My belief is still about that person, even if that person happens to be Jesus.

What about Johnson's view that it is only the present that matters or, more modestly, that to whatever extent the past matters, it is acceptable to base one's views about the past solely on one's present experiences, with no constraints on how one should interpret those experiences? To me, this does not sound right either. Johnson uses an analogy to try to explain what he means. He says, "The situation with the Christians' memory of Jesus is not like that of a long-ago lover who died and whose short time with us is treasured," but, "like that of a lover who continues to live with the beloved in a growing and maturing relationship." Then, drawing on his own personal experience, he says that even though he experiences the love shown him by his wife as continuous with the love that she showed him in the early years of their relationship, "in no way do I find that love dependent on the right interpretation of those earlier experiences."[11] But unless Johnson is an *extremely* unusual person, I doubt that he means what he says—that is, that his current love for his wife *"in no way"* depends on how he interprets their past together. Suppose, for instance (with apologies for the example), that one day, while rummaging around in the attic of his house, he were to discover a large envelope full of correspondence between his wife and another man. . . .

Let's change the example. Suppose, to take the focus off of Johnson, that *you* are a middle-aged man who believes himself to have been happily married for twenty years to your current wife and that one day, while rummaging around in the attic of your house, you discover a large envelope full of "love letters" between your wife and another man, all bearing postmarks from the first ten years of your marriage. How would you react? Imagine that you were to read the letters. Perhaps initially you would read them in shock, unable to believe what you were reading. Your mind would race in search of comforting explanations—the letters are a hoax, and so on. But eventually what you had discovered would reassert itself. The truth could no longer be denied: During the first ten years of your marriage, your wife had had a secret lover in a nearby town. Among other reactions you might naturally have, probably you would rethink a great many things you remember your wife having said to you during those years, such as that she loved only you. Up until a few minutes ago, her having said such things had always been deeply significant to you. Now you imagine that during the same time she was telling you that, she was telling her secret lover the same thing.

Would your discovery affect your feelings toward your wife or would you simply disregard your discovery as an irrelevant part of the dead past, not as a "vibrant part of the living present"? If you are a normal human being, with normal emotions, *of course* your discovery would affect your feelings. It would matter deeply. The "love" shown to you now by your wife would not only be experienced by you as continuous with the love she showed you in the earlier years of your marriage, but *in many ways* how you experienced her love in the present would be deeply "*dependent* on the right interpretation of those earlier experiences." The moral of this alternative version of Johnson's own example is that contrary to what he has suggested, to virtually everyone, probably even including Johnson, history matters. And the history that matters is not history constructed entirely independently of ordinary historical evidence, but history determined largely, if not solely, on the basis of ordinary historical evidence. In the case of our example, this evidence would include the letters. To suggest, as Johnson does, that history determined by ordinary means does not in general matter is to reveal that in this respect one's theories are out of touch with the actual bases of one's emotional life, or at least of most people's emotional lives.

I say these things not to reject the *religious experience* version of the Only Faith response. My goal, rather, is to show what is involved in being committed to that version of the response. In my view, part of what often (but not necessarily always) is involved, as in Johnson's self-characterization, is the *illusion* that we are mentally compartmentalized in ways that few of us actually are. For most of us, I suspect, our experiences in the present are not segregated and insulated from our interpretations of the past, any more than our interpretations of the past are segregated and insulated either from our experiences in the present or from what we learn on the basis of ordinary historical evidence. Everything goes into the same hopper.

Although the human capacity for self-deception sometimes seems boundless, for the most part we are holistic enough that we want some sort of harmony, first, between how we interpret our present experiences and our views of the past and, second, between our views of the past and whatever ordinary evidence we are aware of about what happened in the past. Were we not this way, we would have a much more difficult time making sense of our lives than we actually do, and whatever sense we did make of them would be merely personal. Such personal histories could not easily be integrated with the personal histories of others, say, family members and coworkers, into a shared representation of what happened.

The fact is that almost all of us believe that at least in most of our lives there are constraints on what it is acceptable to believe about what happened. And ordinary historical evidence, together with personal memories (not only our own but also those of others), is the backbone of these constraints. We could, of course, decide that although it is appropriate for these constraints to be in place when it comes to determining most of what we believe about the past, when it comes to Jesus, it is all right to throw these constraints to the winds. In effect, this is what Johnson has proposed. But before embracing this proposal, thinking Christians may want to explore other ways to meet the challenges posed by historical scholarship.

In the case of the secular quest for the historical Jesus, we can, if we like, avoid the inconvenience of having to grapple with historical evidence by simply avoiding ever becoming acquainted with that evidence. Most Americans, whether Christians or not, do that for most of history anyway. And all of us do that for at least some portions of history. One cannot be concerned with everything—there is not enough time. However, in the long run, it may not be so easy for most Christians simply to turn away from the secular quest for the historical Jesus. The scholarship being generated by that quest has only recently come into public view. It may be tempting to suppose that if one just ignores this scholarship, it will go away. But how likely is that? As the years and decades roll by, probably it is going to be harder and harder for even ordinary, history-ignorant, television-addicted Americans not to learn what secular historians think about Jesus and why. Whether we like it or not, we are going to get treated to these new, revisionist portraits of Jesus in movies, books, and, yes, even television programs. Eventually almost everyone will find out about them.

Books by secular historians of Jesus are already on the shelves of most shopping-mall bookstores (to see for yourself, go to your local shopping mall bookstore and ask for a book by J. D. Crossan or Marcus Borg). Books by secular historians of Jesus are in most public libraries. Soon they will be in most high school libraries. Movies based on these books will be playing occasionally in neighborhood theaters (remember *The Last Temptation of Christ*). And television series based on these books, at least series made for public television, will continue to be beamed into our living rooms (this has already happened, both in the United States and England). The bottom line is that even if you and I were to choose to ignore the portraits of Jesus that have emerged from secular histories, eventually our children and some of our neighbors are going to notice them. In relatively free societies, there is no way of keeping people, particularly inquisitive young people, from confronting the results of secular scholarship about Jesus. Some of the portraits of Jesus generated by secular scholarship are too sensational to be kept under wraps. Sooner or later they will enter the common culture. And what then?

Note that I am separating two questions here: whether Christians *should* pay any attention to secular scholarship about Jesus, and whether in the long run they will *be able to avoid* paying some attention to it. I am addressing only the second of these questions. What I am suggesting is that for most of us, rejecting ordinary historical evidence in the way Johnson suggests that we should may not, in the long run, be a realistic option. Eventually many of us are going to become aware of the new evidence and interpretations. And eventually many of us are going to understand what it is that we have become aware of. What I am questioning is whether when that time comes many of us will be able simply to give historical evidence the backs of our hands; some will be able to, but how many?

In my view, most of us are too psychologically holistic to segregate and insulate our experiences in the present from our interpretations of the past, and also too holistic to segregate our interpretations of the past from evidence that we are aware of concerning what happened. In other words, what I am suggesting is that even if we wanted to compartmentalize our psyches and our lives so as to keep experiences, interpretations, and evidence completely insulated from each other, most of us are too holistic to succeed in doing it. Just as in the case of the wife example, what most of us think about one important part of our lives and how we experience that part both affects and is affected by what we think about other important parts of our lives and how we experience them—especially parts as big and significant as "the past" and "the present." And what most of us think about "the past" both affects and is affected by whatever evidence we are aware of concerning what actually happened. We can *say* that we are going to keep everything in separate compartments in our minds, isolated and insulated from each other. We can *try* to do that. But neither saying nor trying is the same as actually doing. If we confuse our reach with our grasp, we are simply kidding ourselves.

Johnson has a second answer to the question of how faith should determine what one believes. According to his first answer—*religious experience*—faith alone should determine our view of the past.

Surprisingly, according to his second answer, which I shall call the *Holy Scripture* answer, the past—specifically the New Testament—should determine the content of our faith. In defending his Holy Scripture answer, Johnson says that although "the premise" of the secular search for the historical Jesus is that "the only way to find 'the real Jesus' is to bypass the Jesus found in the canonical Gospels," in fact the very thing that appears to historical Jesus scholars as the core problem is "seen by Christians as the best and truest aspect of the Gospels, namely, their postresurrection perspective." By "the postresurrection perspective," of course, Johnson means the perspectives of the New Testament authors, particularly the authors of the four canonical Gospels. "For a community of faith that lives in the presence of the resurrected One," Johnson continues, "it is absurd, even a betrayal of the truth," to consider the passion of Jesus "apart from" the interpretation of those events given by the Gospels.[12]

Thus in Johnson's Holy Scripture answer, he takes it as axiomatic that the interpretations of Jesus in the four canonical Gospels will assume great importance in a Christian's attempt to understand Jesus. No doubt, to Christians, these Gospel interpretations almost always do assume great importance, but in light of Johnson's first answer, why *should* they? The point of his bringing up the wife example was to reveal what he took to be the irrelevance of the past as well as the irrelevance of how we or anyone else interprets it. Now, it seems, the past together with how we interpret it—in this case, by appropriating the interpretations conveyed in the four canonical Gospels—suddenly are immensely relevant. How did they become so relevant?

The answer, I suspect, is that not even Johnson can stick consistently to his *religious experience* answer. Perhaps he would not want to abandon it altogether. On reflection, he might want to say that religious experience *and* sacred scripture should work together to determine the proper content of a Christian's religious faith: religious experience informing one's reading of Holy Scripture, and one's reading of Holy Scripture nourishing and giving content to one's religious experience. Fair enough, if this is what he really thinks. But would he want to leave it at that? That combined answer would leave the content of a Christian's faith entirely up to the individual Christian, provided that his or her faith was based on an interpretation of the New Testament. Does Johnson really want to give the individual Christian believer that much autonomy? It would seem not.

In defending his Holy Scripture answer, Johnson suggests that it is not up to each of us to arrive at our own interpretation of Jesus in our own way—either on the basis of current experience, Holy Scripture, or anything else—but that interpretations favored by "the community of faith" are somehow normative. But he never explains who is included in "the community of faith" or who gave them the right to decide questions of scriptural interpretation for the individual Christian. This latter is a strange omission for him to make. When the question was that of who gave secular historians the right to decide for "the" community of Christians how they should interpret the New Testament, Johnson is quite definite. His view is that no one gave historians the right to decide what as a matter of faith any community should believe, and until someone who has the authority does give historians that right, they do not have it. On this latter point, I agree entirely with Johnson.

However, Johnson then goes on to say that "without a *community's* commitment to acknowledge 'a more adequate history' as normative, the criticism of tradition carried out by historical research is strictly beside the point." He says that "*Christian faith* and *Christian theology* have never made such a commitment" to secular historians. Instead, he says, they have "made a commitment to the 'history' limned in the texts of the New Testament, and above all to the 'story of Jesus' inscribed in the Gospel narratives."[13] In such remarks, Johnson talks blithely about "the community," "Christian faith," and "Christian theology" as if there were just one Christian community, one version of Christian faith, and one Christian theology, and that this community, faith, and theology are automatically normative for all believing Christians, regardless of whether all Christians acknowledge it as normative. But surely it is not obvious that there is just one community, one faith, and one theology, and even if there is, that each is automatically normative for all believing Christians. At the very least, Johnson needs to tell us why we should assume this with him. In my view, we should not assume it with him because it is not true.

To sum up, Johnson's first answer to the question of how Christians should arrive at an understanding of Jesus—*religious experience*—stresses the importance of the *present*. His second answer—*Holy Scripture*—stresses the importance of the past, in particular the perspectives of the authors of the New Testament. Based on how Johnson defends this second answer, it seems that he may want to combine his first two answers and, in doing so, mix in a third ingredient: the normative-conferring authority of "the community of faith." But if he does want so to combine his answers, surely now he has backed away completely from the simple straightforwardness of his initial endorsement of present experience. Apparently, in his view, it is no longer the case, if it ever was, that anything goes. Far from it. In this part of his remarks, Johnson repeatedly talks approvingly about *community* constraints on individual belief. But which community? Why, of course, the community of *Christian theologians!*

Surprisingly, in defending this—his third—answer, Johnson stresses the importance of *critical thinking*. He says that for "loyalty" to "the Christian tradition" to be "an authentic expression of faith," it "must also be critical." But who gave *him* the right to define when an expression of faith is *authentic*? Johnson seems to assume that "Church theology," which is informed by scholarship and driven by "critical thinking," gave him the right. For instance, he says that while "ultimate human loyalty is appropriately directed to the living God rather than to community memory," "the task of theology in the church is not only discernment of God's word and praise of God's work" but "also critical reflection on the received tradition and the adequacy of the human response to God." Biblical scholarship, he says, plays "a key role" in such critical reflection. Then he stresses—sounding now more than a little like his archenemy, Crossan—that this scholarship must take into account anthropological, historical, literary, and religious perspectives. Appeals to divine inspiration, he continues, are "claims about the ultimate origin of the texts and their authority," not keys to their interpretation. In interpreting the texts, *anthropology* is important, he says, because the texts were written by real people who were interpreting their experience in terms of "available cultural symbols." *History* is important, since the New Testament authors were first-century Mediterranean Jews and, as such, "necessarily interpreted" their experiences and convictions within "a symbolic framework specific to that place and time." *Literature* is important, first, because "the meaning of texts is inextricably connected with their literary construction" and, second, because the final literary form of the New Testament texts was "canonized" (there's that community, exercising its normative power again). *Religion* is important, he continues, since the New Testament texts arose out of religious experiences and convictions, and hence to read them simply for the historical information they provide is to miss what is most important about these texts, namely, "how the experience of the powerful transforming power of God that came through the crucified Messiah Jesus, created not only a new understanding of who Jesus was but, simultaneously, a new understanding of God and God's way with the world."[14]

A striking thing about Johnson's list of relevant considerations, given how anxious he has been to dismiss historical expertise as religiously insignificant, is how much every item on the list, with one possible exception, is a matter about which some historians are experts. For instance, if, as Johnson says, for religious purposes it is crucial to remember that the New Testament authors were first-century Mediterranean Jews and, as such, necessarily interpreted their experiences and convictions within a symbolic framework specific to their place and time, to whom does the religious person turn to discover what that symbolic framework actually involves? Are not secular historians and other social scientists the experts on such matters? And so on, with the other items on the list, except for considering how the texts were influenced by the experience of "the powerful transforming power of God" that came through Jesus. However, if Johnson were to reformulate that latter condition as the need to take into account not how the experience of the transforming power of God influenced the authors of the Gospels, but rather how what the authors of the Gospels *interpreted* as the experience of the transforming power of God influenced them, then we are back again in the arena of secular historical expertise.

One could argue that the historical experts are not *really* experts, a point that Johnson comes close to making. These days, with a few notable exceptions, trashing the expertise of secular historians practically has the status of a pro forma ritual in conservative Christian apologetics. However, a problem with this sort of trashing is that, as we saw earlier in our survey of historians' views, it's clear that the historical experts really are experts. Granted, secular historians sometimes overstep the bounds of their expertise, a point to which I shall return in the next chapter, but their sometimes overstepping their bounds does not strip them of their status as experts when they stay within their bounds.

One final thought about Johnson. In Chapter 6 I argued that secular historians, no matter how much they might try to keep from making assumptions that have theological implications, all but inevitably slip into making them. It is interesting to note that even Johnson—who among living thinkers is as sophisticated and articulate a champion as I have found of the Only Faith response—claims that it is crucial for us to remember that the New Testament authors were first-century Mediterranean Jews and, as such, "necessarily" interpreted their experiences and convictions within a symbolic framework specific to their place and time. My question is this: If the New Testament authors were divinely inspired, as Johnson clearly thinks they were, why is he so quick to assume that *necessarily* they interpreted their experiences in such a restricted way? Surely God has access to broader perspectives, and hence *could have* influenced New Testament authors to transcend their cultural limitations and write from these broader perspectives. In assuming that *necessarily* this did not happen, that is, that *necessarily* New Testament authors were not sufficiently divinely inspired to transcend their cultural limitations, Johnson comes close to assuming that New Testament authors were not divinely inspired at all, which, as we have seen, is what most secular historians, at least in their role as secular historians, also assume.

Quite apart from worries about how the restricted perspectives of New Testament authors might have influenced what they wrote, Johnson goes on to say that there are entirely independent bases for criticizing interpretations in New Testament texts. He says that these texts "can be challenged morally, religiously, and theologically for their adequacy, consistency, and cogency." For instance, he asks whether New Testament texts, when taken at face value, support societal arrangements in which women are oppressed. He answers that if they do, they "can best be criticized, not by constructing an imaginary, alternative history of early Christianity in which women enjoyed equality, but on the basis of theological convictions that God's Spirit has brought to maturity within the church."[15]

Surely Johnson is right that if New Testament texts encourage the oppression of women, probably the texts are not best criticized by constructing imaginary, alternative histories. But how does Johnson know that such secular histories are *imaginary*? From whom did he learn that in first-century Israel there were no traditions of sexual equality, such as the one Schüssler Fiorenza describes, and how did he learn this, if not from secular historians and via processes of ordinary scholarly criticism? Did Johnson learn this on ordinary historical grounds—say, from Meier, whom he so much admires—or did he learn it from faith? And what if Schüssler Fiorenza's version of the facts about Jewish communities of the time is true, rather than imaginary? In Johnson's view, would that make any difference to how New Testament texts could best be criticized?

Or, to take another example, consider the views of the historian Elaine Pagels, who has not written about Jesus per se but about what she takes to be a contrast between early Gnostic Christian communities and those that became identified with the institutional church.[16] Pagels portrays the Gnostic communities as being much more sexually egalitarian. That is, according to her, in many Gnostic communities, in striking contrast to practices in communities fostered by the emerging institutional church, women tended to be treated as equals. Many historians seem to accept at least that much of Pagels's characterization. Is Johnson suggesting that Pagels's history is merely "imaginative," that is, that it is bad history? And, if he is suggesting this, how does he know?

Assume, for the sake of argument, that all histories according to which there was greater equality between the sexes in some subcultures that existed in early Christian times than there was in the emerging institutional church are bad histories. Even so, would the only remaining basis for criticizing New Testament texts for encouraging the oppression of women (supposing that these texts do encourage it) be *theological convictions that God's Spirit has brought to maturity within the church*? Why should one have to turn to theologians, or to the church, for a basis for criticizing the oppression of women? For that matter, why should one have to turn to theologians, or to the church, for a basis for criticizing the oppression of anyone? Does one have to turn to theologians or to the church for a basis for criticizing societies that tolerate slavery or child abuse? Sometimes, it almost seems as if what really irks Johnson is that secular historians have challenged, and perhaps even usurped, the authority that used to be conferred unquestioningly on theologians.

In sum, it seems that Johnson has strayed a long way from his initial posture as one who recommends the Only Faith response. He began by encouraging us to put our faith in our own personal experience. Then he encouraged us to put it instead in the "structure of meaning" ingredient in the canonical Gospels. In the end, he seems to be recommending that we give high marks to the structure of meaning ingredient in the interpretation of history of some group of theologians that he admires—in effect, that we withdraw our faith from, say, the Gospels of Luke and John and put it instead in the gospel of Luke Johnson! If that is the sort of thing he has in mind, it seems a heavy price to pay just to ward off secular historians.

The Only Faith response may be much better than Johnson's defense of it would suggest. However, it is clear from my critique of his defense that those who would defend it need to address six issues. First, they need to be clear about whether in their version of the Only Faith response "anything goes," or instead there are constraints on what one can rationally believe about Jesus on the basis of faith. Second, they need to address the question of whether it is realistic to suppose that what people believe on the basis of faith can effectively be insulated from what they believe on the basis of whatever ordinary historical evidence they are aware of and understand. Third, they need to address the question of whether thus insulating the deliverances of faith from other normal sources of belief is healthy. That is, even if by some sort of disciplined mental compartmentalization we could learn to insulate what we believe on the basis of faith from what we believe on the basis of ordinary historical evidence, would we harm ourselves psychologically by doing it? Fourth, advocates of the Only Faith response have to explain whether everyone's faith, or just their own, is going to be assessed simply on internal criteria. Fifth, they need to respond to the obvious fact that by faith different people come to believe different and even contradictory things. And, finally, since it is of the essence of the Only Faith response that one rejects secular histories of Jesus as irrelevant to what one believes about Jesus, defenders of this response should also ask whether one should also reject secular histories of everyone else—Socrates, say, or the Buddha, or Abraham Lincoln, or a convict who continues to proclaim his innocence—as irrelevant. Or, instead, does one toss out historical studies as irrelevant in assessing one's own cherished beliefs and then bring them back in to assess everyone else's beliefs? And is it just evidence from historical studies that gets the ax? What about evidence from biology or physics—say, evidence that the universe is older than 4004 B.C.E.? Is such evidence also irrelevant?

In sum, in trying to protect Christian religious beliefs from the potential challenge of secular historical studies, the Only Faith response, in effect, insulates and isolates to a remarkable degree what a Christian believes religiously from what he or she believes on other grounds. Some will be willing to pay this price to defend Christian religious beliefs from the challenge of secular historical studies. Others will think that it is too high a price to pay. The latter may well wonder whether there isn't some other way to defend Christian religious beliefs. The answer, of course, is, yes, there are other ways. Whether they fare better has still to be determined. We have seen one version of one of these other ways—although, in my view, not the best version—in the last of Johnson's three responses, and we shall see other versions of it in the next chapter.

9

FAITH SEEKING
UNDERSTANDING

*Whatever God hath revealed is certainly true; no doubt
can be made of it. This is the proper object of faith. But
whether it be a divine revelation or no reason must judge.*

—*John Locke,* Essay Concerning Human Understanding, *1689*

ACCORDING TO THE FAITH SEEKING UNDERSTANDING response, when expert historical opinion conflicts with the prompting of faith or religious experience, some sort of compromise must be worked out in which both faith and reason have to give. But what should determine how the compromise is made? John Locke's famous remark, quoted above, may sound as if it is an answer to this question. But it is hard to tell whether it is an answer without knowing how much room reason leaves for divine revelation. For instance, if Locke is saying that reason always refuses to admit as divine revelation the report of any event that transcends the limits of the workings of nature as understood by science—such as Jesus' miracles and his resurrection—then presumably his proposal would exclude divine revelations, since they would seem to transcend the bounds of ordinary natural processes. But in this interpretation of Locke, faith would give, but reason would not.[1] Hence when it comes to assessing the Faith Seeking Understanding response, a lot depends on how the compromise between faith and reason is made and, in particular, which, if either, gets the upper hand. I want now to illustrate the importance of this issue by considering the views of several thinkers who subscribe to the Faith Seeking Understanding response but make the compromise in different ways.

John Meier

Meier begins by pointing out that for him even to address the question of why, if at all, a Christian should bother with historical evidence in trying to figure out who Jesus was and what he was about, he (Meier) has to doff the hat of the modern, critical historian and don that of the theologian. For the historian, he says, the "real" has to be defined in terms of what exists in the world of space and time; and it has to be capable, in principle, either of being observed by anyone or reasonably inferred from what can be observed by anyone. As a Christian theologian, however, he says that he affirms "ultimate realities," such as "the triune God and the risen Jesus," that may not be capable of being observed or proven rationally. Thus, he says, to ask about the relation between the Jesus who can be reconstructed from modern historical research and the risen Jesus is to pass from the narrower realm of the merely observable and rational into the larger one of faith and theology.[2]

In Meier's view, the historical Jesus "is not and cannot be the object of Christian faith." For one thing, many Christians who do not know much, if anything, about the historical Jesus have believed and still do believe in Christ, "yet no one will deny the validity and strength of their faith." And even if all Christians were acquainted with historical Jesus studies, the church could not make the historical Jesus the object of its preaching and faith, since historians propose different and often contradictory portraits of Jesus and are always modifying their views. So which Jesus should be the object of Christian faith? Beyond that worry, Meier says, there is another, more important one. The object of Christian faith "is not and cannot be an idea or scholarly reconstruction, however reliable," but must be Jesus himself, who lived as a human being on earth in the first century C.E. and "now lives, risen and glorified, forever in the Father's presence." In Meier's view, Christian faith is directed primarily to this real Jesus, the one "existing and living now," the "risen Lord, to whom access is given only through faith" and only secondarily to ideas and affirmations about him.[3]

Why, then, one might ask, should Christians bother their heads at all about historical Jesus studies? Meier says that if we are "asking solely about the direct object of Christian faith," then the answer is that they should not bother; however, if we are asking, in a contemporary cultural setting, about faith seeking understanding, that is, about contemporary theology, then the price Christians will pay for not bothering about historical Jesus studies is to have their views dismissed as irrelevant by educated people, including by many Christians. He says that once a culture has become imbued with a historical-critical approach, as has Western culture since the Enlightenment, theology can speak credibly to that culture only if it takes historical research into account.[4] Thus, in his view, the reason Christians might want to be concerned with historical Jesus studies is to construct a more "credible" theology. He adds that this appropriation by theology of the quest for the historical Jesus is not faddishness, but rather "serves the interest of faith" by its reminding Christians that faith in Christ is neither a vague "existential attitude," nor a way of life, nor adherence to some "mystically divine entity," but rather an affirmation of an actual person, Jesus, who said and did specific things in a particular time and place in human history.[5]

Meier says that Jesus was "as truly and fully human—with all the galling limitations that involves—as any other human being." Against any attempt to domesticate Jesus for the purposes of respectable, middle-class Christians, the quest for the historical Jesus, he says, is a reminder that Jesus was not respectable in that sense: Among other things, Jesus associated with religiously and socially disreputable people and was a critic of merely external religious observances. Finally, in Meier's view, it is useful to view Jesus through the lens of historical research because Jesus was remarkably silent on many social and political issues of his day and "can be turned into a this-worldly political revolutionary only by contorted exegesis and special pleading."[6] In short, "by refusing to fit into the boxes we create for him," the historical Jesus "subverts not just some ideologies but all ideologies," and thereby "remains a constant stimulus to theological renewal."[7]

Implicit in these remarks is the idea that historical Jesus studies put rational constraints on faith. For instance, Meier suggests that one cannot accept on faith that Jesus was a political revolutionary if the historical evidence does not support that conception of Jesus. But why can't Christians simply give the backs of their hands to historical evidence? In particular, since Meier, along with many Christians, thinks that faith provides independent access to truth about Jesus, why, for Christians, should faith give way to reason if there is a conflict between them? Meier does not answer or even address this question except to say that if faith does not give way, Christian theology will cease to be credible. But credible to whom? It will still be credible to those who have faith and do not care about historical evidence. And why should someone with faith care if his or her theology is credible to someone without faith? Chances are that it will not be credible anyway.[8]

C. Stephen Evans

Evans, a religiously conservative Christian, is a professor of philosophy at Calvin College. In his recent book, *The Historical Christ and the Jesus of Faith* (1996), he says that although "the Spirit of God" can quite independently of evidence and arguments produce faith that counts as knowledge, the Spirit can also work through evidence and arguments, and in those who are educated the faith thus formed is enriched by confirmation of its truth.[9] In other words, Evans's view is that what one believes on faith does not have to be integrated with secular learning to be knowledge, but if it is integrated, it may be "enriched."

For expository reasons, Evans imagines a hypothetical Christian, whom he calls *James*, in whom the Spirit has done its work but who nevertheless is threatened by secular historical scholarship. Evans says that because of James's confidence in the original ground of his beliefs, he would have been rationally entitled simply to have ignored historical scholarship. However, having read some secular historians, James now has grounds both for believing and for doubting "the incarnational narrative."[10] Even so, Evans says, James is under no rational obligation to defer to the secular experts. Evans then lists approvingly several reasons for discounting expert opinion, such as that experts often get caught up in fads and address issues that are beyond their narrow areas of expertise. He concludes from his litany of potential problems with expert opinion that even after encountering a challenge from secular historians James may well be on solid ground, so far as rational considerations are concerned, in simply ignoring the evidence and clinging to his original beliefs.[11]

But wouldn't it depend rather on which of James's historical beliefs we are talking about, and on how much and what kinds of evidence against his beliefs historians provide? Consider an analogy. Suppose that before a murder trial even begins, a juror is disposed to believe "on faith" that the defendant is innocent. The juror simply accepts the defendant's word that at the time of the murder he was nowhere near the scene of the crime. Subsequently, on the basis of historical evidence, the prosecution shows conclusively that at the time of the murder the defendant was at the scene of the crime. Is the juror rationally entitled *on his original grounds* to continue believing in the innocence of the defendant? It would seem not. But a murder trial *is* a historical inquiry. Hence if such a juror would not be rationally entitled on his original grounds to continue believing in the innocence of the defendant, why in the case of a conflict between what James accepted initially on faith and what historians show on the basis of evidence is James nevertheless entitled to persist in his beliefs?

If, in Evans's view, James is rationally entitled simply to dismiss the views of the historians, then Evans faces the same sorts of questions that we saw arising for those who appeal to the Only Faith response to the challenge posed by secular historical studies: How far may James go in clinging to his original beliefs? Does anything go, or are there limits? If there are limits, what are they, and what is their source and scope? If, say, James is convinced that the Spirit of God is working through him in producing his religious beliefs, would he be entitled, without sullying his claim to be a rational person, to cling, say, to his biblically inspired belief that the universe was created in 4004 B.C.E.? Would he be entitled to believe that David Koresh is Jesus?

I am *not* suggesting that Evans would want to answer the latter two questions in the affirmative. My point, rather, is that there seems to be nothing in his account of rational belief that would block affirmative answers to them. Indeed, there is nothing in his account that would block the result that if James thought the Spirit of God was working through him in generating some consistent belief, James would be rationally entitled to persist in the belief, no matter what it was, in the teeth of *any amount* and *any kind* of contrary evidence from merely secular sources. If Evans does not want his view to sanction affirmative answers to such questions, then he needs to tell us where to draw the line, and on what basis, between what James is and is not rationally entitled to believe. Then we might be able to determine whether James's dismissing the views of historians would be justified. But instead of telling us where he would draw that line, Evans leaves it to us to draw that line for ourselves. The result of this strategy of silence is that his view is much less interesting than it might otherwise have been.[12]

On the surface, Evans may come across as more moderate than he does in my characterization of his views. For instance, he concedes that James may realize, on reflection, that his belief in the reliability of the New Testament accounts is motivated by factors that are not conducive to truth, such as wish-fulfillment. However, he may also realize that his skeptical doubts are similarly motivated. So, in Evans's view, James's best option, in the absence of further evidence, is "simply to examine the situation as honestly as he can," and then to believe whatever seems to be true on the basis of that examination.[13] Fair enough. But in examining his situation, what exactly is it that James is supposed to review?

We have already seen some of the things James might examine in questioning the credentials and pronouncements of the so-called historical experts. Later in his account, Evans even extends his list of the potential problems with expert opinion. But what should James examine on *his* side of the ledger? Evans mentions only "wish-fulfillment." But that is not nearly enough. In fact, wish-fulfillment may not even be a problem, since there is nothing wrong with wanting your beliefs to be true, so long as your wanting them to be true does not cause you to ignore or misconstrue evidence. James's recognition of the fact that he wants the New Testament accounts to be reliable would not be a reason for him to reject them, any more than a historian's wanting his thesis to be true would be a reason for the historian to reject his own thesis.

Yet we *can* say what would be rational grounds for a *historian* to dismiss his own thesis: *evidence* or *reasons* on the basis of which some competing hypothesis emerges as more likely. What sort of evidence or reasons? The sorts I canvassed earlier in my characterizations of the views of Sanders, Meier, Schüssler Fiorenza, Crossan, Borg, and Wright and that routinely emerge in the course of scholarly debate over the merits of competing historical interpretations. No reputable historian ever publicly dismisses another historian's views just because he or she does not like them. Rather, historians always give *reasons* for dismissing others' views—evidence that they think the other historian has overlooked or assessed incorrectly, well-confirmed theories that they think the other historian has failed to take into account or to weight properly, and so on.[14] What, then, would be good reasons for James to dismiss his original view? Evans does not say.

Evans does explain why James came to accept his original view in the first place. He accepted it, Evans says, on the basis of "the total circumstances of his life in which the truth of the Gospel has become evident as he has responded in faith to the assertions, promises and demands he perceives God to be making upon him in Jesus." Evans says that the question is whether these beliefs on James's part continue to be reasonable after they have been challenged by critical historical scholarship. He answers that they do: "In this case the disagreements within critical historical scholarship undermine any pretension that historical criticism has some strong claim to be a sure authority for the layperson and leave the original ground for the belief undefeated."[15] Perhaps so. I shall return to the issue of disagreement among historians. The problem for now is that what Evans has identified as the question and then answered is not the question for which we wanted an answer. We wanted to know what might give James rationally persuasive grounds to conclude, in the light of historical scholarship, that what he had accepted until now on the basis of faith he should abandon. Evans's assertion that James does not *have* to abandon anything does not answer this question.

It might have been helpful if Evans had been more explicit about James's grounds for those of his beliefs that he accepts on faith. His characterizing these grounds as "the total circumstances of James' life" is not informative, for it includes too much to shed any light on what *in particular* James should be reevaluating when he reevaluates his grounds. Later, Evans is more explicit. He says that James "might for example be impressed by the lives of the people that he has encountered" in his local church "or by his own experiences with church life." Evans supposes that James "has acquired a strong consciousness of meeting God in the communion services, or a strong sense of God's presence in times of prayer with others." He says that "through these kinds of experiences James might well reasonably come to believe that the church is a visible instrument of the work of God and conclude that its teachings are likely to be reliable."[16] Such reasons, Evans concludes, are enough to defeat the challenge posed by secular historical scholarship.

But are they? What Evans is asking us to accept is that James's being "impressed" with people he has met at church or by his "experiences with church life" is as likely to make him a good judge of historical truth as the special training and knowledge of professional historians. But if James can in this way override expert opinion with respect to history, then presumably he can in the same way override expert opinion in other areas as well. If what Evans is suggesting were true, it would be a good reason for shutting down the history departments in all of the schools in the land. Instead of going through the arduous and expensive business of acquiring professional training, we could just ask students who "impresses" them. Since Evans puts no restrictions on what it is about the others that is impressive, he has left the door wide open for all sorts of absurdity. We are back to the problem of "anything goes."

Evans seems to think that disagreement among the experts, in effect, disqualifies them as experts with respect to issues about which they disagree. Yet he never then addresses the question of whether, in his view, what James is rationally entitled to believe would be more constrained if the experts were to agree. Instead, it is sufficient for Evans—and is of overwhelming importance, judging from how often he brings it up—that the historians of Jesus do in fact disagree. In his view, disagreement among historians, in effect, levels the playing field: Since the people who most of us might have thought were the experts are not worthy of being believed, everyone, including James, becomes a sort of expert in his or her own right. "One might wonder," Evans asks, whether "it is arrogant of James to rely on his own judgment when by hypothesis he knows much less than the scholars in the field. Should he not defer to the judgments of scholars?" Evans replies that "the illusory force of this rhetorical question dissipates as soon as one asks, 'Which scholars should he trust?'"[17]

But surely there is more to the issue of whose view should be trusted than merely asking whether James should have deferred to this or that historical scholar. Suppose, for instance, that on the basis of "the total circumstances of his life" James thinks that he knows what really happened with respect to some specific issue, even though what really happened is a matter about which expert opinion is directly relevant, the experts do not agree, and James has not even acquainted himself with the evidence that experts ponder in trying to decide the issue. For instance, suppose that what James thinks he knows on faith is that the entire Gospel of Thomas was formed at a later date than everything in the Synoptic Gospels.[18] Wouldn't James be just a tad arrogant if he were to suppose that even though the experts disagree about whether the entire Gospel of Thomas was formed later than everything in the Synoptic Gospels, he, as a non-expert who has not even bothered to acquaint himself with the relevant evidence, does know that Thomas was formed later? In such circumstances, wouldn't it be more reasonable of James to suspend judgment?

Perhaps, though, James has had a dazzling religious experience in which the veil dropped from his eyes and the truth about the Gospel of Thomas was revealed. Fair enough. If that is how James came to his views and he has good reasons for thinking that his revelatory experience was in fact genuine, then, in my opinion, James is rationally entitled to his view. But, according to Evans, perceptions much less than such a revelatory experience—say, James's being "impressed" with people he has met at church—will also entitle James to his view. James in effect becomes his own source of expert opinion—even though the "expertise" on which his opinion about the Gospel of Thomas is based involves no study or training, but only socializing.

Evans says that in addition to simply consulting his own opinion, another option available to James is to appeal to "the authority of the Church." Evans concedes that of course someone may challenge the church's competence to decide such matters. But he quickly dismisses this worry with the observation that "such a challenge can in principle be raised with respect to any authority, including the guild of historical scholars."[19] Yes, and including also mathematicians, physicists, brain surgeons, bridge builders, baseball batting coaches, potters, and so on. Evans takes the fact that such a challenge can be *raised* as being decisive. But isn't it also relevant how the challenge, once raised, is *answered*? Surely the mere fact that a challenge can be raised does not mean, as Evans assumes, that all attempts to answer it are equivalent. For instance, we could challenge the competence of a computer scientist to design some software, even though he has been specifically trained to design it and he is universally regarded by other experts in the field as highly competent to design it. And we could challenge the competence of someone like me, who knows practically nothing about computers, to design the very same software. So far as just the challenges are concerned, the two cases are parallel. But when it comes to the crucial matter of responding to the challenges, surely a better case could be made that the computer scientist is more competent to design the software than I would be. To deny such obvious facts would be to take flight into epistemological la-la land. But then why isn't something analogous also true, and for pretty much the same reasons, when we are comparing the competence of highly trained professional historians to figure out whether certain things really happened in the first century C.E. with James's competence, or the church's competence, to answer the very same questions?

Evans never explains how the church can meet challenges to its competence to be an authority on questions of historical fact as well as trained professional historians can. Nor does he explain whether the church could also meet challenges to its competence to be an authority in other areas where there are also trained professional experts: physics, biology, and so on. Throughout, Evans relies on the idea that trained secular historians obviously *cannot* meet challenges to their competence. For instance, he says that "the answers which the New Testament scholar gives are very largely the result of his own presuppositions and prejudices."[20] Hence, if trained historians are that far beyond the pale, then, when it comes to assessing historical evidence, apparently the church can do at least as well as trained historians. But then why do even good Christian schools, such as Calvin College, have rigorous programs of training for would-be historians comparable to what would-be historians get in a secular institution? Wouldn't it be easier, and cheaper, if we wanted to know what happened with respect to some specific question of history, just to ask the church, or James?[21]

Evans seems to think that James, even without any special training in historical scholarship, could do quite well, if not as a historian per se, then at least as an evaluator of historical scholarship. Evans says that when scholarly disagreement is pervasive it does not imply that no scholar has good grounds for his scholarly beliefs or ever knows that any such disputed beliefs are true.[22] Rather, what it implies, he thinks, is that the scholars' views on such disputed questions "cannot provide a strong basis for other people to form beliefs."[23] I agree. But does it then follow that other people are then free to form their own beliefs on such disputed questions willy-nilly, without thereby undermining their reputations as rational people? Evans, it seems, would answer yes.[24] He says that "if James is or becomes a New Testament scholar himself the situation [i.e., his competence to make judgments on matters historical] does not appreciably change."[25] Apparently it is easy to be a competent historian.

In Evans's view, one of the basic problems with secular historians of Jesus is that in their work as historians they are closet philosophers. That, he seems to think, is what explains their inability to agree. It is also largely why, in crucial respects, James may well be the equal of professional historians. Evans says, for instance, that a "good deal of this disagreement [among historians] is rooted in factors where the scholars in question may not have any special expertise either," such as, "philosophical, theological, and literary assumptions" with respect to some of which "James may be competent to evaluate the views of the scholars."[26] Among the philosophical assumptions that Evans thinks matter is a prejudice that many historians share against the miraculous and, in general, against any supernatural intervention into the natural world, including against prophesy.[27] He points out, for instance, that many historians date Acts after the fall of Jerusalem because they think that otherwise they would have to admit that its author had prophetic powers. In the process of criticizing this particular dating and then arguing for an earlier one, Evans says that it is important to challenge the implicit assumption that accurate "prophesies" must have been made after the events that they prophesied. This assumption, he says, makes it impossible to give the New Testament accounts, with their stories of miracles and prophesies fulfilled, "a fair historical test."

Evans says that one "cannot begin by ruling out as impossible any supernatural knowledge or insight on the part of Jesus, if one wishes fairly to test the claim that God was at work in Jesus in a special way, or that Jesus was actually God incarnate."[28] From my discussion in Chapter 6, it should be clear that I agree with Evans about this. However, after making this plausible methodological criticism Evans not only says almost nothing about how an enlightened historian is supposed to deal with the possibility that Jesus may have had foreknowledge, but, as we saw in Chapter 6, in enthusiastically endorsing Eleanor Stump's interpretation of the story of the raising of Lazarus, he even *presupposes without comment* that on some occasions Jesus did *not* have foreknowledge.[29]

In the previous chapter, I criticized Johnson's defense of the Only Faith response. I did this not to put the Only Faith response down, but to reveal some of the problems that have to be resolved in order to put that response in its strongest form. Johnson's defense of that response is the best contemporary defense of it with which I am familiar, or at least the best that is specifically addressed to the challenges posed by secular historical scholarship. Yet his defense, I argued, is not very good. In this chapter, I have criticized, in the same spirit, Evans's defense of the Faith Seeking Understanding response. Once again, my criticisms are intended not to defeat a version of the Faith Seeking Understanding response that would give faith the upper hand, but to show how problematic it can be and, in particular, that some of the main problems that arise for Evans's defense of it are the same as those that arose for Johnson in his defense of the Only Faith response. What, though, if one were to try to defend the Faith Seeking Understanding response in a way that gives reason the upper hand? We turn now to the views of a philosopher who has done just that.

Basil Mitchell

Mitchell is a professor of the philosophy of the Christian religion at Oxford University. He is the author of many widely discussed papers and books, including *Law, Morality, and Religion in a Secular Society* (1967), *The Justification of Religious Belief* (1973), and *Faith and Criticism* (1994).[30] The latter book is devoted to explaining how liberal theologians can solve a problem that Mitchell says arises in their view of Christianity. The problem is that while they assume that Christianity has a truth to impart about the world on the basis of which salvation is to be understood, they also assume that there are other sources of truth, such as science and historical studies, which sometimes yield results that conflict with what was assumed to be a truth of Christianity.[31] Conservative theologians, Mitchell says, avoid this problem simply by rejecting claims to truth that conflict with what they take to be truths of Christianity.[32] Mitchell says that he agrees with the conservatives that as Christians, we "hear God speaking to us in the Bible and in the tradition of the Church." He adds, however, that "simply to repeat what is said in the Bible without any attempt to understand it" is neither really listening to it nor sufficiently respectful of the word of God. In addition, he says, simply repeating ignores "the instruction of scripture itself to 'mark, learn, and inwardly digest.'" In any case, he claims, since the Bible is not always consistent with itself, there has to be a process of subordinating some parts of it to others.[33]

In defending liberal theologians, Mitchell first points out that usually the contrast between the faith of theologians and the reason of scientists is overdrawn. There is faith too in science, he says, which shows itself in scientists' persevering in their commitment to theories even when they acknowledge that there are problems with the theories that they do not know how to solve. He says that this persevering behavior, although often shown in the physical sciences, is more prevalent in the social sciences and the humanities. There, he says, it is evident that, as a rule, convictions do not change radically as a consequence of particular pieces of evidence. Rather, when in the social sciences and humanities convictions change, it is as a result of steadily accumulating considerations that collectively persuade theorists that their approaches are no longer viable. In such processes of change, Mitchell says, strong emotions, entrenched habits, and even loyalty, say, to like-minded colleagues, play their parts. Thus, until the case against a theory has become very clear, which may not happen until a competing theory has been established beyond reasonable doubt, theorists may feel that they should not act on their doubts about their theories, for fear of hurting others. And, Mitchell says, when it comes to the attachments that people develop to their philosophies of life, which by their own admission often afford them "a faith to live by," it is even more obvious that this is how reason works.[34]

Thus, Mitchell, like Evans, believes that a certain amount of persistence in sticking to one's beliefs in the face of criticism is a good thing. However, their attitudes toward the tension between reason and faith are entirely different. Evans is combative, anxious to make sure that reason does not get the upper hand. Mitchell is conciliatory, anxious to show that the seeming opposition between faith and reason is largely illusory. In Mitchell's view, what we take to be reason is up to its neck in commitments that are born of faith. But, he thinks, even though reason includes faith, reason still has teeth of its own. In recognition of this, he says that in the pursuit of truth it is essential that the overall state of the evidence be continually reviewed since otherwise theoretical problems will not be acknowledged, and hence needed corrections will not be made. Evans, you will recall, stressed that it would have been completely all right for James simply to have ignored evidence from historical studies that is contrary to his beliefs.

Another difference is that Evans is intent on questioning the expertise of historians. He is worried that scholarship may deplete faith of some of its content. His strategy, in part, in protecting faith from historical Jesus scholarship, is to argue that since this scholarship is next to worthless, faith can afford to ignore it. Mitchell, on the other hand, has a high regard for historical Jesus scholarship. He even argues that without it, religious faith becomes stagnant. How, then, does Mitchell protect religious faith from scholarship? In part, he protects it by arguing that one has a right to persist in one's faith, and so one does not have to cave in right away, even in the face of legitimate scholarly criticisms. In his view, religious faith has a right to persist not because of anything special having to do with faith but because that is how reason works across the board, including in historical studies. He says that although there is such a thing as unreasoning prejudice, it does not make sense to be constantly changing one's stance; hence, at the very least, we need to adhere to our convictions long enough to put them to the test and into practice, to see what becomes of them.[35]

But even if one accepts Mitchell's argument to this point, it would seem to support only a kind of delaying action. What about in the long run? That is, what protects religious faith from *eventually* succumbing to the criticisms of scholars? Mitchell concedes that in the *very* long run, nothing protects faith from historical scholarship. But he counters that faith does not need that much protection. He says that the sort of perseverance that is necessary in intellectual pursuits and in the practical affairs of life is of a piece with what is necessary in the case of a person's adherence to his or her religious beliefs. In all of these cases, he says, often the faith that is required is not one that is merely tentative and provisional, but is "persistent and deeply committed" and capable of governing a person's whole life.[36] He says that for commitment to be genuine it does not have to be blind to criticism, but just to be persistent. And rationality already endorses a faith that is persistent enough to last a lifetime.

But when, then, should faith be abandoned? Mitchell says that what is accepted as knowledge has credentials of varying strength, and these differences of degree affect how it is rational for a person of faith to respond to knowledge claims. For instance, if a scientific theory is so well justified that no reputable scientist would think of disputing it, such as, say, the broad outlines of the Darwinian theory of natural selection, then, says Mitchell, theologians must accept it. But if scientific findings are in dispute, then theologians are not required to accept the majority view.[37] He says, for instance, that contemporary physiologists tend to adopt as a methodological assumption that all mental events consist of changes in the brain, and may, for that reason, subscribe in their philosophies of life to some form of scientific determinism. But Christian theologians and others who emphasize human freedom and responsibility are not bound to accept this view.[38]

Here Mitchell seems to be conflating two issues: whether the experts agree, and, if they do, their reasons for agreeing. Consider first the matter of whether the experts agree. To keep things simple, consider only questions about which almost everyone would agree that one needs expertise to form a responsible independent opinion. Most, I suppose, would concede that when there is a substantial amount of disagreement among the experts even about such matters, no one is under any obligation to believe what only a slight majority of the experts favor. For instance, although all historians of Jesus agree that he spoke Aramaic, suppose that a slight majority of them think that he also spoke Greek and hence was bilingual. Then, it would seem, nonexperts are under no rational obligation to go along with the majority view. However, that does not mean, as Mitchell sometimes (and Evans almost always) seems to suggest, that when it comes to the question of what language Jesus spoke, nonexperts are thereby entitled to believe whatever they want. If agreement among experts puts constraints on what a nonexpert may rationally believe, then so, it would seem, does disagreement.

Suppose, for instance, that on the question of what language, or languages, Jesus spoke, 45 percent of the experts think that Jesus spoke only Aramaic, and 55 percent of them think that Jesus spoke both Aramaic and Greek. Suppose, further, that the question of what languages Jesus spoke is one that requires expertise to decide on the basis of primary evidence. Finally, suppose that nonexperts have no access to information relevant to answering the question other than knowledge about how expert opinion is divided (and perhaps also the evidence that the experts have access to). Under these circumstances, it would seem, there are only two responses that nonexperts can have that would be rationally permissible. The first would be to suspend judgment on the issue (since the experts are substantially divided). The second would be to believe that Jesus was bilingual (since a majority of the experts believe that). It would not be rational, under these circumstances, for nonexperts to believe that Jesus spoke only Aramaic (since it would be arbitrary of them to side with the minority expert view).

There is an unfortunate tendency among those who would defend religious faith against historical scholarship to think that if the experts disagree, then anything goes. One can understand this in the case of someone like Evans who seems to think that anything goes regardless of whether the experts agree. It is enough for him if James, for whatever reason, is "impressed" by the people he has met at church. However, this attitude is harder to understand in the case of someone like Mitchell, who has a high regard for expert opinion. If one places a high value on expert opinion, then (with one qualification, to be discussed in a moment) regardless of whether the experts agree, expert opinion will be consequential to what it is rational for nonexperts to believe. If the experts *dis*agree, the consequences for nonexperts will be different than if the experts agree, but that does not mean that there will be no consequences.

The qualification is that it matters *why* the experts agree or disagree. This is the second of the two issues that Mitchell conflates. In particular, it matters whether the experts agree for methodological or for substantive reasons, that is, because they think that assuming the claim in question will facilitate their inquiry (methodological reasons) or because they think that the claim in question has been shown to be true on the basis of evidence (substantive reasons). Thus a historian may for *methodological* reasons, and strictly *for the purpose* of doing "scientific" history, *assume* that Jesus was neither God nor divinely inspired because he or she does not see how it is possible to do scientific history on any other basis. Yet the historian may want to leave open the question of whether Jesus actually was either God or divinely inspired. But no historian would assume as a matter of historical methodology that Jesus spoke only Aramaic or that Jesus spoke both Aramaic and Greek. If a historian has a professionally held view on this question, it will be because he or she believes that it is supported by historical evidence.

Mitchell is quite right to think that nonexperts are under no obligation to believe what scientists or historians assume for methodological reasons. But the absence of any such obligation has nothing to do with whether scientists or historians *agree* among themselves about the methodological desirability of making the assumption in question. Even if the experts all were to agree that it is methodologically desirable to make the assumption, nonexperts would still be under no obligation to go along. The reason they would be under no obligation is that the thing about which the experts agree is not something that they have *shown* on the basis of evidence, but something that they have *assumed* for the purpose of getting on with their investigations in what they take to be the best way.

In fairness to Mitchell, later in his discussion he considers the point that some of the things that historians agree about they have merely assumed for methodological reasons. In such cases, he says, others are under no obligation to go along. The Resurrection, he thinks, is a case in point. Liberal theologians, he says, often argue that scientific history cannot acknowledge supernatural causes, and so cannot allow for the occurrence of the Resurrection as it is traditionally understood. Hence, in their view, the evidence of testimony in the reports of early Christians is irrelevant. The Resurrection either has to be accepted entirely on faith or else "demythologized," that is, interpreted as the expression of a change in attitude on the part of early Christians to Jesus' death, but not as implying his actually being raised from the dead. "However," Mitchell says, "to argue in this way is to ignore entirely the crucial difference that is made to our evaluation of the historical evidence by belief in the creative power of God." He says that "scientific" history, *for good reason,* does not take into account the creative power of God; however, "this methodological restriction on the part of historians does not permit them to claim, on the basis of the evidence, that the Resurrection did not happen" but at most that, "given entirely naturalistic assumptions, some other explanation is to be preferred" or that "it is impossible to settle the question."

Mitchell points out that many theologians as well as many ordinary Christians both believe and think they are justified in believing that there is a God who created and sustains the world, and acts within it for its redemption. Given this assumption, which Mitchell says many Christians rightly think they have independent reasons for accepting, "they both can and should take [historical] evidence as showing that God raised Jesus from the dead." Mitchell says that historical evidence, and with it all that goes to make up the critical scholar's apparatus, has its own integrity and cannot be made to support equally any thesis whatever. But when it comes to choosing between overall interpretations it becomes a matter of judgment how much final weight to give to the various elements in it. It simply will not do to leave it to the historians to decide what actually happened and to require theologians to accept their decision as final, as determining definitely the basic historical foundations on which they have to build.[39]

I agree. All that I would add to this is, first, that the reason it would not do to leave it to the historians to decide such questions has nothing to do with whether historians agree but, rather, with the fact that they agree, if they do, as a matter of *historical methodology,* not as a matter of *substantive result.* And, second, even if Mitchell is right, all that he has established is that Christians do not have to accept the results of historical work that is based on methodological assumptions that Christians would reject as substantive truths. This is an important point, but it is, in effect, only the point that Christians are rationally entitled to strike a balance between the claims of faith and those of secular rationality. Mitchell's point leaves untouched the crucial question of *how* Christians should strike that balance.

On a related issue, when the theologian, in believing something, disagrees with the scientist or historian, is the theologian's commitment to his belief merely tentative, or is it unconditional? As we have seen, Mitchell stresses that even if in the long run the theologian's commitment is tentative, it may be long-lasting in that he would be entitled to stick with it throughout his life, and it may be total in the sense that "he stakes his whole being" on the correctness of his opinion. Mitchell says that the theologian's commitment to what he accepts on faith can be like Shakespeare's commitment to the reality of love: Although Shakespeare concedes the theoretical possibility that he might be mistaken, he bets his life that he is not.[40]

Still, it might be objected, this means only that the theologian's faith may be total, in the sense that it is wholehearted. It does not imply that his faith may be unconditional. Mitchell answers that he has been talking all along about faith as if it were always a question of believing, say, that there is a God, who created us, loves us, and so on. Mitchell says that there is another dimension to faith that has to do not with believing but with "trusting reliance upon God" and that this trust may well be unconditional.[41] Indeed, Mitchell claims, it is just the unconditional nature of this trust that allows the theologian to expose his faith to criticism. The theologian assumes that "if we are honest in our search for truth and at the same time loyal to the signs we have been given, we shall not ultimately be misled."[42] Mitchell asks which attitude shows greater trust in God—one that refuses to submit traditional beliefs to criticism, or one that is confident that if we put our traditional beliefs to the test of reason and experience, we shall be led in the end to understand them better and be more firmly convinced of their truth?[43]

How, then, should the compromise between faith and reason be struck? In Mitchell's view, if I understand him correctly, it should be struck in a way that, in the long run at least, leaves secular reason in the driver's seat. However, reason is in the driver's seat only with respect to those results of secular reasoning that are free of methodological assumptions that Christians are entitled to reject. Except for what I have already summarized, Mitchell does not elaborate on how this works out in practice.

N. T. Wright

Wright, though in many ways as religiously conservative as Evans, is more wholeheartedly in the Faith Seeking Understanding camp. It is central to his view that Christian faith is inextricably rooted in history. And for him this means that historians not only can but also should question the claims of faith, and people of faith not only can but also should listen to their criticisms. He says that if Jesus was as Reimarus, or Schweitzer, or even Sanders has portrayed him, then Christians would need to revise their faith quite substantially.[44] However, Wright says that Christians often imagine that in defending themselves against historians they are defending Christianity, when what they are actually defending is just a pre-Enlightenment worldview that is no more specifically Christian than any other.[45] What Christians need to do, he thinks, is not to attach themselves slavishly to the outmoded worldview of early Christians but to discover a modern worldview that "makes sense of the world as we know it" and "stands in appropriate and recognizable continuity" with earlier Christian worldviews.[46]

It is past time, Wright thinks, to get beyond the idea that the story of the historical Jesus must be told only from the perspective of religious faith. Fundamentalists, he says, in insisting on this approach, divorce the New Testament from the intentions of its authors and, in

effect, interpret it to support their own views of its call to a particular sort of spirituality or lifestyle. For them, he says, the New Testament is a sort of "magic book" that exists "to sustain the soul," but
"not to stretch the mind." Wright says that it is also past time to get
beyond the idea that the story of the historical Jesus should be told
only from the perspective of secular history. Most New Testament
academic scholars, he says, in officially subscribing to this approach,
think they are reading the New Testament in a thoroughly historical
way, "without inflicting on it the burden of being theologically normative." But, he says, all historians of the New Testament and early
Christianity known to him, "without exception," have begun with
their own ideas about the importance of the events under discussion,
and rather than remaining "content with bare description," have
tried to make their stories relevant to the present.[47]

Wright says that when it comes to historical Jesus studies, the
most salient question is not that of whether to do either theology *or*
history, but of how properly to mix theology *and* history.[48] One of
the intended purposes of his own work as a historian is to show that
"rigorous history" and "rigorous theology" belong together, and
never more so than in the discussion of Jesus. He says that if this
means that we need a new metaphysic, then "so be it." He says that
"it would be pleasant if, for once, the historians and the theologians
could set the agenda for the philosophers, instead of vice versa."[49]

How, then, for the purposes of historical Jesus studies, would
Wright mix theology and history? He says that he would employ a
new approach, one that is a creative synthesis of the premodern
(fundamentalist) emphasis on the text as in some sense authoritative;
the modern emphasis on the text and indeed all of Christianity, including its theology, as irreducibly integrated into history; and the
postmodern emphasis on the reading of the text.[50] His hopes for this
new approach are not only that it will contribute to private edification and academic satisfaction but also that it will advance "the
kingdom of God"![51]

Wright answers the question of how his new approach is supposed
to work in two different ways. One is in a long, philosophical preface in which he answers it directly. The other is in his historical
work itself, which exemplifies his new approach. So far as the philosophy is concerned, he begins by endorsing an epistemological
view that he calls *critical realism,* which is a view that fully acknowledges both the independent reality of the thing known and that our

only access to this independent reality is through interpretive structures that are internal to us. These structures, Wright says, confine the knower to fewer points of view than are available, and they are colored by the knower's expectations, hopes, and so on. They also have a great deal to do with the communities to which the knower belongs. Wright says that just as there is no such thing as a *neutral* or *objective* knower, so also there is no such thing as a *detached* knower.[52]

Historical interpretations, Wright says, always reflect the world-views of their authors, which contain irreducibly narrative components. Wright thinks that our most fundamental stories underlie our explicitly formulated beliefs, including our theological beliefs. When human beings try to assimilate new information, he says, they do it by trying to integrate the information into preexisting story forms. When the new information is itself a story, then for someone to assimilate the information the new story must be close enough to stories the hearer already believes for a spark to jump between them, yet far enough away that the spark, "in jumping, illuminates for a moment the whole area around, changing perceptions as it does so." Tell someone to do something, Wright says, and you change his or her day. Tell people a story, and you change their life. Get everyone to believe the same story, he might have added, and you change the world. Get everyone to believe the same true story, and you advance the kingdom of God.[53]

How does one tell whether a story is true? Not by proving it neutrally or objectively. There are no such "proofs," Wright says. Rather, the story we are asked to believe must make more sense, both as a whole and in detail, than competing stories. "Simplicity of outline, elegance in handling the details within it, the inclusion of all the parts of the story, and the ability of the story to make sense beyond its immediate subject matter: these are what count."[54] In sum, Wright recommends, within the larger model of worldviews, a critical-realist theory of knowledge that acknowledges the essentially "storied" nature of human knowing, thinking, and living. In his view, even though there is an external world to be known that can be known, all knowledge of it takes place within the framework of a worldview, of which stories are an essential part.

Knowledge of the world progresses, Wright says, by setting up as hypotheses competing stories about the world or parts of it, and then testing these stories by assessing their "fit" with stories that are already accepted. Although experience plays a role in this process, neither it nor anything else is foundational. There are no foundations. Wright says that the larger stories to which we subscribe, which themselves form the framework for more specific views we have, including his own critical-realist epistemology, "are tested not by their coherence with a fixed point agreed in advance," but "by their simplicity and their ability to make sense of a wide scope of experiences and events." In the end, he says, "the proof of the pudding remains in the eating."[55]

The rest of Wright's answer to how the theological/historical approach he recommends actually works is his historical work itself. In Chapter 7 I sketched some of his main methods and results. Suffice it to say here that the differences that matter most between Wright and other historians are not so much in their views of what they are doing as in their doing of it, that is, in their historical interpretations themselves. And the main difference here between Wright and more secular historians is that in trying to decide how best to explain some event, such as the resurrection, Wright assigns a much higher initial probability to certain theological explanations than would secular historians. When all of the competing *naturalistic* explanations are weak, a more secular historian would either choose the best among them or else just admit that he or she does not know. Wright, on the other hand, is often willing to adopt a theological explanation.

History and Theology Revisited

Everyone who subscribes to the Faith Seeking Understanding response agrees that when expert opinion or empirical evidence conflicts with the prompting of faith, some sort of compromise needs to be worked out in which both faith and reason have to give. They disagree among themselves about how the compromise is to be struck. Conservatives such as Evans are eager to strike it in a way that gives faith the upper hand. The problem for them is basically the same as the problem for those who would defend the Only Faith response: Anything goes. Liberals such as Mitchell (some of the time) are ready to strike the compromise in a way that gives reason the upper hand. The problem for them is basically the same as the problem for those who would defend the Only Reason response: Not enough goes. If anything goes, then there are few, if any, rational constraints on what one can believe. If not enough goes, then religious faith becomes at best a thin veneer on an otherwise wholly secular view, which is itself committed to a secular faith. Between these two extremes are the views of someone like Mitchell (most of the time) and Wright (all of the time), who try to strike a more even-handed balance between the claims of faith and reason. The problem for those in this middle group is to explain specifically how the compromise is to be struck without sliding into a version of their views that incurs either the anything-goes objection or the not-enough-goes objection. Such problems are not necessarily insuperable, but they are predictable and chronic. When a proponent of one version or another of the Faith Seeking Understanding response tries to solve the characteristic problem with his version of the response, almost inevitably he compromises his version in ways that bring it closer to one of the other approaches, along with its characteristic problem.

As we have seen, Mitchell argued in favor of striking a compromise between faith and reason, but beyond saying that people of faith are not required to accept views whose justification depends essentially on methodological assumptions they reject, he gave precious little guidance about how the compromise between faith and reason should be struck. Much the same is true of Wright. He gave a fuller explanation than did Mitchell of why people of faith do not need to cave in to the demands of Only Reason types, but when it came to the question of how the compromise between faith and reason should be struck, he resorted in the end to vague talk of coherence and puddings. Although his account is both insightful and promising, and will surely serve as a useful point of departure for further reflection, in my view, when it comes down to the hard question of how the compromise between faith and reason should be struck, he comes up short. Yet I don't know of anyone who has done any better. One is reminded of the ancient Chinese curse, "May you live in interesting times." For Christians who would try to figure out how they should respond to historical Jesus studies, these are interesting times.

10

ONLY REASON

WE HAVE ALREADY CONSIDERED two responses to the challenge posed by secular historical scholarship to traditional Christian beliefs. The first—Only Faith—was to reject secular scholarship whenever it contradicts the claims of religious faith. The second—Faith Seeking Understanding—was to integrate the diverse claims of secular scholarship and religious faith into a single coherent account. A third response—Only Reason—is the polar opposite of Only Faith. Only Reason enjoins Christians to be totally submissive to the agreed-upon *expert* opinions of secular historians (but not to the opinions experts express that transcend their areas of expertise). In addition to Only Reason, in this chapter I want to consider a related response that results from taking a small but crucial step beyond Only Reason. This latter response is actually a version of Faith Seeking Understanding, but one that differs significantly from the others considered thus far in the way it is related to the Only Reason response. I call it *multiperspectivalism*.

As we saw in the previous two chapters, although there is something to be said for the Only Faith and Faith Seeking Understanding responses to the challenge posed by secular historical scholarship to traditional Christian beliefs, each also has its drawbacks. The main things to be said in favor of the Only Faith response is that it respects the autonomy of religious faith and preserves its character as total commitment. Its main drawback is that because it completely denies the claims of secular scholarship, it is vulnerable to the criticism that "anything goes." An additional drawback, perhaps not of Only Faith itself but of the way it is almost always defended, is that its proponents, from Tertullian to Luke Johnson, have had a hard time sticking to it consistently. Because it is such an extreme view, they tend, in defending it, to soften its edges by denying its implications.

The main thing to be said for the Faith Seeking Understanding response is that it acknowledges the value of both religious faith *and* secular reason. Its main drawback is that out of the infinite number of ways in which a genuine compromise between religious faith and secular reason might be struck, there seems to be no good reason for striking it one way rather than another. A possible additional drawback is the difficulty in this response of preserving for religious faith its character as total commitment.[1] Finally, there is a tendency on the part of some proponents of the Faith Seeking Understanding response to understand it in a way that gives faith the upper hand, hence making it vulnerable to the same problems as the Only Faith response, and on the part of other of its proponents to give reason the upper hand, hence making it vulnerable to the same problems as the Only Reason response, to which we now turn.

Only Reason

Historically, Only Reason has been not so much a response to the challenge posed to Christianity by secular historical scholarship as to what gave rise to that challenge in the first place. Only Reason depends for its plausibility on acceptance of the assumption that secular rationality is our only source of knowledge, from which it follows, first, that if our objective is knowledge, then in conflicts between secular rationality and religious faith, secular rationality always prevails; and, second, that even when there is no conflict, religious faith is not an additional source of knowledge. Not surprisingly, Only Reason is the view of secular critics of traditional Christian beliefs.[2] However, for those who have never looked into the matter, it can be surprising to learn how popular Only Reason has been even among Christian theologians and clergy. It is, for instance, implicit in Rudolf Bultmann's demythologizing approach to early Christianity, and it is deeply implicated in Bishop Spong's more recent reinterpretations of traditional Christian beliefs.[3] Somehow, the wolf got inside the door.

The Only Reason response has three main advantages. One is that if everything can be explained naturalistically, then by excluding, from the beginning, consideration of possible "non-natural" sources of influence, this response tremendously simplifies and hence facilitates the search for historical explanations. In fact, it is exactly this simplification in the realm of the physical world that led to the development of modern science in the first place. And many think that a similar simplification is required in order to have truly scientific historical studies. Another advantage is that in Only Reason we seem to know, at least implicitly, what the rules are on the basis of which we should evaluate competing historical interpretations. Very roughly, the rules are, first, to toss out interpretations that cannot be justified except by appeal to religious faith, and second, to test the others in accordance with the same procedures that are used in secular historical studies generally (that would be used, for instance, in trying to reconstruct the history of Alexander the Great). A final advantage of Only Reason is that these standard procedures, in bringing competing interpretations before the bar of empirical evidence and testing them there, are relatively well grounded.

The main drawback of the Only Reason response, particularly in the case of historical Jesus studies, is that its simplifying assumption that everything can be explained naturalistically may be false. When its proponents insist that this assumption is not false, Only Reason becomes vulnerable to the charge of *epistemological imperialism,* that is, of closing off possibilities that ought to be left open. Although the proponents of Only Reason often do this under the guise of remaining theologically neutral, as we have seen, far from being theologically neutral, they are committed in advance to a form of naturalism that implies that Jesus was neither God nor divinely empowered (by "in advance" I mean not as a result of historical scholarship on Jesus, but rather as a presupposition of even engaging in that scholarship).

One could, of course, subscribe to an exclusively naturalist approach to historical studies only methodologically, for the purpose of doing so-called scientific history, but as we have also seen, it is not clear what the advantages are of closing the door even methodologically to non-natural influences when there are alternative methodologies available that would leave the door open without inviting methodological chaos. And in any case, most who subscribe to Only Reason as a response to the challenge posed to Christianity by secular historical scholarship go beyond merely subscribing to it methodologically, and subscribe to it substantively as well. That is, they subscribe to it not only for the purpose of composing histories, but also because they are committed to its being true. And therein lies the main problem: In the context of historical Jesus studies, proponents of Only Reason assert, as a matter of *secular faith,* that knowledge of Jesus can be obtained only through historical scholarship that is free of *religious faith.* As a consequence, the real contest between Only Reason and the other two responses is not between reason and faith, as proponents of Only Reason would have it, but between, on the one hand, a secular approach that *presupposes* the denial of religious faith and, on the other, approaches that are more hospitable to religious faith. But in presupposing the denial of *religious* faith, Only Reason is not thereby free of faith, since secular reason, while an alternative to *religious* faith, is not an alternative to *faith altogether.*

Even if Only Reason were not guilty of imperialistically asserting the superiority of secular faith over every version of religious faith, the main challenge that it poses for traditional Christian belief is not, as its proponents often claim, wholesale revisionism, but rather skepticism. To see why the challenge is mainly skepticism, remember that the vast majority of us who are interested in who Jesus was and what he was about are not expert historians. Hence if we base our beliefs about Jesus on historical evidence alone, the evidence upon which we have to make a decision about what to believe depends crucially on the testimony of expert historians, who, on many important points of interpretation, disagree among themselves. Hence, in accordance with Only Reason, the most rational response for us nonexperts is *not* to subscribe to the interpretation of any particular historian (say, Crossan) or even any group of historians (say, the liberals) but to suspend belief on any question about which naturalistically inclined historians as a group tend to disagree. Of the historians whose interpretations we have considered in the present book, the only one whose interpretation would clearly be excluded from consideration is Wright, though suspicious glances would also have to be cast toward Dunn and Borg.

So far as nonexperts are concerned, in the Only Reason response the views of conservative, naturalistically inclined historians, such as Sanders and Meier, would not be rejected altogether. Hence even on its own terms, in the Only Reason response few traditional Christian beliefs are actually *shown* to be mistaken. Rather, what is shown is that if we suspend judgment about whether liberal or conservative interpretations of Jesus are more reliable on issues about which liberal and conservative historical Jesus scholars disagree, then we cannot know, on historical grounds alone, that many traditional Christian beliefs are true. In other words, with two notable exceptions, the challenge posed by historical Jesus studies to traditional Christian beliefs is skepticism rather than revisionism. The exceptions are that virtually all secular historians agree, first, in dismissing the birth narratives in the Gospels of Matthew and Luke as fictional and, second, in rejecting as nonhistorical the portrait of Jesus in the Gospel of John. But if a Christian can accept these findings, then his or her religious views about the historical (pre-Easter) Jesus can fairly comfortably be accommodated to the findings of secular scholarship. As a consequence, even in the Only Reason response the challenge posed to Christianity by secular historical studies may not seem that threatening.

The Only Reason response is guilty of epistemological imperialism, however, in its excluding from consideration unabashedly religious interpretations of Jesus. Currently, with the exception of the views of N. T. Wright, there are no unabashedly religious interpretations of Jesus that among educated people have achieved all that much visibility, and hence (for all practical purposes) are even available as candidates to be believed. So, for the nonexpert who is aware only of highly visible contributions to historical Jesus studies, currently (for all practical purposes) the Only Reason response is vulnerable to the charge of epistemological imperialism only in excluding Wright's interpretation from consideration.

In my view, one of the reasons Wright's interpretation of Jesus is so valuable is that he is so deeply erudite that his views cannot be dismissed out of hand even by more naturalistically inclined secular historians, and yet he challenges their interpretations not just on their own turf but also in insisting that the contest among historical interpretations of Jesus be held in an enlarged arena. For secular historians the price of admission to this larger arena is their admitting that their commitment to naturalism is merely a dogma of secular faith. One could make the case, even if there were no N. T. Wright, that secular historians ought to be more forthcoming about admitting this. But one can make this case much more forcefully because of Wright's work. Without his interpretation of Jesus, secular historians might be able to ask rhetorically what is the alternative to proceeding as we are proceeding—the unspoken implication being that there is none. With Wright's interpretation of Jesus on the table, however, the question is hollow and its unspoken implication obviously false. The alternative, one can reply, pointing to Wright's impressive tomes, is this!

However, it does not take much sophistication to see that even Wright is involved in a form of epistemological imperialism of his own. In my view, it is not quite as bad as that of the proponents of Only Reason, but almost. What makes it not quite as bad is that Wright cheerfully admits that he is taking a lot for granted and perhaps even arguing in a circle. His defense is that since there is no alternative to doing this, it is not just his own practice: Everyone is taking a lot for granted and arguing in a circle.[4] Even so, by inviting his readers to join him in asserting the superiority of his own interpretation, Wright is inviting his readers to take with him a leap of faith. If one accepts this invitation and asserts on faith the superiority of his interpretation, or even the superiority of his approach, how is this any less imperialistic than the secular historians' asserting on faith the superiority of their interpretations or their approach over Wright's? In my view, it isn't. If Wright, or someone else, were to reply that there is no alternative to taking a leap of faith and asserting the superiority of some interpretation or other, or at least of some approach or other, he would be wrong. There is an alternative.

Multiperspectivalism

Just as the Only Reason response would require nonexperts to suspend belief among competing secular interpretations but *exclude* religiously inspired interpretations from consideration, one can easily envisage an approach that would require nonexperts to suspend belief among all kinds of expert interpretations, *including* religiously inspired ones. In other words, instead of viewing the historical Jesus only from the perspective of naturalism, one can take a more relaxed, multiperspectival view that spans the gap between narrowly naturalistic interpretations and more expanded approaches.

There is nothing radical in general about recommending multiperspectivalism. In fact, the widely acknowledged desirability of taking a multiperspectival view in the humanities generally, and in historical studies in particular, is arguably one of the "defining" differences between science and the humanities.[5] Suppose, for instance, that you were to go to a professional historian seeking the "true interpretation" of the American Revolution. In all likelihood, and certainly if the historian responded in the best way, he would not recommend just one book—say Gordon Wood's *The Radicalism of the American Revolution*—and not even just several books written from a single interpretive perspective.[6] If he responded in the best way, he would not even do this if he were Gordon Wood, or a proponent of one particular interpretive perspective. Rather, a historian who responded to your question in the best way would first point out that it is naive of you to suppose that there is just one "true interpretation" of the American Revolution, and that if you want to understand the Revolution, you will have to study several books, written from *different* interpretive perspectives. Then, if the historian really wanted to be helpful, he would recommend several books that collectively cover the range of interpretive approaches that expert historians of the period currently think are worthwhile. In the case of the American Revolution, no one would regard such a historian's advice as bizarre.[7] Instead, most of us would regard his advice as wise. But if, in the case of the American Revolution, such a multiperspectival approach can be wise, why not also when it comes to historical Jesus studies?

One might think that because of the great importance of the difference between naturalistic and non-naturalistic interpretations, interpretations of Jesus are not analogous to those of the American Revolution. I doubt that this is so. There may be problems in a *historian's* thinking that he could do history without taking some stand or other on most of the issues he considers; recall, for instance, the problems that Meier encountered in trying to remain theologically neutral. But for *students of history* the situation is different. My suggestion is that nonexperts can approach historical Jesus studies so as to leave it *genuinely* open whether Jesus had "supernatural" powers. They can do this not by committing themselves to a single interpretation, whether that of Meier or of anyone else, but instead by adopting a multiperspectival approach that embraces a variety of interpretations on both sides of the naturalism divide. Quite reasonably, they can take the view that understanding Jesus historically is best achieved not from the perspective of only one interpretation, or even from only one kind of interpretation, or even from only naturalistic interpretations, but from the perspectives of a more inclusive range of interpretive approaches.

Adopting such a multiperspectival approach in historical Jesus studies is analogous to what many of us might do if we personally witnessed, say, a shaman apparently doing something that, so far as science is concerned, cannot be done. Suppose, for instance, that while attending a Native American "spirit quest," you saw something apparently happen that according to science cannot happen—say, an ordinary person walking through a closed wooden door without altering either the person or the door. On the one hand, if all the internal and external conditions under which you made this observation were favorable (you were well rested and free of drugs and alcohol, the lighting was good, others present claimed to have seen what you think you saw, etc.), then since you seemed to see the impossible happen, you might take seriously the possibility that what you seemed to see happen actually did happen. On the other hand, since you "know"—suppose—that such things as you think you saw cannot possibly happen, you might question whether, in this instance, you should trust your own eyes. In the end, rather than resolving this conflict, you might hold both of these two incompatible accounts of what happened before your mind, in a kind of uneasy equilibrium, neither affirming nor denying either. And, so far as your *understanding* of what happened is concerned, in doing this you might be at least as well off, if not better off, as you would be if you felt compelled to choose, on the basis of both what you know from science and your own observation, between incompatible accounts of what you saw.

In the case of historical Jesus studies, then, the chief advantage of a multiperspectival approach, at least for nonexperts, lies in its honest acknowledgment of two realities: First, there is a great difference between expert historians of the first century C.E. and nonexperts; the experts are much more competent to form a judgment, based mainly if not exclusively on primary historical evidence, about what actually happened. Second, on matters about which the experts widely disagree, nonexperts who want to form their views on the basis of historical evidence are not in a good position to say which experts are right and which are wrong. Of course, in the exclusively naturalistic Only Reason approach one also has these advantages, but only by incurring the considerable disadvantage of making one's view vulnerable to the charge of epistemological imperialism. In multiperspectivalism, one can have these advantages seemingly without being vulnerable to the charge of epistemological imperialism.

An additional advantage of a multiperspectival approach, especially for Christians, is that the rationale for adopting it applies equally to everyone, including to secular historians who are committed to naturalism. Hence the rationale for adopting a multiperspectival approach is also a defense of the legitimacy of interpretations that are constructed from non-naturalistic perspectives, such as Wright's. Thus, in adopting a multiperspectival approach to historical Jesus studies, Christians could get out of a defensive posture. In other words, they would be in a good position not only to *answer* more naturalistically inclined critics of traditional Christian beliefs, but also to *object* to the naturalism that is a central tenet of the secular faith of most academic historians, including Sanders and Crossan. One of the reasons Christians would be in a good position to make this objection is that presumably they would then not be vulnerable themselves to the charge of epistemological imperialism. Other Christians, who have committed themselves (in the last analysis, on faith) to the superiority of religiously inspired interpretations of Jesus, such as Wright's, have lost this advantage.

From the point of view of a Christian, there are two possible drawbacks to multiperspectivalism. First, one might feel that if one is *not* going to choose among competing interpretations, then there is no point in even considering historical Jesus studies in the first place. In my view, the answer to this objection is that although in following a multiperspectival approach one may not ever be led by historical Jesus studies to commit to the one and only "true" interpretation of Jesus, nevertheless one can reasonably expect to enhance considerably one's *understanding* of the historical Jesus. By analogy, when we refrain from choosing even between two competing *naturalistic* interpretations of Jesus—say, those of Sanders and Crossan—we are not then left with nothing. In studying these two interpretations, we may have learned a lot. For one thing, Sanders and Crossan agree on many things, and we are under no obligation to suspend judgment on matters about which they agree. But even on matters about which they disagree, we would have learned a lot—perhaps not about who Jesus *actually* was and what he was *actually* about, but who he *might* have been and what he *might* have been about. In other words, in trying to learn who Jesus actually was and what he was about, we would have learned something important about what are the most plausible options.

Naturally, we long for more than that. We want answers. But if the best we can do on the basis of historical evidence is to learn what are the most plausible options, then *we do not learn anything more by committing ourselves to one interpretation or to one kind of interpretation.* Rather, we merely take an arbitrary stand. Such commitments are commonly thought to be more psychologically satisfying. In my own case, I do not find this to be true. I find it more psychologically satisfying not to pretend. But even if it were true that committing oneself to one interpretation or to one kind of interpretation of Jesus were more satisfying, doing so still would not enhance one's *understanding* of Jesus one whit. One does not enhance one's understanding by pretending to know what one does not know.

From the point of view of a Christian, another possible drawback to the multiperspectival response is that it may seem that it requires one to suspend judgment about some truth that one thinks one knows, such as that Jesus rose from the dead. I think this criticism points to a way in which even multiperspectivalism is vulnerable to the charge of epistemological imperialism. Although multiperspectivalism does not enjoin Christians to make their decision about what to believe on the basis of historical evidence alone, purged of the influence of all religious faith, it does enjoin them not to assert the superiority of the perspective of their religious faith over that of secular reason. In other words, whereas multiperspectivalism makes room for the consideration of religiously inspired interpretations, such as Wright's, it does not allow that any such interpretation should ever prevail. Hence, although multiperspectivalism does not close the door on religiously inspired historical Jesus studies as firmly as does the Only Reason response, it does not open the door as widely as do some versions of the Faith Seeking Understanding response.[8] In other words, multiperspectivalism substitutes for the secular faith of Only Reason a more relaxed kind of methodological, multiperspectival faith and becomes, in effect, one among many versions of Faith Seeking Understanding, with no resources for showing that its way of striking the balance between faith and reason is superior to competing ways.

The Bottom Line

In earlier times the problem of how a Christian might respond to the challenge posed by secular historical scholarship to traditional Christian beliefs seemed simpler. It seemed then that there was religious belief on the one hand and science on the other. Science was radically different from religious belief. Whereas religious belief was nourished by faith, science was nourished only by secular reason, which had been purged of faith. In those days, science seemed to be solid ground, and we all knew how to stand firmly on it. The only question was whether our heads could then reach to the heavens, that is, whether we could on naturalistic grounds alone justify religious truths.[9] Determining whether this could be done was the challenge bequeathed to us by the Enlightenment.

Times have changed. The source of tension is still the contest between religious faith and secular reason. But now secular reason looks more like religious faith than it used to. In fact, to many, secular reason looks as if it includes at its core a kind of secular faith. If it does, that makes all the difference. It is then no longer a question of planting our feet on the solid ground of science purged of faith and seeing if our heads will reach to the heavens, for as N. T. Wright so aptly put it, there is no solid ground. We have to make assumptions even to get the knowledge enterprise going, and if we are going to make some assumptions that we cannot prove, why not also make others that we cannot prove? Of course the assumptions we make, taken together, have to be capable of sustaining a coherent account of ourselves and the world. But there are many different kinds of coherent accounts, some naturalistic, some not, some Christian, some not, and many different kinds of assumptions that will serve as the basis for coherent accounts of each of these kinds. So, how to proceed?

On all sides, it seems, we are encouraged, first, to leap, and then to assert the superiority of the view that results from our leaping.[10] In following this procedure some of us will leap one way, some another. Naturally, then, we will end up in different places, at different bottom lines. And what then? If we assert the superiority of our various leaps, and hence also of our destinations, what have we gained? Certainly not knowledge or understanding. And we have thereby become guilty of epistemological imperialism. But if we refrain from asserting the superiority of our leaps, and even from asserting the superiority of our refraining from doing that, then we are not vulnerable to the charge of epistemological imperialism. And what then? From that vantage point, the bottom line is that there is no bottom line.

NOTES

Chapter 1

1. Bertrand Russell, "A Free Man's Worship," *The Independent Review,* December 1903. Subsequently reprinted numerous times, including in *The Basic Writings of Bertrand Russell,* ed. Robert E. Egner and Lester E. Denonn (New York: Simon and Schuster, 1961), p. 67.

2. Bultmann, Rudolf, "New Testament and Mythology," in his *Kerygma and Myth,* ed. H. W. Bartsch (New York: Harper & Row, 1961), p. 5. See also John Meier, *A Marginal Jew: Rethinking the Historical Jesus* (New York: Doubleday, 1991–1994), vol. 2, p. 533, n. 40.

3. John Shelby Spong, *Born of a Woman: A Bishop Rethinks the Birth of Jesus* (San Francisco: HarperSanFrancisco, 1992), p. 31. See also Spong's other best-selling books, including *Resurrection: Myth or Reality* (San Francisco: HarperSanFrancisco, 1994). The historian N. T. Wright, whose interpretation of the historical Jesus I shall consider in Chapter 7, has responded vigorously to Spong's views; see Wright's *Who Was Jesus?* (London: SPCK, 1992).

4. Meier, *A Marginal Jew,* vol. 2, pp. 520–521.

5. See, for instance, Kelley Clark, ed., *Philosophers Who Believe: The Spiritual Journey of Eleven Leading Thinkers* (Downers Grove, IL: InterVarsity Press, 1993); Thomas V. Morris, *God and the Philosophers: The Reconciliation of Faith and Reason* (Oxford: Oxford University Press, 1994); and the journal *Faith and Philosophy.*

6. It is impossible to work daily in a major philosophy department and not realize that among intellectuals generally, Christianity is on the way back. See, for instance, H. Margenau and R. Varglese, eds., *Cosmos, Bios, Theos: Scientists Reflect on Science, God, and the Origins of the Universe, Life, and Homo Sapiens* (Chicago: Open Court, 1992); Monroe Kelley, *Finding God at Harvard: Spiritual Journeys of Christian Thinkers* (Grand Rapids, MI: Zondervan Publishing House, 1996); and R. J. Berry, *Real Science, Real Faith* (Eastbourne, England: Monarch, 1991).

7. I shall return to this topic in Chapter 7, in which I consider the views of Marcus J. Borg and N. T. Wright.

Chapter 2

1. John Meier, for instance, has said that a biography of Jesus is "out of the question," since the "real Jesus," "unknown and unknowable," is "not available and never will be"; see Meier's *A Marginal Jew* (New York: Doubleday, 1991–1994), vol. 1, p. 22. See also E. P. Sanders, *The Historical Figure of Jesus* (New York: Penguin Books), 1993, p. 75. But compare N. T. Wright, who says, "The gospels are biographies," in his *Who Was Jesus?* (London: SPCK, 1992), p. 74.

2. Traditionally scholars have thought that Jesus spoke only Aramaic, but now many think that he may have been bilingual and even have taught in Greek. See, for instance, Meier, *A Marginal Jew*, vol. 1, pp. 255–268, and vol. 2, p. 1040; and Robert Funk, *Honest to Jesus: Jesus for a New Millennium* (San Francisco: HarperSanFrancisco, 1996), p.79.

3. Sanders, for instance, has written that "scholars have not and, in my judgment, will not agree on the authenticity of the sayings material, either in whole *or in part*," in *Jesus and Judaism* (Philadelphia: Fortress Press, 1985), p. 4 (emphasis added). Sanders's skepticism on this point is endorsed by the religiously conservative historian N. T. Wright, in *Jesus and the Victory of God* (London: SPCK, 1996), p. 85, n. 2.

4. See, for instance, Sanders, *The Historical Figure of Jesus*, pp. 61–62.

5. On information about Jesus from the letters of Paul, see Tom [N. T.] Wright, *What Paul Really Said* (Oxford: Lion Publishing, 1997), and James D.G. Dunn, *Jesus, Paul, and the Law: Studies in Mark and Galatians* (London: SPCK, 1990), and *The Theology of Paul the Apostle* (Edinburgh: T. T. Clark, 1998), chapter 4, section 8.

6. The oldest biblical manuscript for any one of the Gospels is Papyrus 52, which dates from around 125 C.E. and contains a small fragment of John, chapter 18. Papyrus Egerton, which contains fragments of an unknown, noncanonical gospel referred to as the Egerton Gospel, is about the same age. See Stephen J. Patterson, "Sources for a Life of Jesus," in Hershel Shanks et al., *The Search for Jesus: Modern Scholarship Looks at the Gospels* (Washington, DC: Biblical Archaeology Society, 1994).

7. Sanders, *The Historical Figure of Jesus*, p. 64; E. P. Sanders and Margaret Davies, *Studying the Synoptic Gospels* (Philadelphia: Trinity Press International, 1989), pp. 7–15, 21–24.

8. See, for instance, Kurt Aland, *Synopsis of the Four Gospels*, 2d ed. (1975), as quoted in Sanders and Davies, *Studying the Synoptic Gospels*, pp. 55–56.

9. This suggestion was made by Robert W. Funk, Roy W. Hoover, and the Jesus Seminar, in *The Five Gospels: The Search for the Authentic Words of Jesus* (New York: Macmillan, 1993), p. xx.

10. J. D. Crossan, *Jesus: A Revolutionary Biography* (San Francisco: HarperSanFrancisco, 1994), p. x.

11. Meier, *A Marginal Jew,* vol. 1, pp. 41–42.

12. Albert Lord, as he reports in *The Singer of Tales* (Cambridge, MA: Harvard University Press, 1960), interviewed and recorded bards from Yugoslavia, who were believed (by themselves and others) to have memorized verbatim long tales and ballads that had been passed down unchanged for centuries. When Lord compared recordings of different performances of what were supposed to be the same songs, he discovered radical differences. Confronted with the evidence, the bards themselves did not dispute Lord's findings. See Walter Ong, *Orality and Literacy: The Technologizing of the Word* (New York: Methuen, 1982).

13. However, a number of prominent New Testament scholars hold that John's Gospel contains a very early "signs gospel." See John Robinson, *The Priority of John* (London: SCM, 1985).

14. All biblical quotations are from the New Revised Standard Version.

15. Sanders and Davies, *Studying the Synoptic Gospels,* pp. 56–57.

16. For readable, nontechnical accounts of the Synoptic Problem, see Robert Stein, *The Synoptic Problem* (Grand Rapids, MI: Baker Book House, 1987), and the overview in *The New Jerome Biblical Commentary* (New York: G. Chapman, 1995). One should be aware that there is still debate over whether our Gospel of Mark has lost its original ending. On this question, see Robert Gundry, *Mark: A Commentary on His Apology for the Cross* (Grand Rapids, MI: Eerdmans, 1993).

17. B. H. Streeter, *The Four Gospels* (London: Macmillan, 1924).

18. Sanders and Davies, *Studying the Synoptic Gospels,* p. 62.

19. Ibid., p. 102.

20. For instance, Sanders and Davies, *Studying the Synoptic Gospels,* p. 116.

21. W. R. Farmer, *The Synoptic Problem* (New York: Macmillan, 1964).

22. However, the recent discovery of the Gospel of Thomas, which is exclusively a "sayings gospel," considerably bolsters the case for Q.

23. Marcus J. Borg, "The Historical Study of Jesus and Christian Origins," in *Jesus at 2000,* ed. Marcus J. Borg (Boulder: Westview Press, 1997), p. 168, n. 16.

Chapter 3

1. Albert Schweitzer, *The Quest of the Historical Jesus: A Critical Study of Its Progress from Reimarus to Wrede* (New York: Macmillan, 1957 [1906]), p. 26.

2. For naturalist methods to have become available for use in reconstructing the life of Jesus, first there had to be science, in the modern sense of the term. Science arrived in the sixteenth and seventeenth centuries, astronomy first and then physics. Then thinkers had to develop a naturalized approach to historical inquiry, and to biblical studies in particular. That is, they had to adapt the methods that physical scientists had used, or were thought to have used, in investigating nature, to the study of the human past. This happened in the seventeenth century. Finally, this naturalized approach to historical studies had to be applied specifically to accounts of Jesus in the New Testament. This too began to happen toward the end of the seventeenth century and continued unabated during the early eighteenth century.

3. Benedict de Spinoza, *Theologico-Political Treatise*, 1670, in *The Chief Works of Benedict de Spinoza*, 2 vols., trans. R.H.M. Elwes (New York: Dover, 1951), vol. 1, p. 7.

4. Ibid., p. 41.

5. Ibid., pp. 101–103.

6. Ibid., p. 83.

7. Pierre Bayle's *Dictionnaire historique et critique* was later translated by J. P. Bernard, T. Birch, and J. Lockman as *A General Dictionary, Historical and Critical*, 10 vols. (London: J. Bettenham, 1734–1741).

8. John Toland, *Christianity Not Mysterious* (London, 1696; reprinted, New York: Garland Publishing, 1978). There is reason to believe that Reimarus was influenced by Toland. See Colin Brown, *Jesus in European Protestant Thought, 1778–1860 (Durham, NC: The Labyrinth Press,* 1985).

9. In a later essay entitled "Hodegus," Toland got into additional hot water by giving naturalistic explanations of Old Testament miracles and because in one passage of his *Life of Milton* (1698) he was thought to have questioned the authenticity of the New Testament as a whole. See *Encyclopedia of Philosophy,* ed. Paul Edwards (New York: Macmillan, 1967), vol. 8, p. 142.

10. Anthony Collins, *A Discourse on the Grounds and Reasons of the Christian Religion* (London, 1724); *The Scheme of Literal Prophesy Consider'd* (London, 1727).

11. Colin Brown, *Jesus in European Protestant Thought, 1778–1860* (Durham, NC: Labyrinth Press, 1985), p. 52.

12. David Hume, "Of Miracles," in *An Enquiry Concerning Human Understanding,* ed. L. A. Selby-Bigge (Oxford: Clarendon Press, 1975 [originally published 1776]).

13. A good selection of both historical and contemporary contributions to the debate over Hume's argument may be found in Richard Swinburne, ed., *Miracles* (New York: Macmillan, 1989).

14. See Brown, *Jesus in European Protestant Thought,* pp. 1–55.

15. Hermann Samuel Reimarus, *The Intention of Jesus and His Followers*, trans. G. W. Buchanan (Leiden: E. J. Brill, 1970).

16. See *Reimarus: Fragments*, ed. C. H. Talbert, trans. R. S. Frazer (Philadelphia: Fortress Press, 1970), pp. 249–250.

17. Ibid., p. 151.

18. The works in question were by J. J. Hess, F. V. Reinhard, E. A. Opitz, J. A. Jokobi, J. G. Herder, K. A. Hase, H. E. G. Paulus, and others. See Schweitzer, *The Quest of the Historical Jesus*, pp. 23–26, and C. Brown, *Jesus in Protestant Thought*, pp. 8–16.

19. Schweitzer, *The Quest of the Historical Jesus*, pp. 38–47. While there is little evidence for such fanciful speculations, they had the advantage—a very important one at the time (and, for many, even in our own times)—of explaining away the Gospel stories of miraculous events without endangering naturalism. A. N. Wilson, the contemporary popular historian of Jesus, in his book entitled *Jesus* (London: Sinclair-Stevenson, 1992), sometimes travels down this same road. For instance, he explains some the resurrection reports as the disciples' mistaking Jesus' brother, James, for Jesus himself: "[If] the stranger were not the dear friend, but the dear friend's brother, who bore a strong resemblance, then this is just the sort of 'double take' which we should expect" (p. 244).

20. David Friedrich Strauss, *The Life of Jesus Critically Examined*, trans. and ed. P. C. Hodgson (Philadelphia: Fortress Press, 1972).

21. Brown, *Jesus in European Protestant Thought*, p. 187.

22. Strauss, *Life of Jesus*, pp. 56–57.

23. Ibid., pp. 56–57, 71, 188–189.

24. Brown, *Jesus in European Protestant Thought*, pp. 203–204; P. C. Hodgson, "Strauss' Theological Development," in Strauss, *Life of Jesus*, p. xlvi.

25. B. Bauer, *Criticism of the Gospels and History of Their Origin*, 2 vols. (Berlin: 1850–1851). In our own times G. A. Wells has taken up the cudgels for the thesis that Jesus of Nazareth is a mythical figure rather than a real person. See Wells's *The Jesus Legend* (Chicago: Open Court, 1996) and *The Jesus Myth* (Chicago: Open Court, 1998).

26. E. Renan, *La Vie de Jésus* (Paris: Michel Lévy Frères, 1863).

27. F. W. Farrar's *Life of Christ* (New York: E. P. Dutton, 1874). The quotations in the text are from the revised edition, published by Dutton in 1894. Another notable history of this sort, from about the same period, is Alfred Edersheim's *The Life and Times of Jesus the Messiah*, 2 vols., 8th ed. (New York: Longmans, Greenman, 1896).

28. Farrar, *Life of Christ*, p. 118.

29. Johannes Weiss, *Jesus' Proclamation of the Kingdom of God* [1892], trans. Richard Hiers and David Holland (Philadelphia: Fortress Press, 1971).

30. Schweitzer, *The Quest of the Historical Jesus*, pp. 9, 23.

31. Marcus J. Borg, *Jesus in Contemporary Scholarship* (Valley Forge: Trinity Press International), pp. 11–12; and Stephen J. Patterson, *The God of Jesus: The Historical Jesus and the Search for Meaning* (Harrisburg, PA: Trinity Press International, 1998), chapter 5. See also Howard Clark Kee, "A Century of Quests for the Culturally Compatible Jesus," *Theology Today*, vol. 52 (1995), pp. 17–28; and Paula Fredriksen, "What You See Is What You Get: Context and Content in Current Research on the Historical Jesus," *Theology Today*, vol. 52 (1995), pp. 75–97.

32. What are the believer's options for responding to this claim from historical studies? There are basically three, the same three as those for dealing with any of the ways in which historical studies challenge Christian faith: Stick with one's faith and dismiss historical scholarship; work out a compromise between what one accepts on faith and what one learns through historical scholarship; or let historical scholarship dictate the content of one's "faith." In the last three chapters of the present book, we shall explore these options in detail.

33. Schweitzer, *The Quest of the Historical Jesus*, p. 403.

34. Ibid., p. 399.

35. W. Wrede, *The Messianic Secret*, trans. J.D.G. Greig (Greenwood, SC: Attic, 1971), p. 131.

36. Martin Kähler, *The So-Called Historical Jesus and the Historic, Biblical Christ* [1896], trans. and ed. Carl E. Braaten (Philadelphia: Fortress Press, 1988, p. 74).

37. R. Bultmann, *Jesus and the Word* [1934], trans. L. P. Smith and E. H. Lantero (New York: Scribner's, 1958). On Wrede's influence on Bultmann, see Stephen Neill and Tom Wright, *The Interpretation of the New Testament, 1861–1986*, 2d ed. (New York: Oxford University Press, 1964), p. 267.

38. R. Bultmann, *Theology of the New Testament*, trans. K. Grobel (New York: Scribner's, 1951), vol. 1, p. 21.

39. R. Bultmann, "Is Exegesis Without Presuppositions Possible?" in *Existence and Faith: Shorter Writings of Rudolf Bultmann*, ed. and trans. S.M.M. Ogden (New York: World, 1966), pp. 289–291.

40. E. Käsemann, *Essays on New Testament Themes* (1964), pp. 46–47, quoted in Neill and Wright, *Interpretation of the New Testament*, p. 290.

41. Neill and Wright, *The Interpretation of the New Testament*, p. 291.

42. On redaction criticism, see N. Perrin, *What Is Redaction Criticism?* (Philadelphia: Fortress Press, 1969); R. H. Stein, *Gospels and Tradition: Studies on Redaction Criticism of the Synoptic Gospels* (Grand Rapids, MI: Baker Book House, 1992).

43. Günther Bornkamm, *Jesus of Nazareth*, trans. I. McLuskey, F. McLuskey, and J. Robinson (New York: Harper & Row, 1960); J. Jere-

mias, *Jesus' Promise to the Nations,* trans. S. H. Hooke (London: SCM, 1958), and *The Proclamation of Jesus,* vol. 1, in *New Testament Theology,* trans. J. Bowden (London: Scribner's, 1971); and E. Schillebeeckx, *Jesus: An Experiment in Christology,* trans. H. Hoskins (New York: Seabury Press, 1979). I've relied in my survey of these works on N. T. Wright, "Quest for the Historical Jesus," *The Anchor Bible Dictionary,* vol. 3, ed. David Noel Freedman (New York: Doubleday, 1992), and his *Jesus and the Victory of God,* vol. 2 of *Christian Origins and the Question of God* (London: SPCK, 1996), pp. 13–27.

44. To get a feeling for the variety of ways in which commentators have tried to divide up the contemporary interpretational pie, compare: Neill and Wright, *Interpretation of the New Testament,* chapter 9; Borg, *Jesus in Contemporary Scholarship,* pp. 3–43, and *Meeting Jesus Again for the First Time: The Historical Jesus and the Heart of Contemporary Faith* (San Francisco: HarperSanFrancisco, 1994), pp. 28–29; James H. Charlesworth, *Jesus Within Judaism* (New York: Doubleday, 1988), pp. 9–29; Ben Witherington III, *The Jesus Quest: The Third Search for the Jew of Nazareth* (Downers Grove, IL: InterVarsity Press, 1995); John Meier, *Jesus: A Marginal Jew* (New York: Doubleday, 1994), vol. 2, pp. 1–2; Gregory A. Boyd, *Cynic Sage or Son of God?* (Wheaton, IL: Victor Books, 1995), chapter 2; Robert W. Funk, *Honest to Jesus: Jesus for a New Millennium* (San Francisco: HarperSanFrancisco, 1996), pp. 62–76; Stephen J. Patterson, "Sources for a Life of Jesus," pp. 9–34 in Hershel Shanks et al., *The Search for Jesus: Modern Scholarship Looks at the Gospels* (Washington, DC: Biblical Archaeology Society, 1994), p. 27; and Stephen J. Patterson, *The God of Jesus: The Historical Jesus and the Search for Meaning* (Harrisburg, PA: Trinity Press International, 1998), pp. 38–45.

Chapter 4

1. For a brief characterization, from the point of view of a liberal, of a central difference between Sanders and Meier as conservatives and the views of some well-known liberals, see Marcus J. Borg's introduction to the revised edition of his *Conflict, Holiness, and Politics in the Teachings of Jesus* (Harrisburg, PA: Trinity Press International, 1988 [1st ed., 1984]), pp. 3–4.

2. E. P. Sanders, *Jesus and Judaism* (Philadelphia: Fortress Press, 1985); *The Historical Figure of Jesus* (New York: Penguin Books, 1993).

3. John Koenig, review of *Jesus and Judaism, New York Times Book Review,* December 22, 1985, p. 1.

4. In his later book, however, Sanders gives more weight—and gives it sooner—to sayings material. Also the two books have different tones. In

the earlier book Sanders sounds a more skeptical note about what can be known about Jesus. In the later book he is more optimistic; after admitting that the "remarkably diverse" interpretations of Jesus that have been proposed by historians have led many to the view that "we do not really know anything," he stresses that "this is an overreaction" and that "we know quite a lot," especially about the effects of what Jesus did and taught. Sanders says that from this knowledge he will try to infer what Jesus "thought, deep inside." However, by his own admission, even in the later book, he cannot infer much about what Jesus thought. See Sanders, *The Historical Figure*, pp. 5, 10, 54, 76, 280.

5. Ibid., p. 77.

6. Ibid., pp. 36–37.

7. Ibid., pp. 42–45.

8. Ibid., pp. 80–81.

9. Ibid., p. 83.

10. Ibid., pp. 85–88.

11. Ibid., p. 94.

12. Ibid., p. 64.

13. Ibid., p. 76.

14. Ibid., pp. 136, 143.

15. Ibid., p. 91.

16. Sanders, *Jesus and Judaism*, p. 11. In the later book Sanders begins with a longer, slightly modified list: Jesus was born around 4 B.C.E., near the time of the death of Herod the Great; he spent his childhood and early adult years in Nazareth; he was baptized by John the Baptist; he called disciples; he taught in the towns, villages, and countryside of Galilee (not the cities); he preached "the kingdom of God"; in about the year 30, he went to Jerusalem for Passover; he created a disturbance in the Temple area; he had a final meal with his disciples; he was arrested and interrogated by Jewish authorities, specifically the high priest; he was executed on the orders of the Roman prefect Pontius Pilate; his disciples at first fled, then (in some sense) saw him after his death, as a consequence of which they believed that he would return to found the kingdom, formed a community to await his return, and sought to win others to faith in Jesus as God's Messiah. *The Historical Figure*, pp. 10–11.

17. Sanders, *The Historical Figure*, pp. 13–15.

18. Ibid., pp. 85–86.

19. Sanders says that the urge to revise Luke's text arises in the first place only because people assume that the text must be true; if they revise it, they think they can still claim that it is true. But if it needs to be revised, Sanders says, then it is not true.

20. Ibid., p. 86.

21. Ibid., p. 100.

22. Ibid., p. 108.

23. Ibid., pp. 117–124. My sketch of Sanders's results is based primarily on his later book. For present purposes, doing this is harmless. In a more critical study, though, it would be worth discussing some troubling inconsistencies between Sanders's two accounts. For instance, he says in his earlier book, "The call of the early disciples, so forcefully presented in the synoptics (Matt. 4.18–22/Mark 1.16–20; Luke 5.1–15) is intended for the edification of the church and gives us *no knowledge* about how Jesus gathered about himself a small group of followers, at least some of whom turned out to be devoted to him after his death" (*Jesus and Judaism*, p. 103, emphasis added). (This negative judgment of authenticity coincides with the majority view of the Jesus Seminar, in Robert W. Funk, Roy W. Hoover, et al., *The Five Gospels* [New York: Macmillan, 1993], pp. 41, 135, 281–282.) However, in Sanders's later, less skeptical book, he says of this very same passage, "I regard the basic story (Matt 4.18–22/Mk 1.16–20) as historically reliable: the earliest disciples were Galilean fishermen; among them were Peter, Andrew, James and John; they left their nets to follow Jesus" (*The Historical Figure*, pp. 118–119). Compare also *Jesus and Judaism*, p. 222 n. 1, and p. 395 n. 1, with *The Historical Figure*, p. 103.

24. Sanders, *The Historical Figure*, pp. 140–141, 145.

25. Ibid., p. 163.

26. Ibid., p. 168.

27. Ibid., pp. 149, 153.

28. Ibid., pp. 182–183.

29. Ibid., pp. 192–193.

30. Ibid., p. 194.

31. Ibid., p. 195.

32. Ibid., pp. 202–204.

33. Ibid., pp. 205, 238.

34. Ibid., pp. 210, 220, 234.

35. Ibid., pp. 236–237.

36. Ibid., p. 243.

37. Ibid., p. 248.

38. Ibid., p. 265.

39. Ibid., pp. 269, 273–274.

40. Ibid., pp. 274–275.

41. Ibid., pp. 276–280.

42. John P. Meier, *A Marginal Jew*, 2 vols. (New York: Doubleday, 1991–1994).

43. The author of the first remark is Jack Dean Kingsbury, of the Union Theological Seminary in Virginia, and of the second remark, Rabbi Burton Visotzky, of the Jewish Theological Seminary of America. The quotations are taken from the book jacket.

44. Ibid., vol. 2, p. 1046.

45. Ibid., vol. 1, p. 1; vol. 2, pp. 4–5. Meier has been criticized on the grounds that if he means to enhance objectivity by including people with different points of view, he should also include both conservative and liberal Catholics and Protestants as well as Hindus, Buddhists, and Muslims— by C. Stephen Evans, in *The Historical Christ and the Jesus of Faith* (New York: Oxford, 1996), who asks, "Is there any reason to hope that such [an expanded] conclave would actually agree on anything?" (p. 41n).

46. Meier, *A Marginal Jew*, vol. 1, pp. 124–127.

47. Ibid., vol. 1, p. 128; Helmut Koester, *Introduction to the New Testament* (New York: DeGruyter, 1982).

48. Meier, *A Marginal Jew*, vol. 1, p. 138.

49. Ibid., vol. 1, pp. 168–183.

50. Ibid., vol. 1, pp. 173, 184; vol. 2, p. 237.

51. Ibid., vol. 1, pp. 6–9. Among the historians whose views we shall consider, Meier is the only one who claims that Jesus was celibate, though, so far as I can determine, he offers no argument in favor of this claim.

52. Ibid., vol. 2, p. 3.

53. Ibid., vol. 2, pp. 108, 116. What of John the Baptist's view of Jesus? Meier thinks that at the time of Jesus' baptism, probably John did not have an individualized view of Jesus. He says that the Baptist's testimony to Jesus, in the Gospels of Matthew and John, are "clearly later Christian theology," designed to take the sting out of the embarrassment of Jesus' having been baptized. Meier also doubts that Antipas's second wife, Herodias, had previously been the wife of Antipas's half brother, Philip. Instead, he thinks, John met a violent death of a different sort than that depicted in the Gospels, but still at the hands of the (ostensibly) Jewish ruler of Galilee, the very place where Jesus was beginning his ministry. Meier concludes that Jesus knew the dangers of what he was doing (vol. 2, pp. 116, 172, 175).

54. Ibid., vol. 2, pp. 264–265, 349.

55. Ibid., vol. 2, pp. 331, 338, 348, 350.

56. Ibid., vol. 2, pp. 450–454.

57. Ibid., vol. 2, pp. 9–10.

58. As we shall see, liberals have an answer to this argument.

59. Ibid., vol. 2, p. 1045.

60. Ibid., vol. 2, pp. 1045–1046.

61. Ibid., vol. 2, pp. 539–540, 548–549.

62. In response to Crossan's enthusiastic endorsement of the suggestion by the Jewish historian Geza Vermes that Jesus should be lumped with Honi the Circle-Drawer and Hanina ben Dosa, Meier replies that we do not know enough about either of the latter two to make a comparison. See ibid., vol. 2, pp. 581, 630, 970.

63. Ibid., vol. 2, pp. 628, 630, 970.

Chapter 5

1. J. D. Crossan, *The Historical Jesus: The Life of a Mediterranean Jewish Peasant* (San Francisco: HarperSanFrancisco, 1991), p. xxvii.

2. S.G.F. Brandon, *Jesus and the Zealots* (Manchester: University Press, 1967).

3. Morton Smith, *Jesus the Magician* (San Francisco: Harper & Row, 1978).

4. Geza Vermes, *Jesus the Jew: A Historian's Reading of the Gospels* (New York: Macmillan, 1973; rev. ed., Philadelphia: Fortress Press, 1981), and *Jesus and the World of Judaism* (Philadelphia: Fortress Press, 1984); Marcus J. Borg, *Jesus: A New Vision* (San Francisco: Harper & Row, 1987), *Conflict, Holiness, and Politics in the Teachings of Jesus* (New York: Edwin Mellen, 1994), and *Meeting Jesus Again for the First Time* (San Francisco: HarperSanFrancisco, 1994).

5. Bruce Chilton, ed., *The Kingdom of God in the Teaching of Jesus* (Philadelphia: Fortress Press, 1984).

6. Harvey Falk, *Jesus the Pharisee: A New Look at the Jewishness of Jesus* (New York: Paulist Press, 1985).

7. Falk, *Jesus the Pharisee*; Barbara Theiring, *Jesus the Man: A New Interpretation of the Dead Sea Scrolls* (London: Doubleday, 1992).

8. Elisabeth Schüssler Fiorenza, *In Memory of Her: A Feminist Theological Reconstruction of Christian Origins* (New York: Crossroad, 1984), and *Jesus: Miriam's Child, Sophia's Prophet: Critical Issues in Feminist Christology* (New York: Continuum, 1994).

9. Richard Horsley and John S. Hanson, *Bandits, Prophets, and Messiahs: Popular Movements at the Time of Jesus* (Minneapolis: Winston, 1985); Richard Horsley, *Jesus and the Spiral of Violence* (San Francisco: Harper and Row, 1987), *The Liberation of Christmas: The Infancy Narratives in Social Context* (New York: Crossroad, 1989), and *Sociology and the Jesus Movement* (New York: Crossroad, 1989); Burton L. Mack, *A Myth of Innocence: Mark and Christian Origins* (Philadelphia: Fortress Press, 1988); J. D. Crossan, *The Historical Jesus*, and *Jesus: A Revolutionary Biography* (San Francisco: HarperSanFrancisco, 1994).

10. E. P. Sanders, *Jesus and Judaism* (Philadelphia: Fortress Press, 1985), and *The Historical Figure of Jesus* (New York: Penguin Books, 1993); John P. Meier, *A Marginal Jew*, 2 vols. (New York: Doubleday, 1991–1994); for overviews, see Daniel J. Harrington, "The Jewishness of Jesus," *Bible Review*, vol. 3 (1987), pp. 33–41; Marcus J. Borg, *Jesus in Contemporary Scholarship* (Valley Forge, NY: Trinity Press International, 1994), pp. 18–43; Ben Witherington III, *The Jesus Quest: The Third Search for the Jew of Nazareth* (Downers Grove, IL: InterVarsity Press, 1995).

11. See, for instance, Borg, *Meeting Jesus Again*, p. 2.

12. See note 8.

13. For instance, Elisabeth Schüssler Fiorenza, *Bread, Not Stone: The Challenge of Feminist Biblical Interpretation* (Boston: Beacon Press, 1984; 2d ed., with a new "Afterword," 1995), and *But She Said: Feminist Practices of Biblical Interpretation* (Boston: Beacon Press, 1992).

14. Schüssler Fiorenza, *Bread, Not Stone*, pp. xvii, 3, 32, 35.

15. *Androcentricism*, in the sense used here, refers to a mind-set that understands everything from a male perspective. *Patriarchy* refers to objective political and social relations in which power is sharply stratified and only some men have most of it.

16. Schüssler Fiorenza, *Bread, Not Stone*, pp. 41, 102.

17. Ibid., pp. 42–43.

18. Ibid., pp. 45–46.

19. Ibid., p. 45.

20. Ibid., pp. 46–47. In Schüssler Fiorenza's view, Andronicus and Junia, a man and woman, were an "influential missionary team who were acknowledged as apostles."

21. Ibid., p. 50.

22. Ibid., p. 52.

23. Ibid., p. 60.

24. Ibid., pp. 142–143.

25. Ibid., pp. 134–135.

26. Ibid., p. 153.

27. Ibid., pp. 153–154.

28. Ibid., p. 152.

29. Ibid., pp. 119–120; also pp. 111–112, 121.

30. Ibid., pp. 134–135.

31. Ibid., p. 107.

32. Ibid., p. 143; compare Ben Witherington III, *The Jesus Quest*, p. 169.

33. Schüssler Fiorenza, *Bread, Not Stone*, p. 148.

34. Ibid., pp. 110–115, 120–121.

35. See note 9.

36. Borg, *Jesus in Contemporary Scholarship*, p. 33; Marcus J. Borg, ed., *Jesus at 2000* (Boulder: Westview Press, 1997), p. 21.

37. N. T. Wright, *Jesus and the Victory of God* (London: SPCK, 1996), pp. 44, 65. However, after showering Crossan's *The Historical Jesus* with praise, Wright ends the paragraph by remarking, "It is all the more frustrating, therefore, to have to conclude that [Crossan's] book is almost entirely wrong." Of course, Crossan has had other critics as well. For a good sampling of this criticism together with Crossan's replies to it, see Jeffrey Carlson and Robert A. Ludwig, eds., *Jesus and Faith: A Conversation on the Work of John Dominic Crossan* (Maryknoll, NY: Orbis Books, 1994). See also Birger Pearson, "The Gospel According to the Jesus Seminar," *Reli-*

gion, vol. 25 (1995), pp. 317–338; and for criticism of Crossan from an evangelical perspective, see Gregory A. Boyd, *Cynic Sage or Son of God?* (Wheaton, IL: BridgePoint Books, 1995).

38. Crossan, *The Historical Jesus,* pp. xxviii–xxix; and "Jesus and the Kingdom: Itinerants and Householders in Earliest Christianity," in Borg, ed., *Jesus at 2000, p.* 22.

39. Crossan, *The Historical Jesus,* p. xxix; "Jesus and the Kingdom," in Borg, ed., *Jesus at 2000, pp.* 22, 29–30.

40. Crossan, *Jesus: A Revolutionary Biography,* p. 20.

41. Ibid., p. 20.

42. Crossan's notation is "Koester 1982:2.112," which indicates Helmut Koester's *Introduction to the New Testament* (Philadelphia: Fortress Press), vol. 2, p. 112.

43. Crossan, *The Historical Jesus,* p. 430.

44. Crossan, *Jesus: A Revolutionary Biography,* p. xi.

45. F. G. Downing, *Jesus and the Threat of Freedom* (London: SCM, 1987), and *The Christ and the Cynics* (Sheffield: Sheffield Academic Press, 1988); Burton Mack, *A Myth of Innocence: Mark and Christian Origins* (Philadelphia: Fortress Press, 1988).

46. Borg, in *Jesus in Contemporary Scholarship,* p. 22, quotes from unpublished papers of Mack.

47. Crossan, "Jesus and the Kingdom," in Borg, ed., *Jesus at 2000, p.* 25.

48. Crossan, *Jesus: A Revolutionary Biography,* p. 122.

49. Crossan, "Jesus and the Kingdom," in Borg, ed., *Jesus at 2000, p.* 104; Crossan, *The Historical Jesus,* p. 138; Crossan, *Jesus: A Revolutionary Biography,* pp. 37–38.

50. Crossan, *Jesus: A Revolutionary Biography,* pp. 94–95.

51. Ibid., pp. 66–74.

52. But, as we shall see in Chapter 7, some conservatives, such as N. T. Wright, have a different view of Jesus' eschatology.

53. Crossan, *Jesus: A Revolutionary Biography,* p. 48.

54. Ibid., pp. 49–50.

55. Ibid., pp. 130–131.

56. Crossan, *Jesus: A Revolutionary Biography,* p. 152.

57. Ibid., pp. 153–154.

58. Ibid., p. 145.

59. Ibid., pp. 165–166, 170.

60. Sanders, *The Historical Figure,* pp. 198–200, 263.

61. What this means is that in the opinion of the Fellows of the Seminar, "Jesus did not say this, but the ideas contained in it are close to his own." Robert W. Funk et al., *The Five Gospels* (New York: Macmillan, 1993), pp. 36, 88.

62. Ibid., pp. 88–89.

63. Meier, *A Marginal Jew,* vol. 1, p. 128.
64. Ibid., pp. 129–138.
65. Ibid., p. 133.
66. Ibid., p. 138.

Chapter 6

1. W. Boussett, *Kyrios Christos* (Göttingen: Vandenhoeck and Ruprech, 1913 [trans. 1970]); quoted in E. P. Sanders, *Jesus and Judaism* (Philadelphia: Fortress Press, 1985), p. 25. For an explanation of why Boussett was so well respected, see Stephen Neill and Tom Wright, *The Interpretation of the New Testament, 1861–1986,* 2d ed. (New York: Oxford University Press, 1988; [1st ed., 1966]), pp. 175–178.
2. Sanders, *Jesus and Judaism,* p. 24.
3. J. D. Crossan, *Jesus: A Revolutionary Biography* (San Francisco: HarperSanFrancisco, 1994), p. xi.
4. Ibid., p. 23.
5. Ibid., p. 26.
6. Ibid., pp. 26–27.
7. Ibid., p. 82.
8. Ibid., p. 170.
9. In a later essay Crossan says that he never formulates the questions about Jesus that he investigates in terms of the Jesus of history and the Christ of faith but instead asks: What did Jesus do and say in the late 20s C.E. that led some to say, "He is criminal; we must execute him," and others to say, "He is divine; we must follow him." Crossan says that this way of asking the question "avoids the Jesus/Christ dichotomy, with its twin extremes of pro- or antidogma, theology, or faith that simply skew the discussion in opposite ways" ("Jesus and the Kingdom: Itinerants and Householders in Earliest Christianity," pp. 21–53 in Marcus J. Borg, ed., *Jesus at 2000 [Boulder: Westview Press,* 1997], p. 22). But in assuming that Jesus could not have performed miracles, Crossan has ruled out one possible explanation of why some people responded to Jesus by saying, "He is divine; we must follow him." Hence Crossan has not avoided, as he seems to think he has, taking a stand against an important aspect of the faith of many Christians. Yet it would seem that Crossan did not intend to contradict faith, but did so in spite of himself; for instance, in his remarks to critics in Jeffrey Carlson and Robert A. Ludwig, eds., *Jesus and Faith: A Conversation on the work of John Dominic Crossan* (Maryknoll, NY: Orbis Books, 1994), he says that the only thing "more pathetic than the dogmatic search" for the historical Jesus is "the antidogmatic one" (p. 153). In this latter opinion, I am in complete agreement with Crossan.

10. J. D. Crossan, *The Historical Jesus: The Life of a Mediterranean Jewish Peasant* (San Francisco: HarperSanFrancisco, 1992), pp. 423–426; *Jesus: A Revolutionary Biography*, pp. 199–201. Crossan's formula is sometimes quoted favorably by others; see, for instance, Stephen J. Patterson, *The God of Jesus: The Historical Jesus and the Search for Meaning* (Harrisburg, PA: Trinity Press International, 1998), p. 48.

11. Crossan, *Jesus: A Revolutionary Biography*, p. 200, emphasis added.

12. In *The Historical Jesus* Crossan reminded Christians that they should not reject the results of secular historical scholarship, presumably including the results of his own scholarship, merely because those results are reconstructions, "as if reconstruction invalidated somehow the entire project. Because there is only reconstruction. For a believing Christian both the life of the Word of God and the text of the Word of God are alike a graded process of historical reconstruction." Hence "if you cannot believe in something produced by reconstruction, you may have nothing left to believe in" (p. 426). But however respectable on secular grounds such a view may be, it begs the question against certain sorts of believing Christians. Even if every account is a reconstruction, it may be that some accounts, such as Crossan's, are *mere* reconstructions and hence dismissible whereas others, such as those of Mark, Matthew, Luke, and John, are *divinely inspired* reconstructions and hence the word of God. I do not say that this is so, but only that Crossan has not explained why he is entitled to assume that it is not so.

13. E. P. Sanders and Margaret Davies, *Studying the Synoptic Gospels* (Philadelphia: Trinity Press International, 1989), p. 45. N. T. Wright, in *The New Testament and the People of God* (London: SPCK, 1992), chastens Sanders for what Wright takes to be Sanders's naive commitment to positivist assumptions (p. 82, n. 3).

14. E. P. Sanders, *The Historical Figure of Jesus* (New York: Penguin Books, 1993), pp. 83, 91.

15. E. P. Sanders, *Jesus and Judaism* (Philadelphia: Fortress Press, 1985), p. 331.

16. Sanders, *The Historical Figure of Jesus*, p. 183.

17. Ibid., p. 187.

18. Ibid., 1993, p. 225.

19. Ibid., 1993, p. 136; see also p. 143.

20. Ben Witherington III, *The Jesus Quest: The Third Search for the Jew of Nazareth* (Downers Grove, IL: InterVarsity Press, 1995), p. 124.

21. John P. Meier, *A Marginal Jew* (New York: Doubleday, 1991–1994), vol. 2, p. 11.

22. Ibid.

23. Ibid.; see also p. 788.

24. More precisely: In the context of writing a history of Jesus, it is natural to suppose that if Jesus could perform miracles, then it is because he is God or was divinely empowered. As a historian, Meier clearly wants to remain neutral on the question of whether Jesus is God or was divinely empowered. Does he succeed in remaining neutral?

25. Meier, *A Marginal Jew,* vol. 2, pp. 106, 110; see also p. 175.

26. Ibid., p. 253.

27. Ibid., p. 407.

28. The *physiologoi* included most of those whom historians of philosophy usually think of as the "pre-Socratics."

29. I am indebted throughout this paragraph to Gregory Vlastos, *Plato's Universe* (Seattle: University of Washington Press, 1975), chapters 1–3.

30. See, for example, the views of George M. Marsden's critics, as quoted by him in his *The Outrageous Idea of Christian Scholarship* (New York: Oxford University Press, 1997). For a discussion of similar issues in a Jewish context, see David Weiss Halivni, *Revelation Restored: Divine Writ and Critical Responses* (Boulder: Westview Press, 1997).

31. Although I gave a rough-and-ready definition of naturalism earlier, defining naturalism precisely can be a tricky business. I am assuming, for the sake of this discussion, that we know what it means to explain naturalistically.

32. Meier, *A Marginal Jew,* vol. 2, pp. 515–517.

33. See, for example, Wallace Black Elk and William S. Lyon, *Black Elk: The Sacred Ways of a Lakota* (San Francisco: HarperSanFrancisco, 1995).

34. Morton Smith, "Historical Method in the Study of Religion," *History and Theory,* vol. 8 (1968), pp. 12–14.

35. C. Stephen Evans, *The Historical Christ and the Jesus of Faith* (Oxford: Oxford University Press, 1996), p. 332.

36. Evans points out, for instance, that many secular historians of Jesus date Acts after the fall of Jerusalem because they think that otherwise they would have to admit that the author of Acts had prophetic powers. Evans argues for an earlier dating, noting that "it is important to challenge the implicit assumption that any accurate 'prophecy' must have been made after the events in question," since "such an assumption makes it impossible to give the incarnational narrative, with its ineradicable miraculous elements, a fair historical test" (ibid., p. 33).

37. Ibid., p. 332.

38. Ibid., p. 341.

39. Ibid., pp. 333–334.

40. J.D.G. Dunn, *Baptism in the Holy Spirit* (London: SCM, 1970); *Jesus and the Spirit: A Study of the Religious and Charismatic Experience of Jesus and the First Christians As Reflected in the New Testament* (London:

SCM, 1975); *The Evidence for Jesus* (Louisville, KY: Westminster Press, 1985).

41. Dunn, *The Evidence for Jesus,* pp. 103, 107.

42. Ibid., p. 1.

43. Ibid., pp. 53–54.

44. Ibid., p. 56.

45. Ibid., pp. 56–63.

46. Ibid.

47. Ibid., pp. 62–63.

48. Ibid., pp. 65–68.

49. Ibid., pp. 71–72.

50. Ibid., pp. 74–75.

51. In Chapters 7 and 9 I shall discuss the interesting possibility that Marcus J. Borg and N. T. Wright are exceptions to this rule.

Chapter 7

1. Citing books by L. Johnson, M. Wilkins and J. Moreland, B. Witherington, and G. Boyd, Borg has written that the Jesus Seminar has "become the target of considerable criticism and attack. . . . Criticism of any scholarly position is, of course, warranted. But both the tone and content of many of these criticisms seem unfair. As one who has been deeply involved with the seminar for the past ten years, I must say that I simply do not recognize the group of scholars portrayed by some of our critics." In Marcus J. Borg, ed., *Jesus at 2000 (Boulder: Westview Press, 1997)*, p. 157, n. 7.

2. The sort of apocalyptic interpretations that Borg *primarily* criticizes are not the sort that Wright defends. The latter sort, as it happens, fit rather comfortably into Borg's very Jewish portrait of Jesus. For a brief but fascinating discussion of these differences between Borg and Wright, see Wright's remarks on pp. xxiii–xxiv of his foreword to the revised edition of Borg's *Conflict, Holiness, and Politics in the Teachings of Jesus* (Harrisburg, PA: Trinity Press International, 1998 [1st ed., 1984]).

3. *Jesus, A New Vision: Spirit, Culture, and the Life of Discipleship* (London: SPCK, 1987); *Jesus in Contemporary Scholarship* (Valley Forge: Trinity Press International, 1994); and *Meeting Jesus Again for the First Time: The Historical Jesus and the Heart of Contemporary Faith* (San Francisco: HarperSanFrancisco, 1994).

4. Borg, *Meeting Jesus,* pp. 23–25.

5. Ibid., p. 26.

6. Jesus' message was not eschatological in the sense that it was not about "the supernatural coming of the Kingdom of God as a world-ending event in his own generation" (ibid., p. 29).

7. Ibid., pp. 30–31. Borg thinks that Jesus' wisdom originated in an "enlightenment experience" similar to those that other great sages are said to have had (ibid., pp. 66–88).

8. Ibid., p. 32.

9. Ibid., pp. 32–33.

10. Ibid., p. 34.

11. Ibid., pp. 46–58.

12. Ibid., pp. 11–12.

13. Ibid., p. 12.

14. Ibid., p. 13.

15. Ibid., p. 13.

16. Ibid., p. 14.

17. Ibid., p. 15.

18. Ibid., pp. 16–17.

19. For one of the most sophisticated (but also most abstract) defenses ever of the claim that one would be justified in believing that to some, God is actually presented in experience, see William P. Alston, *Perceiving God: The Epistemology of Religious Experience* (Ithaca: Cornell University Press, 1991).

20. More precisely, Borg said that in his role as academic historian it would have been "inappropriate" for him to have approached the study of Jesus with specifically Christian presuppositions in mind or with concern for Jesus' significance for Christian faith. But surely what he meant (or at least should have meant) is that it would have been inappropriate for him to have had *any* "specifically" theological presuppositions in mind. See, for instance, Marcus J. Borg, "The Palestinian Background for a Life of Jesus," pp. 37–57 in Hershel Shanks et al., *The Search for Jesus: Modern Scholarship Looks at the Gospels* (Washington, DC: Biblical Archaeology Society).

21. *Jesus, A New Vision,* pp. 67–71.

22. In saying that no one "knows," I mean that no one has sufficient, non-question-begging reasons for believing. I am aware, of course, that in the so-called reliability accounts of knowledge, one might know without having reasons. See, for example, Fred Dretske, *Seeing and Knowing* (Chicago: University of Chicago Press, 1969); David Armstrong, *Belief, Truth, and Knowledge* (Cambridge: Cambridge University Press, 1973); and Robert Fogelin, *Pyrrhonian Reflections on Knowledge and Justification* (New York: Oxford University Press, 1994). For an explanation of how such accounts of knowledge can impinge on discussions specifically of historical knowledge, see my "Critical Study: Joyce Appleby, Lynn Hunt, and Margaret Jacob, *Telling the Truth About History,*" *History and Theory,* vol. 34 (1995), pp. 320–329.

23. *Jesus, A New Vision,* pp. 7–8.

24. N. T. Wright also publishes under the name Tom Wright.

25. For a sample of this traditional approach, see the quotation from W. Boussett at the beginning of Chapter 6.

26. Wright, *Jesus, A New Vision,* p. 98.

27. Wright, *Who Was Jesus?* (London: SPCK, 1992), pp. 97–98.

28. Wright, *Jesus and the Victory of God* (London: SPCK, 1996), p. 93. In *Who Was Jesus?* Wright says, "The great achievement of Marcus Borg, in my judgment, is to have demonstrated that the severe warning which the gospels attribute to Jesus have little or nothing to do with either hell-fire after death or with the end of the world, in the sense of the end of the space-time universe. Instead, the warnings are to be read as typical pieces of Jewish 'apocalyptic' language, as prophecies about a *this-worldly* judgment which is to be *interpreted* as the judgment of Israel's God" (p. 15).

29. Wright, *Who Was Jesus?* p. 58; see also Wright's summation of Jesus' message about the kingdom of God in *Jesus and the Victory of God,* pp. 96–98.

30. Wright, *Jesus and the Victory of God,* p. 98.

31. Ibid., p. 103.

32. Ibid., p. 104.

33. Wright, *Who Was Jesus?* pp. 100–101.

34. Ibid.

35. Ibid., p. 102.

36. Wright, *Jesus and the Victory of God,* p. 108.

37. Ibid., pp. 413–417.

38. Ibid., pp. 111–112.

39. Ibid., pp. 110–111; see also Wright, *The New Testament and the People of God* (London: SPCK, 1992), pp. 456, 458, 476; quoted in Wright, *Jesus and the Victory of God,* p. 110. Wright also mentions a fifth question: Why are the Gospels what they are? He says that the way to find the historical Jesus is by "a pincer movement: forwards from the picture of first-century Judaism; backwards from the gospels." In asking this fifth question about the gospels, he sees himself as being on one (temporally remote) edge of a giant jigsaw puzzle, the middle of which is an accurate portrait of Jesus. However, he does not try to answer this question about why the Gospels are as they are on the grounds that it would take another whole book to do so. He mentions the question, he says, to make the point that "it would enormously strengthen an interpretation of Jesus if it also explained why the gospels are what they are." See *Jesus and the Victory of God,* pp. 112–113.

40. In Wright's view, it is necessary to invent "new categories" that will transcend the distinction between history and theology, without collapsing either into the other, and yet also do justice to historical Jesus studies. Wright, *The New Testament and the People of God,* p. 25.

41. Wright, *Who Was Jesus?* p. 48.

42. Ibid., p. 18.

43. Ibid., p. 40.

44. Ibid., p. 80.

45. Ibid., p. 81. For instance, Wright says that when the Bible reports that God told Adam and Eve to "be fruitful and multiply," it is highlighting the fact that God put "into their inmost beings, as creatures made to reflect his image into his world, a deep desire for one another, and a deep longing to create and nurture order and beauty within creation." In remarks like this, it can look as if Wright is playing the old accommodation game, in which traditional Christian beliefs are reinterpreted to make them compatible with science. But compare what he says about miracles in such discussions as the one in *The New Testament and the People of God,* p. 93.

46. Wright says that he has heard it seriously argued that we can no longer believe in the virgin birth now that, with the aid of modern medical research, we know so much about the process of conception and birth. He says that writers who say this sometimes say that because the ancients lacked modern science they were open to the possibility of all sorts of odd things happening. Wright counters that this "simply misses the point." Conceding that we do, of course, know much more about conception and childbirth than people did in the first century, he says that first-century Jews knew as well as we do that babies are produced by sexual intercourse. He adds that "when, in Matthew's version of the story, Joseph heard about Mary's pregnancy, his problem arose not because he didn't know the facts of life, but because he did." In *Who Was Jesus?* p. 79.

47. Ibid., p. 85.

48. Ibid., pp. 61–62.

49. Ibid., pp. 62–63.

50. Ibid., pp. 81–82.

51. Ibid.

Chapter 8

1. I shall suggest that there is also a variation on the Only Reason response, according to which Christians should be totally *sub*missive *to* the expert opinions not just of secular historians but also of historians more generally. Toward the end of the final chapter, I shall explain how this response works.

2. Kierkegaard's views are best expressed in his *Concluding Unscientific Postscript,* trans. David F. Swenson; introduction, notes, and completion of translation by Walter Lowrie (Princeton: Princeton University Press, 1941). For a well-known critique of Kierkegaard's views by a prominent Christian philosopher, see Robert Merrihew Adams, "Kierkegaard's Arguments

Against Objective Reasoning in Religion," *Monist,* vol. 60 (1977), pp. 228–243. The twentieth-century theologian Paul Tillich took the view not so much that secular rationality per se is irrelevant to Christian religious belief but that historical scholarship is irrelevant. See, for instance, his *Systematic Theology* (Chicago: University of Chicago Press, 1951–1963) and *The Dynamics of Faith* (New York: Harper & Row, 1957). It would seem that Tillich's view of Christian belief is too mystical for most Christians, including most Christian intellectuals. His response to the challenge posed to Christian belief by historical scholarship is widely regarded more as a way of avoiding the problem than as a way of solving it.

3. In the rural, conservative area where I live, I sometimes see displayed on a car my favorite bumper sticker: *Jesus Said It. I Believe It. That Settles It.* I imagine—rightly or wrongly—that the mental landscape of the person who would display such a sticker is neatly divided into straight, definite lines: No probably's or probably not's, no maybe's, no I don't know's, no fuzzy lines—just yes's and no's. I also imagine that he is an Only Faith type.

4. Luke Johnson, *The Real Jesus* (Boulder: Westview Press, 1996).

5. Ibid., pp. 127–128.

6. Ibid., p. 132.

7. Ibid., pp. 132–133.

8. Ibid., p. 172.

9. Ibid., p. 141.

10. Ibid., pp. 142–143.

11. Ibid., p. 143.

12. Ibid., pp. 144–146.

13. Ibid., p. 175, emphasis added.

14. Ibid., pp. 171–173.

15. Ibid., pp. 173–175.

16. Elaine Pagels, *The Gnostic Gospels* (New York: Random House, 1979).

Chapter 9

1. This may have been Locke's view. See, for instance, John Locke, *An Essay Concerning Human Understanding,* ed. Peter H. Nidditch (Oxford: Oxford University Press, 1975), book 4, chapter 17, section 24, pp. 687–688.

2. John P. Meier, *A Marginal Jew,* 2 vols. (New York: Doubleday, 1991–1994), vol. 1, p. 197.

3. Ibid. Here, for the same sort of reasons that I explained in connection with my criticism of Luke Johnson in Chapter 8, it seems to me that Meier is confusing two questions: that of where information about Jesus comes

from, and that of whom the information is about. Even if you get your information about Jesus from historians, the object of your faith could still be, and presumably would be, not the information itself, but Jesus.

4. Ibid., p. 198.

5. Meier's slap at "existentialism" is no doubt meant for followers of Rudolf Bultmann. For an interesting footnote to Bultmann's lingering influence, see N. T. Wright's criticism of Marcus J. Borg, on p. xx of his foreword to the revised edition of Borg's *Conflict, Holiness, and Politics in the Teachings of Jesus,* rev. ed. (Harrisburg, PA: Trinity Press International, 1998 [1st ed., 1984]).

6. For an alternative to this view, see Wright's foreword to Borg's *Conflict, Holiness, and Politics,* in which Wright endorses Borg's view that Jesus was a political revolutionary but expresses some differences with Borg about Jesus' views and activity. For more on Wright's views on this topic, see his *The New Testament and the People of God* (London: SPCK, 1992), pp. 185–203. And for criticism of Wright's view, see J. D. Crossan, "What Victory? What God?" *Scottish Journal of Theology,* vol. 50 (1997), pp. 345–358.

7. Meier, *A Marginal Jew,* vol. 1, p. 199.

8. Suppose, to switch examples, that through faith a believer "knows" that the world was created in 4004 B.C.E., and through reason, unguided by faith, he or she knows that the world must be much older than that. Why, in such a believer's mind, should faith give way to reason? Is it because believers, in addition to having faith in what they take to be divine revelation, also have faith in reason or in the harmony of faith and reason? But is the latter true of all believers or just some? For those, apparently like Meier, who do have faith in the harmony of religious faith and reason, does that faith in harmony include just one's own religious faith, or the religious faiths of other people also? If it includes the religious faiths of other people, how does one reconcile the conflicting things that people believe on faith? So far as I know, Meier does not address such questions.

9. C. Stephen Evans, *The Historical Christ and the Jesus of Faith* (Oxford: Oxford University Press, 1996), p. 355.

10. Ibid., p. 315.

11. Ibid., p. 316.

12. In other words, what I am suggesting is that since Evans thinks that James is rationally entitled to subscribe to the extreme Only Faith response, naturally James is rationally entitled to subscribe to the more moderate Faith Seeking Understanding response. Evans's procedure is a little like that of a trapeze artist who, practicing his art with an imposing safety net firmly in place, brags that he can try his hand at more and more difficult tricks without ever hitting the ground. True, one might observe, but with the safety net so firmly in place, it would be more impressive if he were to actually hit the ground.

13. Evans, *The Historical Christ and the Jesus of Faith,* p. 316.

14. For an analysis of examples, this time not from religious history but from controversies over various interpretations of the American Revolution, see my "The Essential Difference Between History and Science," *History and Theory,* vol. 36 (1997), pp. 1–14, and "Progress in Historical Studies," *History and Theory,* vol. 37 (1998), pp. 14–39.

15. Evans, *The Historical Christ and the Jesus of Faith,* p. 327.

16. Ibid., p. 318.

17. Ibid., p. 327.

18. See the evidence described earlier, in Chapter 4.

19. Evans, *The Historical Christ and the Jesus of Faith,* p. 317.

20. Ibid., p. 339.

21. Such questions as Evans does ask about professional expertise need to be sorted out. When he suggests that the church can meet challenges to its competence to be an authority on questions of history as well as trained professional historians can, does he mean on questions of history when the answers to those questons are determined solely on the basis of ordinary historical evidence, or does he mean on questions of history when the answers are determined at least partly on the basis of Christian theology? If he means the former, his view seems a little silly—after all, trained professional historians do seem to know their business better than people who lack their training. On the other hand, if Evans means the latter, then he is surely right. The church would be at least as good—probably better—at determining *through the lenses of its own particular theology* the answers to historical questions than would trained secular historians. But then other churches and adherents of other theologies would also be better qualified to determine historical truth through their particular theological lenses. In my view, it seems that in all of this historian bashing, something crucial is being lost: So far as competence at doing history is concerned, everyone is not in the same boat. In general, professional secular historians seem to be doing what they do better than theological historians—or James—could do it. Amazingly, Evans seems to have his doubts. But see his conciliatory remarks, ibid., pp. viii–ix.

22. Evans says that a striking fact that will be evident even on a superficial examination of secular historical scholarship is "the fundamental and radical disagreements that permeate it" (*The Historical Christ and the Jesus of Faith,* p. 321).

23. Evans makes this point by drawing on an analogy between philosophy and history (ibid., p. 325).

24. Evans apparently thinks that the scholarly qualifications of trained professional historians, even those acknowledged to be, so to speak, at the top of their game, are so shaky that he does not hesitate to enter the game himself. He disputes specific interpretations of historians on various diffi-

cult questions and endorses those of other historians (or of himself) on other difficult questions. See, for instance, *The Historical Christ and the Jesus of Faith,* pp. 329, 337, 338; pp. 342–344, 353–354.

25. Ibid., p. 345.

26. Ibid., p. 332.

27. Ibid.

28. Ibid., p. 33.

29. In other ways too, Evans's discussion is flawed. For instance, he says at one point that it seems overwhelmingly likely that if the authors of the New Testament Gospels preserved, as some of them did, material that is embarrassing and unhelpful, then they are even more likely to preserve authentic material that supports their agendas (ibid., p. 336). True enough, but who denies it? The more crucial consideration is whether the authors would also preserve material that is inauthentic but that supports their agendas. And if, as almost all secular historians believe, the authors of the New Testament Gospels not only would invent inauthentic material, but for liturgical or evangelical reasons actually did so on numerous occasions, then the fact that a story that appears in only one of the Gospels fits in with the theological agenda of the author of that Gospel obviously counts against the historian's accepting that story as authentic. It is not that the historian necessarily knows that the story is inauthentic, but rather that under the circumstances he or she may not be able to know that the story is authentic and hence, without being overly speculative, may not then be entitled to rely on it importantly in arriving at an overall interpretation of what happened. And while we are on the topic of speculation, it is worth pointing out that Evans seems to employ a double standard. When secular historians speculate, he is critical of them; for instance: "Whatever the outcome of such an endeavor [going "behind the text" to discover earlier sources] and though it certainly leads at times to interesting and helpful findings, it appears inevitably to be a speculative, uncertain enterprise in many cases." But then when it is the religiously inspired interpreters who are doing the speculating: "There is just as much risk in a skeptical [interpretive] policy as in a more trusting policy"; and: "We are being no more cautious or safe in our procedure if we discard doubtful material than if we retain it" (*The Historical Christ and the Jesus of Faith,* pp. 338–339).

30. *Law, Morality, and Religion in a Secular Society* (London: Oxford University Press, 1967); *The Justification of Religious Belief* (London: Macmillan, 1973); *Faith and Criticism* (Oxford: Clarendon Press, 1994). For a bibliography of Mitchell's principal writings through 1985 as well as several papers that discuss issues that arise in his writings, see William J. Abraham and Steven W. Holtzer, eds., *The Rationality of Religious Belief* (Oxford: Clarendon Press, 1987).

31. In Mitchell's view, *within* the liberal camp there is an additional tension between "traditionalists," whose primary concern is to safeguard tradition, ensuring that no truth that it contains is lost, and "progressives," whose primary concern is to acknowledge modern discoveries and contemporary experience. In this debate, Mitchell does not choose sides. The dispute itself, he says, is both unavoidable and desirable, since in the hands of traditionalists alone the tradition would tend to ossify, and in the hands of progressives alone it would tend to dissolve into the secular culture (ibid., p. 3).

32. Mitchell, *Faith and Criticism*, p. 2.

33. Ibid., pp. 54–55.

34. Ibid., pp. 27–28.

35. Ibid., pp. 32–37.

36. Ibid., p. 45.

37. Ibid., p. 59.

38. Ibid., pp. 58–59.

39. Ibid., pp. 59–61.

40. Ibid., p. 65.

41. Ibid.

42. Ibid., p. 66.

43. The question is meant to be rhetorical. In Mitchell's view, even though knowledge of God is not merely a matter of detached theoretical inquiry but rather of direct encounter, it does not follow that there is no need for criticism. By analogy, we have knowledge both of other people and of ourselves that comes from "direct encounters," yet to understand people, including ourselves, we need to approach them in two ways: first, by observing them, and second, by interpreting what we observe "in terms of conceptions of character and personality that are, so far as we can make them, coherent and defensible." Mitchell says that however intuitive the first process may be, it cannot be divorced from the second. We need data that are immediate and intuitive, but also reflection on those data, ultimately including reflection on what it is to be a person. And the views we hold that result from that reflection, Mitchell claims, like the theories of theologians that result from their personal encounters with God, always are and always should be both tentative and subject to criticism (ibid.).

44. N. T. Wright, *The New Testament and the People of God*, p. 22.

45. Ibid., p. 9.

46. Ibid., p. 12.

47. Ibid., p. 16.

48. Ibid., pp. 4–5.

49. N. T. Wright, *Jesus and the Victory of God* (London: SPCK, 1996), p. 8; see also p. 24, and Wright, *Who Was Jesus?* (London: SPCK, 1992), p. 69.

50. Wright, *The New Testament and the People of God,* p. 26.

51. Ibid., p. 27.

52. My way of putting Wright's view is a simplification of his way of putting it, but one that I think captures what is essential to his view. See *The New Testament and the People of God,* pp. 32–36.

53. Ibid., pp. 38–42.

54. Ibid., p. 42.

55. Ibid., pp. 42, 45–46.

Chapter 10

1. This is merely a *possible* additional drawback, because, as we have seen in our discussion of Mitchell's views, it is not clear, first, that in the Faith Seeking Understanding response one cannot preserve for religious faith its character as total commitment, and, second, that even if one can preserve it, one should.

2. Including, for instance, A. N. Wilson, in his book *Jesus* (London: Sinclair-Stevenson, 1992). See also Wilson's *Against Religion* (London: Chatto & Windus, 1991).

3. John Shelby Spong, *Born of a Woman: A Bishop Rethinks the Birth of Jesus* (San Francisco: HarperSanFrancisco), 1992; *Resurrection: Myth or Reality* (San Francisco: HarperSanFrancisco, 1994).

4. See, for instance N. T. Wright's criticism of A. N. Wilson, in Wright, *Who Was Jesus* (London: SPCK, 1992), pp. 44–47, 64.

5. For more on this, see the following papers of mine: "Objectivity and Meaning in Historical Studies: Toward a Post-analytic View," *History and Theory,* vol. 32 (1993), pp. 25–50; "Telling the Truth About History," *History and Theory,* vol. 34 (1995), pp. 320–329; "The Essential Difference Between History and Science," *History and Theory,* vol. 36 (1997), pp. 1–14; "Progress in Historical Studies," *History and Theory,* vol. 37 (1998), pp. 14–39. And as background for these papers, my *The Past Within Us: An Empirical Approach to Philosophy of History* (Princeton: Princeton University Press, 1989).

6. Gordon Wood, *The Radicalism of the American Revolution* (New York: Alfred A. Knopf, 1991).

7. If a historian refused to commit himself to the superiority of just one interpretation or just one interpretive approach, no sensible person would regard him as somehow suffering from "a failure of nerve." Yet in the context of historical Jesus studies those who refrain from committing themselves to the superiority of just one interpretation or just one interpretive approach are sometimes so regarded. But how much nerve does it take to

pretend to know more than one actually knows? And is that sort of "nerve" a good thing?

8. It is tempting to reply that this objection fails, since all that multiperspectivalism commits one to suspending judgment about is the question of what one should believe, on the basis of historical evidence *alone* and on matters about which historians disagree. The multiperspectival approach, it may seem, has nothing to do with what one should believe on the basis of faith. For instance, suppose that a Christian were to think that she does know, on the basis of historical evidence alone, that, say, Jesus rose from the dead, and hence that she shouldn't suspend judgment about that. But *how, on the basis of historical evidence alone,* does she know that Jesus rose from the dead? Perhaps she thinks she knows it as a consequence of having been convinced by Dunn's argument (see Chapter 6). Dunn said that his argument is based on historical evidence alone and makes no appeal to faith. But recall, first, that Dunn's argument was crucially dependent on his claim (among others) that unless we suppose that Jesus rose from the dead, we cannot explain the empty tomb, and second, Crossan's argument that there is little reason to believe that Jesus even had a tomb. If Crossan is right, Dunn's argument collapses. Is Crossan right? Who's to say? Note that this particular disagreement between Dunn and Crossan does not hinge on disputes about the status of naturalism. The question is only whether Jesus was buried in a tomb. Although Dunn claims to be arguing in general on naturalistic grounds alone, even if he were not, presumably the question of whether Jesus was buried in a tomb is one that he would want to settle on naturalistic grounds alone. But if the experts disagree, as they do, about whether Jesus was buried in a tomb, then on what grounds, on the basis of historical evidence alone, is a nonexpert entitled to side with one group of experts against another? Our hypothetical Christian is left with three options: First, she can belief on faith that Jesus rose from the dead; second, she can believe on the basis of historical evidence alone that Jesus rose (or did not rise) from the dead; and third, she can leave open the question of whether Jesus rose from the dead. The first option, it may seem, has nothing to do with the multiperspectival approach, which concerns only what one should believe on the basis of historical evidence alone. The second option is incompatible with the multiperspectival approach, but it requires of a nonexpert that he or she side with one group of experts against another on a question to which their expertise, which the nonexpert lacks, is directly relevant. And the third option is the multiperspectival approach.

9. There have always been—and there still are today—thinkers who claim that our heads can reach as high as the heavens, that is, that on scientific grounds alone one can justify traditional religious beliefs. Among historical Jesus scholars, Dunn, for instance, claims that on the basis of histor-

ical evidence alone, crucial traditional Christian beliefs, such as the Resurrection, can be adequately justified.

10. One is reminded here of Albert Camus: "Let us insist again on the method: it is a matter of persisting. At a certain point on his path the absurd man is tempted. History is not lacking in either religions or prophets, even without gods. He is asked to leap. All he can reply is that he doesn't fully understand, that it is not obvious. Indeed, he does not want to do anything but what he fully understands. He is assured that this is the sin of pride, but he does not understand the notion of sin; that perhaps hell is in store, but he has not enough imagination to visualize that strange future; that he is losing immortal life, but that seems to him an idle consideration. An attempt is made to get him to admit his guilt. He feels innocent. To tell the truth, that is all he feels—his irreparable innocence. This is what allows him everything. Hence, what he demands of himself is to live *solely* with what he knows, to accommodate himself to what is, and to bring in nothing that is not certain. He is told that nothing is. But this at least is a certainty. And it is with this that he is concerned: he wants to find out if it is possible to live *without* appeal." *The Myth of Sisyphus,* trans. Justin O'Brien (New York: Alfred A. Knopf, 1955), p. 39.

INDEX